Bede's *Historiae*

GENRE, RHETORIC, AND THE CONSTRUCTION
OF ANGLO-SAXON CHURCH HISTORY

This book reappraises the impact of Bede's writings. Focusing on genre
and rhetoric, and their respective roles in audience reception and the
construction of a narrative of Anglo-Saxon Church history, the author
explores Bede's text and audience from the perspectives of both literacy
and textual community, using internal evidence from his writings to
illuminate bias and monastic politics.

Dr VICKY GUNN is Senior Lecturer, Learning and Teaching Centre,
University of Glasgow

Bede's *Historiae*
Genre, Rhetoric, and the Construction of Anglo-Saxon Church History

Vicky Gunn

THE BOYDELL PRESS

First published 2009
The Boydell Press, Woodbridge

ISBN 978 1 84383 465 6

The Boydell Press is an imprint of Boydell & Brewer Ltd
PO Box 9, Woodbridge, Suffolk IP12 3DF, UK
and of Boydell & Brewer Inc.
668 Mt Hope Avenue, Rochester, NY 14620, USA
website: www.boydellandbrewer.com

The publisher has no responsibility for the continued existence or accuracy of URLs for external
or third-party internet websites referred to in this book, and does not guarantee that any content
on such websites is, or will remain, accurate or appropriate.

A CIP record for this book is available
from the British Library

This publication is printed on acid-free paper

Printed in Great Britain by
CPI Antony Rowe Ltd, Chippenham and Eastbourne

Contents

Acknowledgements

THIS BOOK HAS BEEN A LONG TIME IN THE MAKING AND INFLUENCED by more scholars and lay folk than I could hope to acknowledge. The intellectual power houses of my undergraduate studies, Mike Kennedy, Patrick Wormald, and Professor Leslie Alcock, are no longer around to see the fruits of their labours, but it is to them that I owe my abiding interest in the Anglo-Saxon Church. Their colleagues and successors at the University of Glasgow continued to stimulate my thinking and thanks go to Stuart Airlie, Professor David Bates, and Andrew Roach. I also gained inspiration from my conversations with academics outwith Medieval History and special thanks go to Catherine Steel and Alice Jenkins, who goaded, cajoled, challenged and even listened to the vagaries of my arguments.

Outside of the University of Glasgow there are numerous people to whom I am indebted. From its first days as an idea in the mind of a raw undergraduate this book was, in part, a product of a chance meeting with Clare Stancliffe and Benedicta Ward at a Cuthbert conference in Durham. Later on Alan Thacker gave invaluable advice and has continued to do so. George Hardin Brown of Stanford University also provided excellent feedback at the review stage of this book and I am particularly grateful to him for straightening some very crooked furrows and updating my bibliographical information in the last stages of revision. The Benedictine nuns of Stanbrook Abbey and the Carmelite sisters at Mansionhouse Road in Glasgow also listened attentively to my meanderings and gave gentle feedback that assisted me greatly.

In terms of daily humour I wish to acknowledge the unsung heroines of this book – my friends – who with ample mixtures of motivation and distraction kept me from falling permanently into my obsession with Bede. Indeed, they rarely batted an eyelid during chats that consisted of me ranting about what I thought Bede said and why, nor did they give up on me when I reached the bottomless pit of the footnote funk. Especial thanks go to Maggie Skinner who not only proofed some of my early tortuous prose but also went out and bought a copy of Bede's *Ecclesiastical History* and read it. Gratitude is due also to Senga B. Angelus and Rosie Elliott who discovered that sharing their lives with me meant sharing their flat with a venerable saint as well (definitely not me). And last but by no means least, thanks must go to Lynn Lavelle and Anne Sinclair for never failing to enquire about Bede, the book, and my health (but not always in that order); Sophie Agrell for sitting on a hot summer's day in a park in Glasgow listening to an abridged version of the text with genuine enthusiasm; and Margaret, Hannah, and Rachel for switching on the light as I completed this text.

I dedicate this book to my Mum, who made it all possible.

V.G.

Abbreviations

AB	*Analecta Bollandiana*
ASE	*Anglo-Saxon England*
BAR	*British Archaeological Reports*
BJRL	*Bulletin of the John Rylands Library*
BLTW	*Bede, His Life, Times and Writings: Essays in Commemoration of the Twelfth Century of his Death*, A. Hamilton Thompson (ed.) (Oxford, 1935)
Campbell, *Essays*	J. Campbell, *Essays in Anglo-Saxon History* (London, 1986)
CCSL	*Corpus Christianorum, Series Latina* (Turnhout)
CSEL	*Corpus Scriptorum Ecclesiasticorum Latinorum* (Vienna)
Cuthbert, Cult & Comm.	*St. Cuthbert, His Cult and His Community to A.D. 1200*, G. Bonner *et al.* (eds) (Woodbridge, 1989)
DTR	*De Temporum Ratione*
EH	*Ecclesiastical History*

GAF	*Gesta Abbatum Fontanellensis*
HA	*History of the Abbots (Historia Abbatum)*
HBS	Henry Bradshaw Society
HE (P)	*Baedae Opera Historica*, C. Plummer (ed.) 2 vols. (Oxford, 1896)
JEH	*Journal of Ecclesiastical History*
LP	*Liber Pontificalis*
MGH : AA	*Monumenta Germaniae Historica: Auctores Antiquissimi*
MGH: SRM	*Monumenta Germaniae Historica: Scriptores Rerum Merovingicarum*
MHE	*Martyrologium Hieronymianum Epternacensis*
OCT	Oxford Classical Texts
OMT	Oxford Medieval Texts
PL	*Patrologia Latina*, J.-P. Migne (ed.)
Wallace-Hadrill, *Comm.*	J. M. Wallace-Hadrill, *Bede's Ecclesiastical History of the English People – A Historical Commentary* (Oxford, 1989)

Introduction
Bede's *Historiae*
in the Late Twentieth Century

THE LATE TWENTIETH CENTURY WITNESSED A WATERSHED IN approaches to Bede's writings. Whilst previous generations of commentators had focused on his straightforward style and sincere truthfulness, theorists of late and post Modernity challenged scholars to scrutinize such assumptions. In the 1980s historians on both sides of the Atlantic reconsidered Bede's *historiae* from a more cynical perspective.[1] The comfort with which one might have read Bede's historiographical writings as those of a consummate and fastidious, if at times quaint, Anglo-Saxon historian was effectively stripped away. Walter Goffart, particularly, left us with evidence of a hidden agenda and a distinctly uncomfortable feeling that Bede was more of a historical manipulator than we wished to see. Subsequent attempts have been made to challenge parts of Goffart's hypothesis, but the overall assumption of innocence with which we might have approached and appreciated Bede's works has been all but lost.[2] The important contributions of James Campbell, Henry Mayr-Harting and Patrick Wormald are products of a learning environment quite different from the post-modern, sceptical university of the late twentieth and early twenty-first centuries in which Goffart's thesis seems so credible.

Correspondingly the 1980s also witnessed a surge in publications examining aspects of the cult of saints as portrayed in early medieval texts in general and in Bede's writings specifically. If 1988 brought a fundamental reconsideration of Bede that effectively transformed the way that subsequent generations would read his *historiae*, then the year 1981 marked an equally important transformation in the study of the cult of saints. The publication, in this year, of Peter Brown's seminal interpretative work, *The Cult of Saints*, is representative of a more general move to take this critical source of understanding for Late Antique and medieval society from the dustbin of relative obscurity to which it had been consigned, to a main place at the table of the discipline of history.[3]

These transformations have certainly influenced the approaches of academics re-examining Bede's writing. Thus Walter Goffart's revision of the motives behind the production of the *Ecclesiastical History (HE)* in particular has forcefully entered the historiographical arena, compelling observers to reconsider their images of Bede as somehow detached from the politics of his day. (Although it is debatable whether we ever really saw Bede as an out-of-touch academic.)[4] Moreover, historians such as Alan Thacker, David Rollason, Susan Ridyard, David Kirby, Stephanie Hollis, Clare Stancliffe, and Catherine Cubitt have all made contributions and stimulated academic debate concerning Bede's images of saints and their cults in his *historiae* texts.[5]

Even allowing for these revisions it is possible to see that in current approaches to Bede there is a seeming polarization in the historiography between those such as Campbell, Wormald, Thacker and, to a certain extent, Ray who look to the role of Bede's life as a monk surrounded by sources, and those such as Goffart, Kirby, and Ian Wood who prefer to see Bede predominantly as a skilful political rhetorician. This book aims to show that in the two polarized groups of secondary literature there is an underestimation of the extent to which Bede's narratives were constructed within generic boundaries and rhetorical limits dependent on non-contemporary, pre-existing frameworks, and that such a method of composition may well have dramatically effected the 'historicity' of his portrayals. For example, the writings of the first group have done much to enhance our understanding of which Late Antique authors influenced Bede, but they have often not fully admitted the consequences of this debt in terms of what we might consider historical reality. Thus, on the one hand, they note the textual influences on Bede, whilst on the other they still choose to focus on offering a more accurate description of events. This apparent paradox has perhaps occurred because the focus has been on attempting to get literal historical information out of texts that were constructed in the conventions of genre and rhetoric. This book endeavours to redress this imbalance and show that not only was Bede consistent in his method of the construction of narratives by drawing on authoritative non-contemporary predecessors (both directly and indirectly), but that the transmission of uniform conventions was actually a primary role of *historiae*.

The second group of studies in the polarization, apparently almost diametrically opposed and somewhat excluding of the first, stress the political motivation behind and political information in Bede's historical texts.[6] Their approach, therefore, has been far less source-comparison based. However, in doing this they too fail to examine the full extent of the impact of Bede's monastic training in terms of generic linking and rhetorical procedures.

Goffart confidently asserted that Bede 'is just about mined out'.[7] In the current academic climate, with its move to understanding the *contingent* nature of the text, the idea that any source is beyond re-reading and reinterpretation is problematic.[8] Essentially, this book is such a 're-reading', seeking to prove that there is still much ground to be covered in our understanding of Bede's *historiae* in terms of the context in which they were produced, his agenda and his portrayal of saints. Indeed, it proposes that for Bede *historia* was a rhetorical exposition governed by rules of construction that differed hugely from modern understandings of history and was aimed at persuading individuals to imitate certain actions perceived as of worth. In this, Bede's concept of *historia* perhaps responds to Gregory's exhortation that 'we ought to transform what we read into our very selves' by providing Bede's audience with something to read that contextualized non-contemporary accounts in a contemporary, chronological framework.[9] It will be shown that experience of the Anglo-Saxon past was described by applying conventional images from Late Antique and biblical texts, using rhetorical devices to build a narrative which exhibited actions worthy of imitation. In this narrative there is also evidence for contemporary monastic rivalry (that shows Bede to be far from isolated) that extended further than just the abasement of Wilfrid and his confederation as focused on by Goffart and that this, whilst important politically, was secondary to the major aim of *historia*. Moreover, in using the same techniques of information manipulation even the issue of inter-monastic competition needs to be viewed with an acknowledgement of the highly constructed textual environment in which it is found.

Without identifying the textual authorities upon which Bede depended in his composition of *historia*, the historian is always faced with making assumptions about passages in his texts that in the end may reveal nothing more than the smooth integration of textual allusion. In a sense this book will be proposing that the application of authoritative sources in the construction of *historia* did indeed distance Bede from the world of his immediate experience, but that they also allowed him to 'read' that immediate experience in a manner similar to those early Church fathers he so respected.[10]

BEDE AND CLASSICAL RHETORIC

From the outset it needs to be acknowledged that this is not the first time rhetorical understandings have been applied to Bede. In a series of articles examining the possible influence of Cicero on Bede, Roger Ray has highlighted the presence of rhetorical assumptions, albeit classical ones, that would themselves have a direct impact on how Bede developed his *historiae*. In 1980 and 1982 Roger Ray dared to hint at what most other Bedan scholars seemed to be avoiding – that Bede was influenced by the classical rhetorical practice of *inventio*.[11] In 1986 he restated this, claiming that it most clearly came through in Bede's *Commentary of the Acts of the Apostles*.[12] Discussing chapter 7, where Stephen misplaces Jacob's burial place, Bede states:

> 'Truly, when speaking to the populace the blessed Stephen followed popular opinion (*vulgi opinionem*) in his discourse. In conflating the two accounts he concentrated less on the arrangement of the historical details than on the point with which he was concerned.'[13]

For Ray this was evidence of Ciceronian inventional theory, particularly the statement of Cicero that a forensic narrative will possess verisimilitude if it draws on various topics like the opinion of the listening audience.[14] Ray pointed out that in the rhetorical textbooks at Bede's disposal only *De Inventione* mentions explicitly the use of audience opinion among the *topoi* of forensic narrative.[15] However, in 1986 Ray was not prepared to go much further than hinting that Bede directly knew Cicero's *De Inventione*.

Just over a decade later Ray was more explicit and in his Jarrow lecture of 1997 he provided three main reasons why he thinks the hypothesis that Bede had access to Ciceronian texts stands. Firstly, that

Bede's *Commentary on I Samuel* offers a remarkable defence of the Christian study of pagan eloquence.[16] Secondly, that, as is shown in his *Commentary on the Acts*, Bede like Jerome (but unlike Augustine) believed that rhetorical pragmatism utilized for an appropriate end was acceptable.[17] Here Ray argues that Bede's practice, rather than being influenced by Jerome's *Epistle to the Galatians*, was in fact given authority directly from Cicero's *De Inventione*. And, thirdly, like Cicero, Bede conceived of history as a rhetorical exposition and that the formula Cicero provides for this in *De Oratore* is one that corresponds to Bede's narrative strategies in *EH*.[18]

In response to Ray's hypothesis it must be noted that no extant manuscript of any of Cicero's works exists from the period in question.[19] Between the fifth and the late eighth century the *Codices Latini Antiquiores* shows a gap, a fact that has not escaped Ray's main critic, Gabrielle Knappe.[20] However, to use an old archaeological cliché, just because the artefact is not evident now does not mean it was not there once. Indeed, Augustine's *De Doctrina Christiana* seems to be an extremely rare text in Anglo-Saxon England, with no copies of it to be found before the end of the eleventh century.[21] Yet we believe that Bede had access to it.

Whilst we can accept at least the possibility of the availability of Ciceronian manuscripts to Bede, it is worth re-examining Ray's other suppositions. Firstly, in Bede's *Commentary on I Samuel* Ray is being optimistic in his belief that Bede was providing a spirited defence of the study of pagan eloquence. This text in fact illustrates quite clearly the tension faced by early medieval authors in trying to explain the use of pagan rhetoric. Bede can thus indicate that knowledge of the Tullian text helped him improve how he wrote, but he was at pains to note that a certain noble teacher of the Church was called to account and even scourged by the Lord for having become not a Christian but a Ciceronian. Like Augustine and Jerome before him Bede goes for the path of reading with moderation and like his patristic forefathers there is an ever-present tension. Indeed, George Brown has gone further to say that Bede censured secular letters more than he promoted them, viewing them as being associated with heresy.[22]

The evidence for a direct textual influence seems almost entirely circumstantial. Where a link with Cicero can be inferred, one can also cite the influence of Jerome, Augustine, Orosius, Eusebius and so on. Ray himself notes the association of the passage in the Samuel commentary with Jerome's Letter 22, and Book 4 of Augustine's *De Doctrina Christiana*.[23] Even in the two texts where Bede makes direct reference to Cicero, *De temporibus* and *De temporum ratione*, the sources of this information are secondary ones.[24] The point is that Ray's argument is dependent on the transmission of assumptions rather than direct inter-textuality. Unfortunately, the presence of assumption doth not an original text make.

We need to avoid oversimplifying what Cicero has to say. It is worth observing, for example, Cicero's definition of *historia* in *De Inventione*. Thus, when discussing the narrative (*Narratio*) Cicero comments that an exposition of events has three forms, *fabula*, *historia*, and *argumentum*.[25] Here Cicero describes *historia* as an account of actual occurrences remote from the recollection of his own age: '*Historia est gesta res, ab aetatis nostrae memoria remota*'.[26] The opening sentence of Isidore of Seville's definition of *historia* in his *Etymologiae*: '*Historia est narratio rei gestae*', sounds like an echo of the first half of Cicero's sentence.[27] Unlike Cicero, of course, Isidore believed history should be a narration of events that happened in sight of the narrator. If Bede had followed this, Ray quite rightly says, he would have written very little.[28] However, Ray's attempts to place a distance between Bede and Isidore, saying that of course Bede is more like Cicero, fail to express the nuances of each of these writers. Firstly, one should not overlook apparent similarities between Isidore and Cicero (of which admittedly there are few). Nor should we ignore what could be read as a contradiction in Cicero between what he says *historia* is (ie actual occurrences) and the rhetorical assumptions on which Ray focuses. In fact, the assumptions upon which Ray centres his argument could lead us to believe that Bede's *historiae* are more *argumentum* (fictitious narrative which nevertheless could be describing actual occurrences) than *historia*.[29] Finally, we need to remember that in his own *History of the Goths*, Isidore was not averse to discussing periods outside his own lived experience, nor to bending the content of his narrative to suit his purpose. What he said in definition and what he did in practice was not always the same.[30]

The challenges to Ray's hypothesis have led Gabrielle Knappe to suggest that to consider the nature of early medieval rhetoric we need to look at two different traditions: firstly, the continuity of the rhetorical tradition of antiquity, and secondly, the tradition of rhetoric in grammar.[31] For her the second of these two traditions provides the answers to Bede's knowledge. During the period in question, she argues, one can discern a blurring of the boundaries between rhetoric and grammar as grammar becomes more important for Biblical exegesis and has, consequently, to widen its scope to include some aspects of textual study hitherto associated with rhetoric. For her there is little evidence regarding the rhetorical tradition of antiquity.[32]

However, perhaps we could add some nuance to her dichotomy. There seems to be a gap between her two traditions – the possibility for the transmission of the rhetorical tradition of antiquity indirectly through mediating texts. It is clear that Bede used directly and alluded to Late Antique patristic writings to imbue the overall framework of his texts with a sense of authority. In so doing, most of his *historiae*, whilst unique in some aspect, can still be placed within genres which gained their status through being products of the revered Fathers of the Church. Bede's intertextual connections in the *Ecclesiastical History* were not, though, just limited to genre considerations. In terms of the characterizations he constructs, this book will illustrate that there are signs of intertextuality which were a major part of his methodology, critical to his comprehension of the role of Christian history, operating on three different levels: direct quotes, variations on apparently Christian literary themes and conventions, and the description of so called eyewitness experiences expressed through established Late Antique literary frameworks.[33]

Bede, like other readers in the early monastic milieu, in some ways saw himself as wholly subject to the texts he took as authoritative and, consequently, he borrowed from them extensively. Having said this, we need not view Bede solely as a prisoner of his sources; rather this book aims to show that he was a talented manipulator of rhetorical tools that he used to introduce textual models into the lives of the individuals he was portraying. Indeed, the dissemination of these, often Late Antique, models in a form and context accessible to the contemporary society around him may have been his primary aim.

The point is that the literary culture of the patristic authors in which Bede was immersed, and from which he drew for his understanding of both rhetoric and grammar, was itself infused with classical rhetorical assumptions that surely would have enabled their continuity though in bastardized form. We should remember the words of Erich Auerbach that 'the rigorists could not destroy the ancient tradition without at the same time making it impossible to transmit the Christian tradition'.[34] As Charles-Edwards has noted, despite their protestations both Jerome and Augustine continued to deploy the techniques of persuasion they learned from the pagan rhetor.[35] Averil Cameron may well be right to state that Christian discourse came to define the boundaries of experience and the means of describing the world, yet what about implicit discourses, those the early Christians themselves could not help but pass on through the medium of their texts?[36] Bede's reading enculturated him into a world of patristic thinking, which was in itself enculturated into aspects of the literary culture of antiquity. The closer Bede read the more he may have been influenced by that which he did not directly recognize as of antiquity.

BEDE'S SIGNS: *HISTORIAE* AND ALLEGORY

In a much neglected piece, Calvin Kendall also examined issues of rhetoric in Bede, albeit with a different focus from Ray, suggesting that Bede's study of rhetoric, particularly as outlined in his *De Schematibus et Tropis*, drew him to include in his *historiae* narrative devices that encouraged allegorical interpretations of some of the events.[37] Despite William McCready's criticism of Kendall's work, where he challenged the notion that Bede expected the *Ecclesiastical History* to be read allegorically, there is still no getting away from the fact that in the text there do seem to be hints that Bede used words and structures open to allegorical, if not typological interpretation.[38] The text is divided into five books, comparing directly with the Pentateuch.[39] As Campbell notes, the style of the *Ecclesiastical History* recalls that of the Gospels.[40] A comparison might also be inferred between his description of the building of the Temple in *De Templo* and the building of the Anglo-Saxon Church in Book I of the *HE*.[41] Moreover, Judith McClure has indicated the importance of the Old Testament in Bede's construction of images concerning certain kings.[42] Such a choice of relevant biblical texts would certainly leave the constructed narrative open to the same allegorical interpretation applied to the original passages even if such an interpretation in non-Biblical texts was frowned upon by some of the patristic Fathers.

When examining the rhetorical and narrative strategies Bede may have applied to *historia* it is also important to take into account his uses of numerology. Whilst Bede's knowledge in this area was established by Plummer, historians have avoided examining whether or not some of the dates Bede uses are not merely numbers with a more important meaning than just the literal, doubtless because of the highly subjective nature of doing so.[43] An illustration of this is to be found in Bede's narration of Hilda's entry into Whitby at the age of 33.[44] There has been some discussion about whether or not this suggests she was a widow, for at 33 she was certainly old enough to be one.[45] However, what if the age of 33 was placed in the text as no more than an offering of an allegorical sign: 33 representing the year of Christ's death and possibly used to signify Hilda's entry into a life 'with Christ' rather than making any literal statement about her age. It could of course be a typological sign.[46] Thus Bede would have chosen to include it in the narrative because he knew it to be a literal truth, with the potential for an interpretation other than the obvious literal one. Mayr-Harting has suggested that Bede omitted Wulfhere from his list of the over-kings not only because of Northumbrian chauvinism, but also because he wanted to use a number of allegorical significance. Numbers have a performative, as well as a literal, role to play in Bede – inspiring links between his writings and Scripture.[47]

A recognition of the impact of this approach on the scriptural exegesis of Bede means that it is difficult to rule out the question of whether it significantly influenced his history writings. Julia Smith has intimated that such a method was employed by the Carolingian hagiographer, Hucbald of St Amand. She demonstrates that Hucbald had transferred this technique of argument common to theological controversy to hagiography.[48] Surely, given Bede's own emphasis on his exegetical texts, it is not impossible to suggest that he preceded Hucbald in this approach. If this can be proved, of course, it has implications for the historical accuracy of his works.

Furthermore, in *De Doctrina Christiana*, Augustine made it clear that being restricted to a literal reading of a sacred text was a form of captivity;[49] that choosing a discourse which did not allow for the interpretation of signs but focused instead on them as things was 'a miserable servitude of the mind'.[50] This statement, however, does supply the observer with a potential caveat concerning the assumption that Bede intended alternative interpretations to be applied to his *historiae*. The *Ecclesiastical History*, for example, was not a sacred text and in his own Biblical commentary, *De Templo*, Bede noted that allegorical readings should be restricted to Scripture.[51] In the *EH*, at least, Bede seems to have contradicted his own strictures and composed a text that he did intend to be subjected to allegorical interpretations. The signs in the text certainly suggest this.

Also of importance in terms of textual accuracy, writing and interpreting allegorically allowed for an easy coexistence in a text of apparent asceticism and rampant materialism. Objects that the modern audience might essentially find to be indicative of a secular society could easily be accommodated in a text by disassociating the materials from their literal truth and seeing them predominantly in terms of something deeper. Mayr-Harting provides an excellent example of this in his description of Gregory the Great's letter to Bishop Natalis of Salona. Here Gregory is seen reprimanding the bishop for his feasting (which the bishop justified by quoting literally from the Bible!). Gregory responded to this by explaining that things done in history had an allegorical significance.[52] In short, seemingly literal events occurred for allegorical reasons, not merely as literal events to be taken and used in justification for all types of behaviour. By changing the emphasis of an event or an object from literal to allegorical the religious author could thereby manage a potential tension in a historical text – between religious and secular values – making it relevant both to a monastic and to an aristocratic audience. By the time Bede was writing, it was a disassociation not only generally accepted in monastic communities in Anglo-Saxon England, but also sanctioned by the authority of Augustine and Gregory the Great.[53]

This book, however, does not seek to reproduce the work of Ray and Kendall. Rather it seeks to examine a different aspect of the application of rhetoric and genre. It demonstrates that Bede's use of pre-existing written textual models to create images of Anglo-Saxon saints was less centred on allegory, than on a new Christian form of *inventio* developed from an immersion in late patristic (not classical) texts, designed not just to prove his point but also to bring authority to the narrative.[54] To do this he not only placed an emphasis on generically identifying certain texts as *historia*; he also applied certain techniques of rhetoric which Diana Greenway has usefully identified (albeit for a twelfth-century text) as authority (that which is directly copied from earlier authors), convention (that which is written to a literary formula) and observation (eyewitness accounts themselves limited and controlled by rhetorical conventions).[55] This book will argue that by utilizing such tools of composition Bede created in the narrative of the *EH* a text that he did not intend to be received as primarily literally historically true by all members of his potential audience. His compositional techniques served as a device whereby he could exhibit the conformity to Rome of the history of certain sections of the Anglo-Saxon Church, particularly Wearmouth and Jarrow, by textually linking them to an earlier Christian period.

In general, when beginning to analyse Bede's *historiae* the researcher needs to take into consideration the fact that monastic and rhetorical priorities may have been placed before the priorities of historical accuracy.[56] Thus, it can be surmised that the history texts written by Bede (possibly excluding the Chronicles) were written with the intention that they could be read at many levels. A text could be read literally, allegorically (as a tool to reveal God), as a framework in which to interpret life, and as a resource of behavioural modification showing the reader how one could be closer to sanctity and, therefore, God.

Having acknowledged this, the texts upon which this book is centred are the *Ecclesiastical History*, *History of the Abbots* (*Historia Abbatum*, *HA*), *Histories of the Saints* (*Historiae Sanctorum*), *The Lesser and Greater Chronicles* (*Chronica Minora*, *Chronica Maiora*) and the *Martyrology* (*Martyrologia*).[57] Through this choice, the book aims to broaden the balance of historiographical analysis that on the whole has centred on the *Ecclesiastical History* and the *Lives of St Cuthbert*. Bede's Chronicles have been a much underutilized resource, only recently receiving translation for the more general perusal of students and mentioned but briefly (if at all) in secondary sources examining Bede's approach to history.[58] The same can be said of the *Martyrology*, which still remains unedited.[59] Even the *HA*, though edited by Plummer and now available in many translations, does not appear to have received much attention from Anglo-Saxon historians.[60]

The approach used is essentially a comparative study of Bede's texts with generically similar writings from patristic, Anglo-Saxon, Irish, and Merovingian authors. The study is directed primarily at texts that are earlier or contemporary to those of Bede in an attempt to place Bede firmly in the discourse context of his own period. Other historians such as Ridyard have tried to build their arguments by placing Bede's *EH* in the context of later Anglo-Saxon hagiographical texts. Whilst this undoubtedly may indicate the insular chronological developments in Anglo-Saxon understandings of the cult of saints it might not necessarily give us an accurate reproduction of Bede's concepts.

The themes of this book will be explored, firstly, through those texts to which we believe Bede had access, either in the library at Wearmouth-Jarrow or from other monasteries, and secondly, through those texts which reflect similar concerns to the ones touched on by Bede but not necessarily known to him, which place him in the context of the wider discourse of Western Christendom. These texts enable us to look at the levels of intertextuality and influence in Bede's works. Moreover, it is a concern here to show not only the influence of particular parts of sources upon Bede's writings but also the impact of generic expectations upon the historicity of his historical works. The book also attempts to place Bede's historiographical works in the context of his other writings, including exegesis, grammar/rhetoric and his poetry. This approach is taken in order to understand more fully how and why he constructed his images of sainthood in the way that he did and what implications this might have for the historicity of his texts.

The key areas of discussion will be an examination of the nature of Bede's audience to stress that the reading and interpretation of his *historiae* texts would have been predominantly limited to a select group (chapter 1); the context in which the cult of saints and the textual material related to it developed in Northumbria (chapter 2); the internal evidence in the text of the *EH* that suggests Bede was intent on promoting his own monastery through his writings (chapter 3); the role that genre played in Bede's development of his *historiae* texts (chapter 4); how Bede effectively created a new sub-genre in the genre of *historia* in his production of the *History of the Abbots* (chapter 5); how Bede made innovations to the genre of historical martyrology whilst still depending upon patristic texts as his models (chapter 6); Bede's method of saintly image construction in the *EH*, and the impact of intertextuality (chapter 7); a comment concerning the implications of Bede's methods (conclusion). In broad terms, this book will examine the extent to which generic placing and textual allusion have had an impact on Bede's historicity. It will be argued that hidden in his well-chosen words and deliberately constructed narratives were subliminal and overt signs designed for the trained eye. Moreover, it will be stated that the monastic context in which these texts were produced was one of competitiveness and that the exhibition of learning as well as the manipulation of monastic history were all part of such inter-monastic rivalry.

There is a major caveat to this approach and it cannot go unmentioned here. Throughout this book it is accepted that the transmission of Bede's *historiae* was fundamentally stable, not prone to the vagaries of scribal error, and that the edited versions we currently possess provide the historian with suitable artefacts upon which to base assumptions concerning historical and rhetorical analysis. This premise is not without its problems. The manuscript scholarship of Michael Lapidge and others has indicated that even the most stable of our texts, Bede's *EH*, shows disagreements between different extant manuscripts.[61] Moreover, the *Martyrology* as we have it, is based on partial, ninth-century manuscripts housed in Europe. There is no autograph manuscript. Ultimately, current opinion that Bede is the originator has been accepted, as has the fact that the list of his works found in the *EH* is accurate and representative of what he personally actually produced. Yet, should we be convinced that the absence of an autograph manuscript is enough to deter the historian from attempting to analyse contemporary documents through the structures provided by theory and historiography? There can be no doubt that one of the many tasks of the early medievalist is to examine the extent to which mistakes, modifications, and dissonances between manuscripts affect the historiographical narrative of a contemporary author. Nonetheless, it is important in this approach that we do not find ourselves giving authority to a process that could lead to the *reductio ad absurdum* of early medieval studies.

Orthographical inconsistencies, grammatical errors, and erroneous syntactical constructions provide a healthy warning with regard to textual corruption, but should not in themselves preclude interpretative textual studies of the documents currently available. We should be wary of prioritizing the empirical notion of textual criticism as primarily pertaining to the ascertaining and reproducing of the author of the text.[62] Such a focus could ultimately lead us to the conclusion that our notions of history are untenable, as we discover that our authors and their autograph manuscripts are ever more invisible (one thinks here of Bede's *Martyrology*, and more generally women's authorship, and the research into the authorship of marginalized groups in society). We should also be on our guard for a reliance on a particular view of literacy and knowledge that places linguistic exactitude as the only essential to the transmission of meaning in a text. A certain level of grammar and orthography does need to be achieved for adequate information transmission, but they do not need to be perfect. Essentially, manuscript analysis that searches for the autograph manuscript and historical analysis which applies modern theoretical and interpretative methods need to be undertaken collaboratively, and, rather than withdrawing into different corners of the same discipline room, historians need to consider the synthesis of these approaches. Until this or some other mediating solution is found in our discipline perhaps we will continue to take sides about what is 'more valid' in the study of early medieval history in general, and Bede in particular.

Chapter 1:
Understanding Bede's Audience

THE AUDIENCES OF THE HAGIOGRAPHICAL AND HISTORIOGRAPHICAL literature of the Late Antique and early medieval period have come under increasing investigation by historians in the last decade.[1] In the fifty years previous to this there had been a notable degree of scepticism concerning the extent to which early medieval Christians understood the nuances of Church teaching. Following Dom Delehaye's assertions that the recipients of hagiography, in particular, were the lowest common denominator of intelligence that depended upon the credulous rather than the historical reality of an individual, it simply was not fashionable to challenge this view. Indeed, were one to read some of Bede's more disparaging comments about the level of learning in contemporary monastic communities, it is easy to see how historians became beguiled by the whole notion of credulity and the subsequent lack of interest in the sources that ensued.[2] Bede, like Delehaye, appreciated learning but had little patience when it was absent. Where audiences are concerned though, issues of reception are not just about one particular type of understanding, but about how different groups in an audience construct different meanings from the same texts.

Interestingly, in relation to Bede there has been more of an assumption that reception of his historiographical texts, at least where the *Ecclesiastical History* is concerned, extended beyond the literate monastic community to that of the king, Ceolwulf.[3] Nonetheless, it is clear that Bede's methods of construction and the messages he wished to disseminate required an intensity of reading beyond the merely literal acceptance of his narrative. This opening chapter aims to examine the recipients of Bede's historiographical texts to illustrate the dangers of taking for granted the idea that the reception of the nuances of Church teaching included in his writings extended beyond an elite and increasingly powerful group of individuals.

To begin this analysis the reader needs to consider not just who the audiences for Bede's *historiae* might have been but also the nature of their understanding of these texts. Peter Brown played a particularly transformative role in initiating a rethink of this issue by shifting the focus from the two-tiered model that differentiated between 'popular' and 'intellectual' belief and, implicitly, the two different types of understanding they perhaps represented. He emphasized that many historians have been pessimistic about the capabilities of the 'masses' to understand changes in religion and theology – i.e. their ability to assimilate new Christian ideas and distinguish them from surviving pagan ones.[4] Thus the historiographical approach has been one of a search for continuity between pagan practices and those of Christians. Against this, Brown asserted that the modern assumption that popular religion represents a continuous tradition has restricted the historian's ability to look for change.[5] Brown tried to undermine the idea of a dichotomy between 'popular' and 'intellectual' religion by noting that rather than looking for continuity, the observer should be looking for discontinuity.[6]

This proposal oversimplifies the complexities of how individuals and groups understand and construct meaning from what they read and hear. From the outset, it is important to note that 'understanding' may itself be contingent on situation and circumstance, and that the notions we use to explain what we mean by understanding of a text now are dependent to a large extent on the context in which we read. Moreover, as has been noted elsewhere, even in an audience from a particular context there might be diverse conceptions of understanding and these conceptions would effect how individuals receive information.[7] Essentially we need to avoid viewing the audience as a monolithic entity, or as is more common amongst early medieval historians, as two separate groups each with their own monolithic identity (popular/intellectual).[8] Such a dichotomy fails to express the complexity of meaning-making in a particular group and will be intersected with multiple influences that we cannot always identify. What we tend to be left with in the historical record is evidence of the ideas and interpretations of a dominant group, representing itself in the face of its own collective hierarchical observation and normalising judgement. In terms of types and levels of understanding our sources arguably reproduce certain codes from the frame of reference of a particular group, but this is not quite the same as giving us evidence of the different ways in which the texts were more broadly read and understood.

Having stated these caveats it is still useful to apply modern conceptions of understanding to get a more sophisticated sense of audience reception. For example, Brown appears to have assumed a universality of access in terms of audience reception to the ideas of the patristic authors and their Merovingian successors. However, where the texts relating to the cult of saints in general and Bede's *historiae* specifically are concerned one must take into account the role of and extent of Latin literacy in the adoption of such refined and exact nuances. Who, fundamentally, was the audience for these works and how widespread was their transmission? One can perhaps accept that Augustine and his contemporaries did write in an educated milieu of secular literacy. However, even here the more sophisticated of their ideas might not have permeated much further than a fairly limited circle (who were themselves engaged in clarifying theological doctrine and therefore had a particular interest in each other's comments).

Moreover, by the early medieval period the culture of secular education had been significantly eroded by the Christian elite who focused their literacy skills in a monastic environment.[9] Whilst there is some evidence from saints' lives to suggest that basic literacy was taught to the children of lay aristocracy there is little evidence that this education went beyond practical literacy for administrative purposes.[10] Is it advisable to conclude, then, that such functional literacy would enable even this audience to comprehend the finer points of theological discourse? Indeed, as Katrien Heene has pointed out, there is little to suggest that even those lay people listening to the readings of the hagiographical material in the Merovingian liturgy necessarily understood the texts that were being recited.[11] This material is hardly suggestive of a widespread ability to understand the Latin of these texts let alone have enough literacy skills to receive the sub-texts embedded in them.

On matters of this kind, Brown's desire to prove a more general understanding of theological nuances reads like a reaction to the provocative judgements made by writers such as Delehaye (who concentrated on the feebleness of the popular mind) rather than a convincing observation of the contemporary documents in their broader societal environment. Basically what both Brown and Delehaye have failed to take into consideration is that different groups and individuals have different ways of framing, defining, and understanding their spiritual, religious, ritual experience despite what the dominant discourse might say. The focus of an intellectual, 'conscious', articulate group of celibate men may determine what we now know about contemporary practice, but this does not mean that their ideas were necessarily universally accepted or understood by contemporaries. This in turn need not deny that the populace had a fairly advanced relationship with the supernatural in their interaction with the cult of saints. The point perhaps is that we should be extremely cautious when generalizing about one group's perceptions and experiences from another group's writings. As historians we are on firmer ground when we try to indicate what the writings seem to show us about the experiences and perceptions of the immediate communities in which the authors produced them.[12]

In his approach Brown was somewhat exclusive, trying to present evidence of a general change in the way individuals perceived their relationship with the human and the divine from texts that were designed to negate any continuity with paganism. However, change and continuity need not necessarily be viewed as mutually exclusive. Instead, perhaps, the observer should be aware of the possibility that 'popular' religion (superstitious or not) could and did co-exist with that of the intellectual elite. This is particularly well shown by two ninth-century sources: firstly, Alcuin's *Life of St Richarius*, in which Heene has identified two distinguishable levels of writing, each with their own audience;[13] and, secondly, in the Preface of the *Life of St Remi* by Hincmar of Rheims. Here Gurevich has noted that although problematic as a source for the early period, it does give insight into how the Church itself perceived the difference between the belief of the populace and the belief of the educated clerics.[14] Thus in the preface Hincmar recommends that when it is read to the people on the feast of St Remi, different parts should be used for different audiences. He clarifies this by stating that he had marked off passages for the *populus* or *simplices* and for the *illuminati*. In this sense, the distinction against which Brown argued is implicit in this early medieval source.

In many ways these comments, derived from Brown's analysis,

are applicable to Bede. Whilst Bede's Latin style in the *EH* is undoubtedly a straightforward one, like his patristic forefather, he was an intellectual, articulate, and incredibly precise author. Bede's *historiae* would have challenged both his pupils' linguistic and their intellectual abilities.[15] As has been implied by the recent research into Bede, there is much evidence of the subtle nuances in terms of political awareness, religious belief, and rhetorical convention that lay hidden in the apparent simplicity of his language. These nuances arguably required a high degree of Latin literacy and erudition to perceive them and the inferences we modern historians now make may have been visible to only a few of Bede's audience.

Indeed, despite Campbell's belief that Bede intended the *EH* for a fairly wide readership one must question to what extent this readership extended outside a monastic environment.[16] Evidence implies, for example, that ignorance of Latin among the Anglo-Saxon clergy was a common and perennial phenomenon.[17] It has also been noted elsewhere that the Anglo-Saxons acquired Latin as a second language, with all of the difficulties that this entailed.[18] The production of grammatical advice in texts such as Bede's *De Orthographia* in the early eighth century might represent attempts to overcome the problems perceived amongst monastic tutors in terms of their students' foreign language proficiency. This is not, of course, to argue that Anglo-Saxon culture was illiterate; the evidence for vernacular literacy shows that this was not the case.[19] Rather there seems to be a distinction between monastic literacy with its focus on Latin and the interpretation of texts, 'hearing literacy' with its focus on the transmission of narratives to listeners (with no expectation that these listeners would necessarily be versed in source analysis or rhetorical structures), and more functional literacy, used for administrative purposes.

To take the last of these groups first, even allowing for the problems of document preservation identified by Patrick Geary, the evidence for functional Latin literacy among the laity in Anglo-Saxon England appears to be far more scarce than for Merovingian Gaul.[20] If one takes, for example, the charter material to exemplify the level of literacy it becomes clear that even in terms of functional reading and writing the laity were limited. Thus, despite her expressed hopes concerning lay (and clerical) literacy, Susan Kelly notes that Anglo-Saxon charters have an absence of any outward mark of validation, and that the lack of lay literacy was overcome by focusing on the ceremony around the charter rather than its actual content, while on one genuine charter she does discuss there is an explicit statement of King Wihtred of Kent's illiteracy.[21] Surely this evidence tends to imply a high degree of Latin illiteracy (as does the translation of the *EH* into Anglo-Saxon) rather more than a general ability to comprehend the hidden messages embedded in Bede's historical works.

Furthermore, the charter evidence perhaps brings into question the actual audience for many of the letters addressed to kings such as Aethelberht, Edwin and Oswiu, that one finds in Bede's *EH*. After all, taken at face value, they seem to imply at least a basic level of Latin literacy on the part of their recipients. Yet in the light of the charter evidence it seems more likely that the ceremony around the reception of the letters may have been of at least equal if not more importance to the kings than the words contained in them. Certainly they did not just land surreptitiously on the floor underneath the royal letterbox and it seems fair to assume that their arrival would have been marked by an occasion of some formality. Gift giving in early medieval society was not without political significance and played a significant role in the rituals and symbolism of a given community.[22] As Aaron Gurevich has noted, the transference of possessions contributed to the acquisition of social prestige and respect.[23] Indeed, on occasion the giving of a gift could involve greater prestige than its retention.

It is of interest here to note that when Aethelberht received his letter from Pope Gregory, Bede says it came along with numerous other gifts.[24] This would make more sense if one viewed the letters as archaeological artefacts that served at least two fundamental purposes. The first of these seems to be reflected in the wording of the texts themselves. Letters seem to be gifts with a role of persuasion from the Bishop of Rome. Though, even here, in terms of persuasion the reader needs to consider to whom the directives were really aimed. It is clear, for example, that letters from clerics and missionaries to kings did not always contain messages favourable to the named recipient. The letter of Boniface to King Aethelbald of Mercia is an excellent example of the admonishing tone letters sent to court could use.[25] Yet, the letters that accompany this apparent correspondence of criticism also illustrate how messages were mediated by other clerics before being read out to the named recipient, so even the immediate persuasive function of received epistles cannot be accepted without caution.[26]

Perhaps, then the second function is the one on which we should focus our attention. Documents from the Pope could act as objects which provided the focal point for a ceremony designed to enhance the recipient's power and standing in his own community by marking him out as special. After all, the *EH* suggests that only bishops, monks, and kings received letters – not the general lay aristocracy. This is pertinent to the *EH*. Like the letters, it was dedicated to a king and it is hard not to ask whether Ceolwulf might have received it in some form of ceremony where the symbolism of the gift exchange was more important to Ceolwulf than the contents of the gift. If the text was completed in 731 this would certainly have been timely, coinciding with a period when Ceolwulf needed all the legitimization as king that he could get. The point, of course, is that if the manuscript had more symbolic than intrinsic value politically there is no need to assume that Ceolwulf could read it. (This is not to say that it did not have any intrinsic value politically at all, merely that the text's own political value was not necessarily related directly to Ceolwulf.)

Professor McKitterick's point that the expense of book production and the status accorded to the possession of books would have made it unlikely an author would 'waste precious parchment and labour on a gift for someone who could not even read' contradicts this.[27] However, if the book was more important symbolically to the recipient than the actual words, the act of giving is what counted.[28] The text need not have been wasted for the king could subsequently store it in an environment where it could be read – such as a monastery – one need only compare the gift of the *EH* with the gift of the book Adomnan made to Aldfrith.[29] If this suggestion does reflect the actuality, it becomes plausible, if not probable, that Anglo-Saxon lay Latin literacy was negligible and consequently, one should be extremely circumspect about pronouncing a wide reading audience for the content of any of the historical narratives we now have at our disposal for this early period (at least in their Latin form).

Sophisticated Latin literacy outside of the ecclesiastical groups was limited and literacy in general may have been expressed more in the vernacular than necessarily in Latin. Indeed, Michael Clanchy, showing slightly more optimism concerning functional literacy among the laity than Susan Kelly, noted that by the time of Augustine's mission in 597 the practice of writing some form of English language is evident in the text of the laws of Aethelberht of Kent.[30] What this seems to imply is that when the laity required practical literacy it wrote and read in a form of Old English rather than Latin. Thus, although functional literacy existed it occurred in the vernacular because of the lack of Latin proficiency outside the monastic establishments. Even allowing then for practical vernacular literacy, the evidence still does not encourage the belief that Latin literacy was widespread nor, consequently, that substantial bodies of text such as *historiae* were intended to be read outside of the monastic environment.

In fact, given this lack of literacy one should perhaps question whether or not Bede actually expected Ceolwulf to read and comment on his *EH*, as stated in its Preface, or if this was merely a rhetorical device.[31] Certainly it would appear that many historians have assumed that it was safe to accept the Preface as literally true and that Bede did expect Ceolwulf to read and use the text whilst king. Thus, Wallace-Hadrill believed Ceolwulf to have read and approved the text. Additionally, Kirby has commented that Bede intended to take royal reaction into consideration in the editing of the *EH* and that Ceolwulf may even have been involved in censoring some of Bede's material.[32] He reiterated this point in his 1992 Jarrow Lecture.[33] Barbara Yorke has also intimated that Ceolwulf may have been expected to derive some 'practical assistance' in his reign from studying the text.[34] However, such an assumption is not without some problems, not only in terms of Latin literacy but also in terms of book ownership.

Firstly then, can one justify maintaining the assumption that Ceolwulf was literate in Latin? Except for the implication of literacy suggested by the Preface of the *EH* (which will be discussed later), Bede is particularly vague about Ceolwulf's abilities and his comments in the letter to Egbert stress Ceolwulf's piety, not his learning. This silence, however, perhaps acts as an indicator that Ceolwulf was not particularly well versed in Latin, for one cannot help thinking that such an ability would have been specifically commented upon by Bede. Essentially historians do not know the levels of royal literacy and consequently cannot make any definitive statements as to whether or not

Ceolwulf could read (and more importantly, interpret) the *EH*. If one places Ceolwulf and the *EH* in the context of the variability of Latin literacy levels as suggested by the recognition of the difficulties of acquiring a second language, the charter evidence, and the need for Anglo-Saxon laws to be written in the vernacular, it seems improbable that many laity, let alone Ceolwulf, could read it. Moreover, even if he could read it literally, there seems absolutely no reason to think that before his entry into Lindisfarne he would have identified the political and rhetorical sub-texts that are present in the narrative.

He might, of course, have heard this text, possibly in translation. After all, Bede makes it clear that Oswald acted as a translator for Aidan. The precedent for translators from one language to another being present at court is therefore established, albeit Irish to Anglo-Saxon. The question still remains as to the extent to which an auditor would be aware of the nuances of the rhetorical manipulation and intertextuality; as does the issue of which sections of the text the translator would focus on for the king. Would Ceolwulf, for example, be viewed as among the *simplices* or the *illuminati*? The point is that Ceolwulf may have received some of the information, but this may itself have been selective without any expectation that he would use the text as a tool for interpretation and analysis.

Secondly, even if he could read it, can one just accept that Ceolwulf did indeed have his own copy of the *EH*?[35] The Preface would certainly suggest that it is a possibility. In general terms, however, lay ownership of books in early Christian Anglo-Saxon England was exceptional.[36] Moreover, if one observes the example that seems to offer the direct possibility of a king possessing his own copy of the *EH*, that of Offa, identified by Susan Kelly, it is clear the evidence is inconclusive.[37] If one scrutinizes the text from which she has drawn her point one can see that it does not actually mention Offa having a copy of the *EH*, rather it reads as if Alcuin were using Bede as an authority to give credence to the argument he is putting forward.[38] In this letter there does not seem to be an expectation that Offa would refer to his own copy to check Alcuin's reference, merely that quoting from Bede gave an argument weight. The observer, then, ought to question the validity of the assumption that Ceolwulf owned his own copy, for it would seem from the evidence that this would be extremely unusual in an Anglo-Saxon context.

Furthermore, if one looks at the actual words of the Preface in the context of a lay environment (as opposed to a monastic one) they seem even more improbable. Thus it is inferable that Bede had sent a copy before and, more pertinently, is sending it again, in Colgrave's words, 'for copying and fuller study, as time may permit' (*et nunc ad transcribendum ac plenius ex tempore meditandum retransmitto*).[39] Whilst in translation these two activities seem fairly innocuous in a secular setting, if one actually looks at what is being asked of the reader it becomes clear that they are more suited to a monastic environment. Manuscript transcribing, after all, was the remit of a scriptorium. Are we to assume that Ceolwulf himself was to copy the text? Or that he had his own scriptorium? Or was it more likely that the text was going directly to a monastery associated with Ceolwulf and that, in fact, though Ceolwulf was named he was not expected to read it? Wallace-Hadrill perhaps implied some of the tension in this phrase in his commentary when he questioned if it would have been sent to Lindisfarne for copying.

This query becomes all the more pertinent when one takes the word *meditandum* into consideration. Although Colgrave's use of the word 'study' is a useful translation it is perhaps inadequate in the specific sense of the way in which Ceolwulf was expected to read the *Ecclesiastical History*. In essence, from Bede's use of this gerund the reader is not told the degree of literacy Ceolwulf exhibits, it merely implies that he might be able follow the stories. This does not automatically mean, however, that Ceolwulf's literacy extended to a point where he could either understand the symbolism and convention in the text or be learned enough to recognize the inter-textual allusions in the narrative. Indeed, it does not even tell the observer whether or not Ceolwulf was to engage in the act of reading or whether he was to hear the stories through a translator. This is a critical point for it must be remembered that literacy *per se* does not necessarily mean that the audience is learned. As Dr Bäuml has commented, 'An educated reader need not be erudite, nor a reader who knows Latin know it well enough to approach the Vulgate without shuddering.'[40] In other words, one cannot take for granted that the word *meditandum* in this context means anything other than a literal reception of the narrative, which could have occurred through hearing the stories.

Taken slightly further, this point also has relevance to Bede's monastic audience. Again, whilst this group may have had the ability to read Latin, this does not equate with them being of a universal standard in terms of understanding or interpreting the texts. Judith McClure has shown that learning in the clerical class was far from being of a uniform nature and misreadings in monastic glosses illustrate that even in the scriptorium mistakes, on a very basic level, could be made.[41] The need for Bede himself to be engaged in translations shows that one needs to question the extent of Latin 'readability'. Thus, though David Rollason has noted that the language and complex scriptural and literary allusions suggest a predominantly ecclesiastical readership for Bede's work as well as other *vitae*, this elite group would surely have exhibited variable standards in terms of Latin literacy.[42] What one should perhaps consider is that in the monastic environment there was a clear scope for a variation in approach to the texts and the consequent forms of comprehension to which these might lead.[43] For example, *lectio* and *emendatio* arguably correspond to surface forms of reading, requiring little sophisticated reflection.[44] *Enarratio* and *iudicium*, on the other hand, require deeper forms of reading and expect the reader to make sense of the text in a profound manner that would require both self-analysis and erudition. The study of poetry in the monasteries is also illustrative of differing levels of sophistication. As Michael Herrin has noted, on a simple level (though itself needing a high level of language literacy) Christian poets employed pagan loan words to express Christian teaching.[45] On a more profound level, however, they would interweave and interpret pagan tales as counterparts to biblical exemplars. Access to this form of reading and reconstruction was surely the preserve of the select elite, not to a wider audience. Though what it does indicate is the potential audience for whom the recognition of subtle messages and undercurrents would be the norm.

In the current climate of deconstruction then an element of caution needs to be raised. Whilst modern learning in the academic environment brings gifts of reading sub-texts and textual manipulations one cannot assume that these were extensively in place in the ecclesiastical communities in which Bede's *historiae* were circulated. As Augustine noted, 'What we teach is one thing, what we tolerate is another, and what we are obliged to put up with is yet another.'[46] This is a sentiment one cannot but think that Bede, on occasion, held with regard to his fellow monks. Throughout the following chapters what may be revealed is more the degree of Bede's own erudition rather than necessarily what the majority of his audience received.

Bede's sophistication, of course, may have had its own symbolic importance. In the wider monastic circles of Northumbria Bede's ability to illustrate such learning may well have enhanced his own reputation and by association that of his monastery.[47] Such erudition in the immediate community of the monastic world (which itself placed an emphasis on the written and read word) would have been valued. As a skill of value, Latin literacy could also be used to enhance one's own monastery in a competitive environment.

There was a gap, then, between an educated elite and the non-literate majority, at least in the context of seventh- and eighth-century Britain. Nonetheless, it is also important to acknowledge that there were different degrees of literacy in a given community's audience and that one needs not only to differentiate between the information gleaned by a non-Latin literate group and that held and understood by the elite, but also have a sense of the potential for different types of meaning-making in each group. Given the apparent variability of literacy one should also regard gifts of Latin texts given to secular authorities in the light of the symbolic ritual that might have surrounded such an exchange. Indeed, such symbolism need not have been limited to gifts going from a monastery to a layman but, as shall be shown in the next chapter, may also have played a part in the giving and receiving of gifts from one monastery to another.

Chapter 2:
The Historical and Contemporary Context of Northumbrian Hagiography and *Historiae* Production

THE IMMEDIATE AUDIENCE FOR BEDE'S *HISTORIAE* WAS predominantly an elite monastic group. The historical context of the production of the texts themselves needs therefore to be placed within the fluctuating fortunes of seven of the institutions in which this elite group lived: Iona, Lindisfarne, Whitby, Ripon, Hexham, York, and Wearmouth-Jarrow. Whilst other monastic houses such as Melrose, Gilling, Lastingham, Coldingham and Bardney clearly played a role, it appears, in textual terms at least, that the seven former monasteries held the predominant positions of authority. Such pre-eminence was not solely a matter of the abilities of their scribes and calligraphers, however. It was primarily dependent on the relationship they had with the secular authorities in Northumbria, most notably the king. The primacy of a particular monastery over the others in what could be considered a fluctuating hierarchy was determined by two critical and inter-related factors: their relationship to royalty; and the success of any cult development programme.[1] As will be shown, the power of the kings was, in its turn, increasingly dependent on the acceptance of the monasteries established by royal predecessors. In short, the connection between the monasteries and the king provided a mutually beneficial situation that both parties could utilize to their advantage. In this sense, whilst it has been argued that there might not have been a widespread audience for the Latin texts of Bede's *historiae*, it is nonetheless clear that the context in which such sources were produced was, in part, the symbiotic relationship between the most powerful monasteries of the kingdom and the members of the ruling house.[2] One cannot deny that authors like Bede would have engaged (both unconsciously and consciously) with their contemporary environment and reflected issues of relevance to secular society in their texts. The extent to which this material would have been received outside the monastic and ecclesiastical community in its Latin form is what has been in question. Essentially, it is suggested that what one views in the Latin texts is a dialogue occurring between members of a particular textual community predominantly composed of monks and clergy. This dialogue may reflect issues of bearing outside those communities but it need not express them in a manner readily available to those not included in the communities.

To understand the context of the production of writings in the late seventh and early eighth centuries, one needs to examine the changing status of these textual communities, particularly those of the Ionan confederation and the 'Roman' monasteries; the subsequent need by incoming kings, especially those acceding to the throne through bloodshed, to gain acceptance by the monastic establishments; and the need of the monasteries themselves to improve their own standing in the ecclesiastical hierarchy.

THE DECLINE OF THE IONAN MONOPOLY

The starting place for any attempt to understand the role that a monastery's status played in the production of narratives that elevated the authority of their particular saint is not Northumbria but Iona. Iona certainly appears to have initiated an insular hagiographic tradition during the abbacy of Segene.[3] There is some debate over the dating of the text that resulted from this initiative, known as the *Liber de Virtutibus Sancti Columbae*, but it would seem fairly safe to assume that it was written some time between 637 and 652.[4] Herbert has suggested that this text was a response to ecclesiastical critics of Iona who questioned the monastery on its Easter practice and, given its admonition of retribution to monarchs, that it was also a caution to secular critics not to attack the kin of Columba.[5] To take the latter point first, such a warning need not have been transmitted to a wide audience in its Latin form, but may have been subject to translation for those outside the Latin literate communities. It need not therefore be evidence of lay Latin literacy. With regards to her first point, whilst the Easter question did become a real issue of contention following Pope John's letter commending change, other political events occurred in the period of the 640s onwards which need to be taken into consideration. These events might have affected the amount of influence and status that the Ionan confederation would have had in Northumbria and, in themselves, may even have precipitated the finalization of a text designed to bolster its authority.

Firstly, the impact of the death of Oswald in 642 should not be underestimated. His relationship with Iona is clearly shown through his decision to ask Iona for assistance in preaching Christianity and subsequently through his close dependency on Aidan. This relationship established a monopolistic situation in Northumbria. It allowed Iona through Lindisfarne to dominate both religious practices and ecclesiastical appointments made throughout Oswald's reign and at the beginning of Oswiu's rule. By inviting Iona's support Oswald clearly established a degree of autonomy for an Ionan daughter house in Northumbria directly attached to the ruling family, thereby giving Lindisfarne a superior status to other foundations in the area, including, it would seem, the Rome-established church at York.

Nonetheless, on the death of Oswald in 642 the Lindisfarne community's status may have seemed more precarious than before, especially as Aidan chose to support Oswine rather than Oswiu, the man who ultimately became the most powerful leader in Northumbria. The impact of this choice should not go unnoticed, for it may well have meant that Oswiu had some reason to be suspicious of Iona's role in power brokering in Northumbria. In turn the Ionan confederation arguably had cause to be more circumspect in its dealings with Oswiu. From this perspective, Oswiu's relationship with the Irish had slightly more nuances than Bede would have his readers believe.

In this context it is worth revisiting Oswiu's gifts following the battle of Winwaed, for they suggest a change in the balance of the relationship between the king and Lindisfarne. Thus rather than making gifts to Lindisfarne, Bede notes that Oswiu gave twelve estates, six in Deira and six in Bernicia, on which monasteries were to be founded in thanks for his victory over Penda.[6] Bede is silent with respect to who established the monasteries on these lands. Bede notes, however, that Oswiu also gave his daughter, Aelfflaed, to be consecrated as a nun. This passage in Bede's narrative (*EH*, III: 24) is not one of the clearest in the *Ecclesiastical History* and it has been assumed in the past that these initial endowments would have included the land upon which both the monasteries of Hartlepool and Whitby were founded.[7] It is clear from Bede's chronology that this is not accurate. Hartlepool was already in existence. It was clearly founded under Aidan's auspices prior to his death in 652.[8] It housed perhaps one of the most invisible women of the text, Heiu, said to be the first Northumbrian woman to take the vows and habit of a nun.[9] It was only following Heiu's retirement that Hilda became its abbess, though again Bede makes it clear that Aidan visited Hilda there. Whitby was founded two years after Aelfflaed's consecration and entry into Hartlepool on another ten hides of land. If Aelfflaed was consecrated following Winwaed (655/6) this would place the foundation of Whitby in the late 650s – certainly subsequent to Aidan's death. In Book IV: 24 Bede hints at the idea that Hilda was forced to undertake the foundation at Whitby. Indeed he injects an element of doubt about the particulars of the foundation at this point, offering the suggestion she may have set in order a monastery already in existence.[10] Whatever the actuality, it seems that in the late 650s the Roman-baptized Hilda was moved from her Aidan-associated Hartlepool to Whitby with Aelfflaed. This raises the question of whether Oswiu was attempting some sort of ecclesiastical realignment within Northumbria. At the Synod of Whitby, Oswiu is portrayed by Bede as having been educated and baptized by the Irish, considering that nothing was better than what they taught.[11] This statement could be seen as a literary embellishment to make the persuasion of the Roman party seem even more effective as the authority of the argument convinced even the most Irish-oriented of kings. Whitby itself might already have been more Romanized than Bede would have had us believe.

Moreover, this was the period when Oswiu's son, Alhfrith, gave Ripon to Wilfrid, expelling the Irish monks to whom he had previously given it. If these endowments are the conclusion of a process in which the Northumbrian king was less enthusiastic than his predecessor with respect to Iona, is it not possible that the production of the *Liber de Virtutibus Sanctae Columbae* and any associated attempt to boost Columba's cult was in part to maintain Iona's status at a time when there had been a perceptible change in its standing?

Whilst the association of the production of the *Liber de Virtutibus Sanctae Columbae* with the reign of Oswiu is purely speculative, it is more than plausible that the status of Lindisfarne and to a certain degree that of Iona was undermined following Oswald's death. While Aidan's stature as a holy man ensured that a degree of status was maintained for the confederation until his death in 652, his successors are not portrayed by Bede as having had such a close connection with the Northumbrian kings. At this point, though, the Irish still had a monopoly in terms of ecclesiastical appointments in the north of England as is shown by Bede's list of the bishops of Lindsey: Diuma, Ceollach and the Irish-educated Trumhere.[12] Whilst the relationship between the king and the Ionans was arguably weakening, the northern Anglo-Saxon church was still dependent on them for senior personnel in the 650s and 660s. The events at the Synod of Whitby may well have been a reaction to such a dependency. Here the key issue for the secular authority may have been less Easter Observance *per se* than the supremacy of 'Columba' and, therefore, the Iona confederacy in Northumbria. After it occurred, non-Iona trained men and members of the Anglo-Saxon-born aristocracy dominated the episcopal appointments in Northumbria rather than Irishmen. Thus Tuda was southern Irish-educated and Eata was of 'the English race'.[13] In terms of text production the important issue to note is that Iona attempted to keep its authority within the ecclesiastical environment by stressing the continued contemporary power of Columba in the production of the *Liber*. This particular hagiographical initiative, like those that followed it, was designed to augment the position of the monastery.

The effect of the Synod of Whitby on the status of Lindisfarne is more complex than on that of Iona. It is hard not to assume, given Lindisfarne's close association with Iona, that Lindisfarne's authority was considerably weakened by the outcome of the Synod of Whitby. Indeed, some evidence certainly suggests that there was a reorientation on the part of the Northumbrian royal family away from Lindisfarne and its Iona roots to York and more Roman ones. Thus, if one is to believe the *Life of St Wilfrid*, both Oswiu and Alhfrith (with the unanimous support of their counsellors) elected Wilfrid to the see vacated by Colman.[14] At this point, however, Stephanus does not clarify exactly where that see is to be located and it is only subsequently (in the next chapter) that the reader learns of Wilfrid being sent back to the see of York after his consecration in Gaul. The implication of this then is that both Oswiu and Alhfrith focused the see of the Northumbrians on York not Lindisfarne following the Synod of Whitby.

Bede, of course, clarifies that the situation was not quite so straightforward. After the Synod, he states that Tuda, following catholic customs, was consecrated bishop of the Northumbrians. He failed, however, to survive the outbreak of plague that year prompting Oswiu and Alhfrith to find another successor to Colman. In Book III:28 Bede seems to imply that rather than Wilfrid being the unanimous choice of these two kings, Alhfrith's support lay with Wilfrid and Oswiu's lay with Chad.[15]

This apparent discrepancy between the *Life of St Wilfrid* and the *EH* has been used by Wallace-Hadrill to suggest that Oswiu was acting aggressively towards his son.[16] In addition to this, Isenberg has stressed that there seems to be a difference of emphasis in Book V:19, where Bede appears to indicate that Oswiu was in full accordance with Alhfrith over his desire to consecrate Wilfrid.[17] This may merely be a consequence of Bede using the *Life of St Wilfrid* as a source in the later book of the *EH*. However, the apparent ambiguity surrounding this part of the text may also be due to an inaccurate reading of what Bede was actually saying.

In the two sections of the *EH* pertaining to Wilfrid, Chad, and the see of York, Bede (like Stephanus, in fact) is, in the first instance, noticeably reticent about naming the site of the bishopric Ahlfrith sought for Wilfrid.[18] Rather he comments that Alhfrith wanted Wilfrid consecrated as bishop 'for himself and his people'.[19] In Book V:19 Bede is similarly vague about an actual episcopal centre for Wilfrid and again the focus is on Wilfrid being consecrated as Alhfrith's bishop: 'Alhfrith sent him to Gaul with the counsel and consent of his father Oswiu, requesting that he should be consecrated as *his* bishop…'.[20] As a result of subsequent events, it is possible observers have wrongly assumed that it was intended from the outset that Wilfrid should be consecrated as the bishop of York.[21] Perhaps the actual plan was that he would be Alhfrith's 'personal' bishop, based at his foundation of Ripon. This is not implausible; after all Oethelwald asked Chad's brother, Bishop Cedd, to found and administer the monastery of Lastingham, as a place where he (Oethelwald) might pray and be buried, and there does not seem to be any assumption that this was an act of usurpation on Oethelwald's part.[22] Also, in Book V:19 Bede places Wilfrid's consecration immediately after he has discussed his ordination to the priesthood at Ripon. Ripon may have been seen as a monastery with a similar connection to its king as Lastingham had with Oethelwald. Moreover, if one reads the passages this way there is far less discrepancy between the two chapters than there seems at first. This need not deny that a power struggle occurred between Oswiu and his son (although there is less reason to believe in this if Oswiu was indeed more reticent in his dealings with the Ionans than Bede would have us believe) but rather that it was initially neither Alhfrith's nor Oswiu's intention that Wilfrid should be bishop of York. It is more likely that Oswiu's appointment of the Irish-educated Chad to York served to mollify Lindisfarne after Whitby at the same time as reorienting the episcopal power base away from Lindisfarne. From this perspective his actions seem less of an aggressive response to a perceived threat from his son and Wilfrid. It also made a symbolic statement that the ruling house of Northumbria was aligning itself to the 'original' Roman foundation of Paulinus and Edwin, rather than maintaining any dependency on Iona that Oswald had established. The importance of all of this in terms of Lindisfarne is, of course, that Oswiu's focus on York meant that it acquired status at Lindisfarne's expense. Moreover, this shift in Lindisfarne's authority is further emphasized in Book III:29 of the *EH* where it is made clear that both Oswiu and Egbert of Kent, acting together, sent Wigheard to be consecrated as the archbishop of Canterbury in Rome.[23] This is a critically symbolic statement by a Northumbrian king, bringing his church closer to Canterbury.

Despite this apparent lowering of Lindisfarne's status it does seem possible to suggest that until the reign of Ecgfrith there was not another monastic house able to compete for the king's favour in terms of resources and prestige in Northumbria. Although the reorientation to York occurred during Oswiu's reign the real impact of this may not have been felt until Ecgfrith's accession as king. Oswiu had nominated a man trained in Ireland and a disciple of Aidan as his bishop for this see, a break in terms of the nationality of the individual but not with the tradition. Furthermore, the *Life of St Wilfrid* implies Chad failed to adorn or repair the church for which he was responsible – as Wilfrid succeeded to a church building that was badly neglected.[24] Even allowing for the partisan nature of the *Life of St Wilfrid* the implication would appear to be that Chad did not undertake any renovations at York and that, in practical terms at least, Oswiu's reorientation towards Rome was not thorough – after all the visual impact of such a 'derelict' building would hardly inspire a sense of York's importance. However, in terms of the appointment it is hardly surprising that Oswiu was forced to choose

an individual connected with Lindisfarne. Except for Whitby, until the
end of his reign, there was not an alternative centre upon which the
Northumbrian king could focus his relationship or from which to draw
ecclesiastical appointees.

In fact, the *Life of St Wilfrid* suggests that a bishop, Wilfrid, rather
than a Northumbrian king, was instrumental in the breaking of
Lindisfarne's monopoly. Certainly, the impressiveness of Wilfrid's
refurbishment of York and his subsequent building programmes at Ripon
and at Hexham suggest that he would have been able to command the
attention of the royal family. Indeed, if one is to believe the *Life of St
Wilfrid*'s version of events in the early years of his reign, Ecgfrith's
successes were due to his obedience to Wilfrid. Thus in chapter 19,
Stephanus alludes to their relationship being similar to that of Joash,
King of Judah and Jehoiada in the *Book of Kings*.[25] In the biblical text
one can see that actually Joash is initially dependent upon Jehoiada to
marshal the forces and to crown and anoint him king.[26] If Stephanus
meant that this allusion should be so identified it is hard not to think that
he was stressing Ecgfrith's dependence upon his 'Jehoiada'. He makes this
allusion more literal when he continues by stating that: 'so when king
Ecgfrith lived in peace with our bishop, the kingdom, as many bear
witness, was increased on every hand by his glorious victories'.[27] How
real this relationship was in practical terms is perhaps questionable. The
Life of St Wilfrid certainly does not imply that Ecgfrith used Wilfrid as
an adviser, merely that by being obedient to him, Ecgfrith's good fortune
was sustained.

A comparison of Ecgfrith's relationship with Wilfrid and his
monasteries with that of Benedict Biscop and his foundations indicates
that any closeness implied by the allusion to Joash and Jehoiada had little
substance. Firstly, whilst Wilfrid was endowed with lands by Ecgfrith
they did not come from Ecgfrith's own lands but rather from lands
deserted by British clergy at the fringes of the Northumbrian kingdom
round Ribble and Yeadon.[28] At Wearmouth quite a different story is
presented. Bede makes it clear that Ecgfrith, so impressed with Biscop,
donated lands from his own personal property (*ut confestim ei terram*).[29]
The quality of this grant is, as Plummer noted, further emphasized in
Bede's *Homily to Benedict*, 'secular rulers, having recognized the zeal of
his virtues, were concerned to give him a place to construct a monastery,

a place not taken away from some lesser persons, but granted from their own personal property'.[30] Bede, of course, wanted to emphasize the superiority of the land gift to Wearmouth.

Secondly, even allowing for Bede's rhetorical strategies, subsequent relations seem to concur with the notion that Ecgfrith and Biscop were close, whereas they certainly do not for Wilfrid; Wilfrid's relationship with Ecgfrith in the early part of the reign seems to an extent determined by the support he gained from Ecgfrith's wife, Aethelthryth. Thus, it is clear that the one significant endowment he received in Bernicia, Hexham, came not directly from the Northumbrian royal family but as a gift from the East Anglian Aethelthryth (as Mayr-Harting so pertinently notes – hardly a pillar of the Northumbrian establishment).[31] Bede indeed emphasises the closeness of this particular friendship in his discussion of St Aethelthryth, noting how Ecgfrith was said to have offered land and money if Wilfrid would persuade Aethelthryth to consummate their marriage, because he [Ecgfrith] 'knew that she loved no man in the world more than him'.[32]

The subsequent veiling of Aethelthryth by Wilfrid suggests there is little reason to question the validity of this friendship. However, it may point to the reason why Wilfrid was less favoured by Ecgfrith and his predecessor, Oswiu. It is clear from the relationship with Aethelthryth that Wilfrid's loyalties did not lie directly with the king but rather with the king's wife. This is true also in Wilfrid's early relationship with Oswiu. At the beginning of the *Life of St Wilfrid* Stephanus asserts that as a youth Wilfrid went, not directly to Oswiu for support, but to Eanflaed, his queen. He then served under her 'counsel and protection' (*consilio et munimine*).[33] It was she who subsequently placed him with Cudda (the king's companion) and she who sent him to King Erconberht in Kent.[34] Wilfrid was, therefore, far more 'her man' than he was Oswiu's. On his return to Northumbria it is perhaps relevant that Wilfrid went not to Oswiu's court but rather to that of his son, Alhfrith. Wilfrid's sphere of influence was among those associated with Oswiu rather than with Oswiu himself.

The significance of this is only illuminated when one compares Wilfrid's early career with that of Benedict Biscop. In the *History of the Abbots*, Bede makes Biscop's links with the Northumbrian kings (as opposed to their queens) explicit. Thus, not only was he one of Oswiu's 'ministers', he, as a nobleman, also received land directly from Oswiu.[35] Moreover, on his return to Northumbria from his third trip to Rome, hearing that the king he was to visit (Cenwalh) was dead, he went to Northumbria, evidently being welcome at the court of Ecgfrith.[36] Biscop, unlike Wilfrid, had not needed to rely upon the support of the queens in Northumbria and, undoubtedly, Biscop's association with Ecgfrith remained notably more friendly than the relationship that existed between Wilfrid and Ecgfrith.

In the case of Wilfrid, despite the wealth he had amassed (as evidenced with the refurbishment of York, and the foundations at Ripon and Hexham), he still did not command enough of Ecgfrith's attention to be as influential as has been supposed. After all, as Kirby has noted, in the final analysis the king's power was superior to that of the bishop.[37] What cannot be in any doubt, however, is that by refurbishing York and by founding Ripon and Hexham, Wilfrid provided Lindisfarne with the first of its serious non-Irish-connected contenders in terms of competing for royal patronage and the consequential cult and text production that was part of this.

ECGFRITH AND THE RISE OF THE 'ROMAN' MONASTERY

Although Wilfrid can be seen as a catalyst in the breaking of Lindisfarne's monopoly in Northumbria, it is to Ecgfrith one must turn to witness an apparently systematic attempt to undermine Lindisfarne's authority. It could be argued that right from the outset of his reign the position Ecgfrith inherited concerning Lindisfarne was quite different from that of his predecessor. On his accession he was not faced with an Irish bishop based at Lindisfarne (as his predecessor had been), rather the present incumbent was the 'Rome'-affiliated Wilfrid. Whilst, as has been noted previously, the association between the two men was not close, Ecgfrith did not immediately expel Wilfrid, and the *Life of St Wilfrid* makes it clear that he did grant some land (albeit poor) to Wilfrid.

The contention here is, however, that the foundation of Wearmouth in 674 marked a critical juncture in Northumbrian ecclesiastical history, for it signalled a concerted attempt on the part of Ecgfrith to separate himself and his family from the previous direct royal association with Lindisfarne. Indeed, it is clear that Ecgfrith had a special relationship with his own foundation. He gave land from his own land;[38] Bede implies that it was through his 'desire and wish' that Wearmouth received the papal privilege from Pope Agatho.[39] It is also indicated that Ecgfrith was involved directly in the foundation of Jarrow, a fact corroborated in the anonymous *Life of St Ceolfrith* which notes that Ecgfrith chose the location of the altar at Jarrow.[40] This chapter of the *Life of St Ceolfrith* supplies further evidence that the relationship between Ecgfrith and Biscop was more than just of a patron king and the abbot of his 'patronage'. It is clear from this *Vita* that Biscop, like great abbesses of royal monastic foundations such as Hilda, worked in an advisory capacity for the king.

There appear to be three main reasons why Ecgfrith chose to endow Wearmouth. Firstly, the wealth Biscop had accumulated on his initial trips to Rome was, if aligned to Ecgfrith, a potential source of status.[41] In chapter 4 of the *HA*, Bede elucidates the information supplied in the opening sentence of the *HA*, noting that on return from his trip to Rome Biscop went to Ecgfrith and told him all that he had done since leaving Northumbria as a young man. Bede describes Biscop's zeal and the objects with which he had returned. He continues with information about the king's donation of land. It is interesting that immediately following his statement concerning the quantity of holy books and relics of the blessed Apostles and martyrs of Christ that Biscop had brought back, Bede goes on to notice that it was at this point Biscop found the 'gracious friendship' of the king, who gave seventy hides of his own royal land (*ei terram septuaginta familiarum*) for the foundation of the monastery.[42] One cannot help thinking that this donation was directly related less to Biscop's great wealth of ecclesiastical and monastic knowledge as to the real material wealth of the sacred objects he brought to the king. Following chapter 6 (which functions like an inventory of great objects) Bede again indicates that Ecgfrith's response to the extensive number of acquisitions was to donate land. Although Bede comments that King Ecgfrith was pleased by Biscop's virtue, industry and devotion, he also mentions the fact that the king could see the land that he had given to the monastery had 'borne fruit'. It is immediately after this note that Bede indicates the next donation of land by Ecgfrith.[43] From this evidence it is easy to infer that Ecgfrith's gifts of land to Biscop were directly related to the sacred objects and, therefore, status symbols Biscop was bringing to Ecgfrith's kingdom.

Secondly, as Wood has recently commented, one must consider the possibility that he was deliberately donating land for a new royal monastery in order to benefit directly from the prayers of that community.[44] In the first instance this may seem a fairly typical move on Ecgfrith's part. It is clear after all that this was one of the motives behind Oethalwald's foundation at Lastingham.[45] This pattern was a common occurrence in Merovingia too. Thus kings such as Dagobert and Clovis II both gave land to individuals with the express purpose of establishing monasteries.[46] What is of particular importance concerning the benefaction of Wearmouth, however, was the closeness of the relationship Ecgfrith was then to have with it. For example, Oswiu certainly founded monasteries rather than just focusing his benefaction on Lindisfarne. Thus, after the death of Oswine, on the instruction of his wife, he founded Gilling.[47] Also, as was noted earlier, following the battle of Winwaed he gave a total of 120 hides of land in Northumbria upon which monasteries were to be founded. The difference, nonetheless, is clear – as far as one can tell there was no particular closeness between Oswiu and these foundations. There is certainly no intimation that these monasteries were founded upon the king's 'private land' – and as Bede specifies this in relation to Wearmouth such a gift had some significance.[48] In terms of the lands given after Winwaed, Bede does not even name the sites of the monasteries that were founded. Ecgfrith's relationship with Wearmouth, on the other hand, is explicitly stated and seems far more reminiscent in type to that of Oethalwald at Lastingham.

Furthermore, previously in Northumbria when kings had founded other monastic establishments they usually depended upon Lindisfarne (either directly or indirectly through individuals who had trained there) to supply them with appropriate founders. At Lastingham Oethalwald used Cedd, and at Ripon Alhfrith initially invited Eata to run his monastery, only later turning to Wilfrid, who himself had spent time training at Lindisfarne. Where founders were chosen from outside Lindisfarne, they still tended to have a link with the Irish, such as Trumhere at Gilling. For Ecgfrith, Wearmouth was to be 'his' monastery and to ensure this he deliberately drew on an individual not only from outside the Lindisfarne enclave but also unlinked to the Irish. Ecgfrith's confidence in reorienting his ecclesiastical focus away from Lindisfarne is exceptionally clear in the case of Biscop.

Thirdly, this last point indicates that there was far more to the foundation at Wearmouth than just the power of its prayer for Ecgfrith's soul or the status afforded by the material wealth the association gave him. (After all, if all he wanted was the status from the material wealth, Wilfrid would surely have suited him as well as Benedict Biscop.) The wider significance of the individual to whom Ecgfrith gave the land is related to Biscop's unequivocal 'Roman' credentials. Thus at the beginning of Biscop's career, when he chose to enter monastic life, he left Northumbria directly for Rome. For him there was no apprenticeship in Lindisfarne, as there had been for Wilfrid. Moreover, on his second trip to Rome the newly consecrated archbishop of Canterbury, Theodore, was placed by the Pope into his care.[49] This relationship subsequently led to him becoming Theodore's abbot at the monastery of St Peter in Canterbury. Biscop's trips to Rome and his connection to Theodore made him a perfect candidate for a king who wished to lessen the power of the Lindisfarne confederation within his kingdom. Biscop, unlike even Wilfrid, had no previous affiliation with this monastic conglomerate. Ecgfrith also enhanced his foundation's links with Rome by desiring and approving a papal privilege of liberty – given by Pope Agatho.[50] Ecgfrith's foundation of Wearmouth was perhaps part of a larger initiative that involved the king firmly aligning the Northumbrian Church to Rome and bringing himself into a closer relationship with the archbishop of Canterbury.

One could of course challenge the proposition that Ecgfrith was in some way pursuing a deliberately Rome-centred approach to matters ecclesiastical. The conflict that arose between himself and the 'noted' Roman sympathizer Wilfrid is perhaps a perfect example of a seeming contradiction. Indeed, following the expulsion of Wilfrid, Ecgfrith had two men consecrated as bishops who had clear Lindisfarne connections. Nevertheless, in an unprecedented move he also had a priest from the monastery of Whitby, Bosa, consecrated. Despite Hilda's apparent Columban sympathies the monastery of Whitby did have its own peculiar Roman connections, most notably Hilda's baptism by Paulinus. Ecgfrith's subsequent appointees confirmed this trend not to depend on Lindisfarne, with Tunberht coming from Gilling, and Trumwine of unknown origin (who, despite apparently knowing Cuthbert and being involved in his elevation to bishop, chose Whitby as his place of retirement rather than Lindisfarne).[51]

In one respect, Ecgfrith's quarrel fits into a pattern of support for a 'Roman' orientation – albeit one interpreted through the desires of Theodore. At the Synod of Hertford, early in Ecgfrith's reign, Theodore had made it clear that as the number of the faithful increased more bishops should be created.[52] Whilst the Synod could not come to an agreement on this issue, Theodore obviously had the division of large episcopal sees in mind. Following Wilfrid's expulsion his own extensive bishopric was indeed divided and Ecgfrith's choice of successors, Eadhaed, Bosa, and Eata were consecrated by Theodore at York.[53] In this case it is hard not to conclude that dissension between Ecgfrith and Wilfrid was to some degree stimulated by Theodore's desires.[54] In Theodore's and Ecgfrith's eyes a bishop's alignment to Rome was not enough to prevent them being deposed; nor, however, does the deposition of a Rome-allied bishop mean that Ecgfrith had any less of an interest in maintaining his own orientation southward rather than towards Lindisfarne. It is after all, noticeable that although Pope Agatho wanted Wilfrid reinstated following this exile, he also agreed with the creation of more bishops in Northumbria.[55]

For the Pope, the fault in this case was not so much the apparent principle behind Ecgfrith's actions as the way he pursued his goal. It is of further relevance here that Ecgfrith's dealings with Wilfrid in 678 do not suggest that he viewed the opinions of the Pope as unimportant. It was perhaps no coincidence that Ecgfrith's adviser, Biscop, happened to be in Rome (his fourth trip) at the same time Wilfrid was pleading his case; nor was it a coincidence that Jarrow was founded in 680 and a Ripon priest, Ceolfrith, given its abbacy. The anonymous *Life of St Ceolfrith* explains that Jarrow was to be for the redemption of Ecgfrith's soul: '*pro redemptione animae suae*'.[56] In some regards this statement is reminiscent of Bede's note concerning the foundation of Gilling. Thus Bede records that the monks of Gilling were to pray for the redemption of both Oswiu and Oswine. The point is that Bede also makes it clear that Oswiu founded Gilling to atone for his crime of murder: '*castigandi huius facinoris*'.[57] Further on in the *EH* Bede reiterates that Gilling was founded to expiate Oswine's unjust death and was granted to one of his near relatives, Trumhere – appeasing a family grievance.[58] Is it possible that Jarrow was founded in similar circumstances, as an act of appeasement to the monastic community of Ripon following Ecgfrith's decision to ignore the papal adjudication on Wilfrid? Of course, the statement, 'pro redemptione animae suae', may merely reflect a standard phrase applied in the literature to such foundations. It is, as Wood noticed, certainly used with regard to Ripon.[59] Yet it is not used by Bede with regard to Lastingham and was clearly not uniformly assigned. In actuality, the evidence concerning the phrase is inconclusive and, as Wood has posited, may represent Jarrow being part of a special royal foundation.[60] Nonetheless, the timing of the endowment of Jarrow and the appointment of Ceolfrith are suggestive. Even though Ecgfrith did both expel Wilfrid and disregard the wishes of the Pope concerning Wilfrid's case, this action was not a pro-Lindisfarne, anti-Roman action. Following Wilfrid's ejection there was no return by the Northumbrian ruling house to a dependence on Lindisfarne for ecclesiastical personnel. Rather, Ecgfrith augmented his own foundation by endowing Jarrow and he strengthened his ties with Theodore, allowing him (in the aftermath of Wilfrid's exclusion) both to consecrate two more bishops and possibly to depose one in 684.[61]

During Ecgfrith's reign there is also evidence to suggest that Whitby realigned itself, shifting away from an apparently pro-Ionan stance towards a more pro-Theodorian one, in an effort to be perceived as more 'Roman'. This is certainly suggested by the unified stance Theodore and Hilda took with regard to Wilfrid's expulsion in 678. The *Life of St Wilfrid* indicates that both the archbishop and the abbess were represented in Rome at Wilfrid's hearing.[62] Moreover, Bede notes that one of Hilda's episcopal products, Oftfor, not only devoted himself to his learning in both Whitby and Hartlepool, but also studied in Kent with Theodore and then in Rome.[63]

Ecgfrith's choice of Bosa as bishop of York reflects this Romanizing process – drawing Whitby and Paulinus's foundation closer together, as well as Hilda and Ecgfrith. Such a change in orientation may have been precipitated by the entry of the widowed Eanflaed, a notable member of the Roman party who had supposedly resolutely refused to practise an Ionan Easter, and who, consequently, brought an official royal link with orthodoxy which Whitby had hitherto been lacking.

Following Hilda's death Whitby's associations with the Rome-

Canterbury-oriented Anglo-Saxon Church became more obvious. Thus, Hilda's familial kinship to Edwin was emphasized. It is noticeable, for instance, that in Bede's chapter dealing with Hilda's life he introduces her as the daughter of Hereric, King Edwin's nephew, and as having been baptized by Paulinus in company with Edwin.[64] Such a direct association with the Roman mission seems to contradict Bede's earlier statement in Book III:25 where, in no uncertain terms, Bede recorded Hilda's Ionan affinities. As shall be shown in chapter 3, in his depiction of Hilda in the *EH*, Bede was pursuing his own agenda and, consequently, underplayed the 'Roman' elements of Hilda's life. The significance for this chapter, however, is that it would appear the source from which Bede derived his material in IV:23 was keen to emphasize that in some regards Hilda was an 'original' Roman-baptized founder whose inviolate faith was initiated by Paulinus not Lindisfarne or Iona.

It is also possible at this juncture that Ecgfrith encouraged his mother and sister to enhance Whitby's reputation as a centre of orthodoxy by tightening its association with Edwin. Alan Thacker has suggested that the translation of Edwin's relics occurred before Ecgfrith's death.[65] If they did so, it is arguable that the movement of Edwin's bones to Whitby happened with Ecgfrith's agreement, if not at his instigation. Whilst the surviving Northumbrian sources do not hint at Ecgfrith's involvement in this event, it should not be ruled out. However, this need not depend purely on the apparent closeness evidenced by Ecgfrith's choice of a Whitby monk as bishop or his desire to promote Roman sites at the expense of Lindisfarne. It is perhaps salient that in two Frankish sources dealing with women who wanted to translate relics, comment is passed on the role of the king. Thus in Gregory of Tours' depiction of Radegund getting relics of the True Cross for Poitiers he notes that she had to gain King Sigibert's written permission to do this.[66] In the later ninth-century Carolingian *Life of St Glodesind*, this is repeated. Thus when nuns wanted to translate Glodesind's relics from the cemetery at Saint Arnulf's to Glodesind's monastery at Subterius it was recorded that none of them dared to act without the king's order or licence. Only after messengers had been sent and had received the king's concession could they undertake the translation.[67] Although neither of these sources are Northumbrian, they point to the possibility of the need for a women's monastery to have the king's approval in actions which would take them outside the monastery itself. In a sense, whilst the abbess had a degree of autonomy within her monastery she was still under the king's authority outside it. Elevating Hilda was an internal affair – Edwin, on the other hand, was lying in lands outside of the monastic site. Consequently, it is conceivable that Ecgfrith played a role. The importance of this elevation should not be understated for, as will be shown, it represented the beginnings of the development of cults in Northumbria which led both to their proliferation and their associated texts.

In summation it appears that Ecgfrith pursued a calculated ecclesiastical policy of Romanization designed to erode further the remains of the monopoly of Lindisfarne and to enhance his own status through an association with Theodore and orthodoxy. To do this he made a substantial grant of land to the most visible Roman supporter in Northumbria on his accession, Wilfrid; established a new monastery through a gift of land given to an individual with unequivocal Roman sympathies and associated with Theodore; drew upon the ideas Theodore outlined at the Synod of Hertford – breaking up the extensive see of Wilfrid, and looking not only to Lindisfarne but also to Whitby for episcopal candidates which he then had Theodore ratify; and extended the size of his own monastic foundation with the development of Jarrow. And, finally, he allowed for the Romanization of Whitby initially through Hilda and then under the auspices of his sister and mother. In these dealings Lindisfarne is noticeably inconspicuous.

It has, of course, been suggested that Ecgfrith's largesse in terms of land grants was not limited to Ripon and Wearmouth-Jarrow but included Lindisfarne as well. This is certainly implied by the *Historia de sancto Cuthberto*.[68] If this were so, it would certainly bring into question the hypothesis being posed – that he deliberately ensured a growth in the status of Whitby and then Wearmouth-Jarrow at the expense of Lindisfarne, particularly in the first decade of his reign (with the intention of identifying himself as distinctly Roman). However, the source itself is a highly problematic one. The *Historia de sancto Cuthberto* is not a contemporary document but one seemingly begun in the Cuthbertine community in Chester-le-Street in the middle of the tenth century and in part compiled by Symeon of Durham in the early twelfth century.[69] Indeed, as Roper has noted, the main difficulty in using this source is to distinguish between those possessions granted to Cuthbert in his lifetime and those made later to the monastic community.[70] Nevertheless, both he and Thacker believed that the grants mentioned in this passage accurately reflect land holdings donated by Ecgfrith.[71]

If one inspects the text more closely, however, the difficulties of accepting it as a credible source for the early period appear insurmountable. Before the text mentions Ecgfrith, it states that, 'Then saintly abbot Boisil immediately made known to King Oswin the sacred vision of blessed Cuthbert, explaining that he was filled with the Holy Spirit. Then the King and all the English magnates gave to saint Cuthbert all that land that lies near the river Bowmont....' [72] As Arnold himself notes and as is reiterated by Ted South this is unhistorical.[73] The donation is made to follow Cuthbert's vision, a vision that was subsequent to the death of Aidan and also, therefore, after the death of Oswine. Arnold views this as suggesting that the story probably arose out of a need for the tenth-century monks at Chester-le-Street to 'invest the original grant of lands which they held with a peculiar sanctity'. In essence he supposes that the monks used Oswine's saintly status to lend authority to their claim. This sounds plausible. However, it assumes that St Oswine had the authoritative status of a saint in the mid-tenth century. This in itself is questionable, and, as shall be argued later in this book, there is actually very little evidence of Oswine being viewed as a saint before his rediscovery and translation at Tynemouth in 1065. In fact, it was not until his second translation in 1103, at which Ranulf Flambard, bishop of Durham, was present, that a *Vita* was produced for him.[74] Given the early twelfth-century dating of Symeon's writings at Durham it is fair to assume that he knew of these events concerning Oswine. This would suggest that the section immediately preceding the information on Ecgfrith was more relevant to the late eleventh century than it was the mid-tenth, let alone the seventh century. Such a point hardly inspires confidence in the reliability of this source to reflect accurately land grants made in the seventh century.

This problem of accuracy is further exacerbated by the chronological inconsistencies in the sections of the text that deal with Ecgfrith. Thus it moves from the land holdings that Cuthbert received after he became bishop in 681, to mentioning another grant supposedly made by Ecgfrith to Cuthbert in the period of 675–679 (Carrum).[75] The inconsistency itself creates doubt as to the accuracy of the information. This doubt is perhaps further enhanced by the fact that neither of the *Vitae* of Saint Cuthbert indicated a close relationship between Ecgfrith and Cuthbert until his accession to the episcopate. Thus whilst there is evidence for the association of Cuthbert with some of the land holdings identified in the texts of Cuthbert's Lives, such as Carlisle, there is certainly no indication that Ecgfrith had granted lands there. Indeed, as an example Carlisle itself presents specific difficulties when one notes that a charter by which Ecgfrith was said to have granted Carlisle to Cuthbert is an obvious forgery that probably dates to the late eleventh or early twelfth century.[76] These sections of the *Historia de sancto Cuthberto* do not then, lend themselves to authenticity concerning the earlier period. Indeed, nor do they necessarily relate to the later sections of the text which Luisella Simpson has identified as of mid-tenth-century origin. The possibility that Ecgfrith made donations of land to Cuthbert must be questioned.

Having acknowledged this, however, one cannot deny the fact that Ecgfrith had an interest in Cuthbert. Cuthbert's consecration as bishop must have augmented Lindisfarne's status and it is clear that Ecgfrith was an active participant in the making of Cuthbert into a bishop. Indeed, the image of Ecgfrith sailing to the island of Farne with Bishop Trumwine and other powerful men to adjure Cuthbert to accept an episcopal see is one of the few direct links with Lindisfarne that can be found for Ecgfrith.[77] Nonetheless, in the *EH* an inconsistency in Book IV:28 appears to intimate that in the first instance Cuthbert was to be consecrated as bishop of Hexham not Lindisfarne. Thus, when he first mentions the Synod at the River Aln, Bede follows the information as given in both his and the anonymous *Life of St Cuthbert* which states that there Cuthbert was elected to the bishopric of the church of Lindisfarne unanimously.[78] However, he subsequently diverges from his sources, noting that Cuthbert's consecration took place at York and that he was elected first to the see of Hexham. It was only subsequently that he was consecrated as bishop of Lindisfarne and then it appears to have been at Cuthbert's own request rather than Ecgfrith's desire.[79] If Ecgfrith's intention had been to have Cuthbert as his bishop at Hexham this would have taken the limelight off Lindisfarne and given it instead to a Rome-associated church. As to why Ecgfrith felt compelled to ask Cuthbert to be a bishop one can only assume that this particular holy man, despite his monastic origins, was just too saintly to be ignored.

By the end of Ecgfrith's reign, therefore, a monastic environment with the potential for competition had been well and truly established. Wearmouth-Jarrow had a particularly close relationship with the Northumbrian ruling house and Whitby also increasingly seems to have become a site of influence. Lindisfarne was once again being shown some favour, although arguably limited, and Wilfrid's confederation had the wealth to interfere in ecclesiastical matters if not political ones. In this context the critical point to consider is that each of these monasteries represented a collective of the aristocracy. Indeed, they may even have been focal points for particular kin groupings each of which had their own authority in the kingdom. This alone does not necessarily answer the question as to why so many cults and so much literature were generated. It does illustrate, however, the establishment of an ecclesiastical environment in which an unexpected change of regime would result in some vying for control if not primacy among the key monasteries.

ECGFRITH'S SUCCESSORS: MONASTIC APPROVAL AND THE ESTABLISHMENT OF A NEW KING

In the previous sections of this chapter, the extent to which Northumbrian monasteries were both dependent upon the king for support and influenced by the king's own ecclesiastical alignment has been shown. Despite the lack of lay Latin literacy, inherent within the sources produced by the Latin writers is the relationship between the king, particularly Ecgfrith, and specific members of the nobility, albeit those in monastic and ecclesiastical positions. In this relationship it appears to be Ecgfrith who held the balance of power, effectively determining the development of real competition for the collective nobility housed in Lindisfarne, and, to a degree, Iona. The result of this is clear. Any pro-Iona successor to the Northumbrian throne would find himself (with the support of Lindisfarne) in a position of needing both to appease and to make himself legitimate in the eyes of the newly powerful groupings of his predecessor's nobility, especially those in Rome-affiliated monasteries. This is particularly evident in the case of Aldfrith. The need to be seen as legitimate by the ecclesiastical nobility is hinted at in Book III, chapter 6 of the anonymous *Life of St Cuthbert*. Here, the author made it clear that Aelfflaed knew from Cuthbert that Aldfrith was to succeed following Ecgfrith's death.[80] Such a prophetic pronunciation coming from the mouth of Cuthbert reads less like an image of things to come than as a retrospective act of legitimization for a king whose accession had not been the outcome of peaceful events. In the historical record at least it seems that Aldfrith and the monastic house with which he was most closely associated wanted his accession to be remembered (by the ecclesiastical if not the secular audience) as the fulfilment of a prophecy, not as the usurpation by a half-Irish product of Iona. The implication of the need to state this, of course, is that Aldfrith was not initially viewed as a legitimate successor.

This desire for acceptance may also explain the apparent delay in any augmentation of the status of Lindisfarne. Thus, although, as Clare Stancliffe has noted, the period of Aldfrith's reign did witness rival church groupings attempting to achieve pre-eminence in Northumbria, the monastic focus of his reign appears to be Lindisfarne and, to an extent, Iona.[81] Despite Aldfrith's brief reconciliation with Wilfrid and the consequent return of Hexham, Ripon, and York to Wilfrid's authority, at least until Adomnan's adoption of Roman practices, there is little evidence to suggest that Aldfrith's allegiance was not centred upon the Ionan confederation. Yet, the elevation of the cult of Cuthbert under Bishop Eadberht, and the connected composition of the anonymous *Life of St Cuthbert* as well as the production of the Lindisfarne Gospels under his successor Eadfrith, did not occur until a decade of Aldfrith's reign had passed.

This necessity for Northumbrian approval, particularly monastic, is illustrated by the fact that Aldfrith and his councillors exchanged three hides of land with Biscop in return for two silk cloaks which had recently been brought back from Rome.[82] As noted in the first chapter, such an exchange had a highly symbolic nature, indicating in this case an initiation of a relationship between the new king and the previous king's advisor, Biscop. Moreover it is clear that at the beginning of his reign Aldfrith went further than this, arranging with Biscop that he was to receive a further eight hides of land for a copy of the *Cosmographia*, an agreement that finally came to fruition during the abbacy of Ceolfrith.[83] These actions were not meaningless but would have involved tangible ritual and served to function as a sign of acceptance.

Indeed, the acceptance of Wearmouth-Jarrow may also have been behind Adomnan's two visits there and his adoption of Roman practices.

If Aldfrith wished to be viewed as a legitimate Northumbrian king what better way to do it than have the abbot of Iona influenced by one of the royal foundations of the previous king? This is not to deny the persuasiveness of the religious argument as put forward by Ceolfrith but to suggest that political expediency may have played at least some part in this decision. If this link between Aldfrith, Adomnan, and the acceptance of the Northumbrian aristocracy were accurate it would explain in part why Columba is portrayed in an overtly orthodox way. As Marie Herbert has shown, as much as Adomnan wanted to justify his actions to his own monastery he also wished to convince the Northumbrian audience of the universal nature of Columba's sanctity.[84] Of course, the subsequent problem for Adomnan was that the monks at Iona refused to accept him – an outcome that clearly mattered less to Aldfrith than acceptance by his Northumbrian monasteries.

In the first few years of his reign Aldfrith's decision to receive Wilfrid back into the kingdom may also have been driven by his need to placate the nobility at Hexham. Thus, according to the *Life of St Wilfrid* he initially gave the possessions of Hexham to Wilfrid: '*et primum coenobium cum possessionibus adhaerentibus in Hagustaldesiae indulgens*'.[85] Only after an interval of time (*et post interuallum*) did he return him to his see of York and monastery at Ripon.[86] This subsequent act, which involved expelling Ecgfrith's choice of incumbents, one of whom came from Lindisfarne, indicates the extent to which Aldfrith was prepared to be seen as pro-Canterbury. Indeed, by acceding to Theodore's conscience-led desires, Aldfrith maintained the relationship with the archbishop of Canterbury that his half-brother had instigated. He then went on to show himself to be acquiescing to the judgements of Pope Agatho – something even his Rome-friendly relative had not done. (This implies the degree of accomplishment Ecgfrith had achieved in realigning the ecclesiastical policy of Northumbria southwards. His nobility had become inextricably reoriented and for Aldfrith to succeed it was a necessity that he maintained continuity.)

In fact, the nature of Aldfrith's accession may hold the key to the subsequent 'Romanization' of both Lindisfarne and Adomnan. One should note that whilst the anonymous *Life of St Cuthbert* implies a foregone conclusion for the Battle of Nechtansmere, this cannot be taken for granted, nor, it appears, can the fact that the Northumbrian aristocracy, (who had under the auspices of Ecgfrith so fully embraced the Canterbury-Rome Church) would accept the Iona-trained Aldfrith as their king. It is conceivable that to ensure his authority in Northumbria, Aldfrith had to prove to the nobles that he was a fully orthodox Northumbrian. To achieve this Lindisfarne needed to be seen as more Northumbrian than Ionan and St Cuthbert needed to be marketed as an orthodox monk. Essentially what was left of Ionan culture visible to an external audience had to be integrated into mainstream Northumbrian aristocratic, monastic practices.

The first hint of this process of integration can be seen in the actions of Cuthbert's successor, Eadberht. It is clear, for example, that Eadberht undertook a programme of rebuilding at Lindisfarne, removing the reed thatch and covering the walls and the roof with lead.[87] The important point here is that Eadberht's amendments to the building covered up an edifice that had been built using the 'Irish' (should one read Ionan?) method: *more Scottorum*, perhaps using lead made the walls look more like stone.

The second lies in the actual texts of the *Vita Columbae* and the anonymous *Life of St Cuthbert*. As has been commented elsewhere, these two texts exhibit close links in terms of resemblances in vocabulary and themes and it is surely possible that they were produced as part of a single initiative under the auspices of Adomnan and Eadfrith respectively.[88] In this context, what is pertinent, however, is that firstly, the anonymous *Life of St Cuthbert* doctors the image of Cuthbert to give him a Petrine tonsure at Ripon rather than the Ionan one at Melrose, thereby assuring his audience of Cuthbert's Roman credentials.[89] Secondly, Marie Herbert has indicated that Adomnan kept his portrayal of St Columba within the literary context of mainstream catholic sanctity.[90] Essentially, both these texts serve to offer images of orthodox saints (who on closer inspection would actually have followed at least some unorthodox practices). There is a sense in which these saints' lives achieved in textual form what Eadberht had achieved with lead – the conscious covering over of Ionan forms to create an image more amenable to the 'Romanized' monastic aristocracy. Walter Goffart was right, then, to suggest that the anonymous *Life of St Cuthbert* originated to fulfil more than merely the spiritual needs of the community at Lindisfarne.[91] However, his assertion that this *Vita* deliberately made Cuthbert respectable in Wilfridian terms especially with regard to the Petrine tonsure and the Rule of Benedict requires modification.[92] It does appear that the anonymous author has attempted to make Cuthbert more 'respectable' or, more appropriately, less Ionan, but this was for a much broader audience than just Wilfrid's confederation. Whitby and Wearmouth-Jarrow also had a claim to view these themes as important. Cuthbert especially, as Donald Bullough noted, could be seen as a great unifier of the two traditions, freeing Lindisfarne from the historical stigma of unorthodoxy, thereby giving it a greater authority in the Northumbrian church.[93] Evidence, nonetheless, suggests that the actuality in the late seventh-century Lindisfarne community itself, at least in terms of liturgical practice, was a continuation of usage related more to Iona than to the monastic houses of Roman foundation.[94]

Arguably, as well as augmenting the status of Lindisfarne, the anonymous *Life of St Cuthbert* served as a record of the legitimacy of Aldfrith's position aimed at the ecclesiastical aristocracy. This alone implies closeness between the monastery and the king. However, it was only after Aldfrith had secured his position that the status of Lindisfarne could be acceptably raised in Northumbria. Initially, to ensure his position he had to appease the monastic houses that had held authority during the reign of Ecgfrith. Yet within seven years of his accession Aldfrith had the power to deprive Wilfrid's church at Ripon of its territories and possessions and subsequently to expel Wilfrid – by this time acceptance of the nobility at Wilfrid's confederation seems not to have been so crucial.[95] Apart from Wilfrid, Aldfrith's relations with the other Northumbrian royal monasteries appear to have remained good. The appointment of John of Beverley (and Whitby) to Hexham in 687 and the return of Bosa to the see of York (c. 692) perhaps indicates that the fortunes of Whitby, of which noticeably little is said by Bede during Aldfrith's reign, were not significantly decreased. This is certainly suggested by the presence of Aelfflaed at Aldfrith's deathbed.[96] Moreover, the *Life of St Wilfrid* presents the image of a king who linked his ecclesiastical policy, as Ecgfrith had done, closely with the archbishops of Canterbury. By the time of Aldfrith's death Lindisfarne's standing in the Northumbrian monastic milieu had increased but it was not returned to the monopolistic position that it once had. Basically, Ecgfrith's actions had ensured that for his successors to remain in power they would have to maintain a relationship with all the royal monastic sites.

The obligation to maintain a relationship with the monasteries of one's predecessor was not limited only to Aldfrith. Indeed, one cannot help wondering if Eadwulf's decision to refuse to allow Wilfrid's return at the beginning of his reign is indicative of a singular lack of appreciation on Eadwulf's part of the necessity for gaining monastic approval from all the main monastic houses. Arguably he focused only on those closest to the councillors who on this occasion advised him and this ignorance, more than anything, may have resulted in his swift departure.[97]

The importance of the monastic groupings is again made visible in the *Life of St Wilfrid*'s account of the Synod of Nidd. Here the boy-king Osred is portrayed as gathering at the Synod with his chief men, his three bishops, their abbots and the Abbess Aefflead.[98] Although Stephanus fails to identify these three bishops it is hard not to assume they represent John of Beverley – Hexham, Eadfrith – Lindisfarne, and Bosa – York. This line-up is interesting purely for the power dynamic that it indicates: that bishops trained at Whitby still held two of the key sees. Moreover, Aelfflaed's presence shows the power base that her monastery clearly had at the beginning of Osred's reign. Lindisfarne is also represented but Wearmouth-Jarrow, lacking a bishop, as implied in the text, is not. It is apparently upon these groupings that the decision to readmit Wilfrid ultimately falls and the impression one gets is of three powerful aristocratic groupings coming to an agreement about another group's leader. Berhtfrith is, however, also a notable player, noted as being second only to the king: '*Berhtfrithus, secundus a rege princeps*', but his acceptance of Wilfrid as representative of the king is not enough to ensure Wilfrid's return.[99] The bishops, and presumably also their monastic communities, had to agree on it, indicating that in this case at least the wishes of the royal boy (Wilfrid's adopted son) were not enough to secure his return. Also of note in Stephanus' record is the fact that the final decision is recorded as being in terms of the Apostolic judgement and that Wilfrid's leading protagonist in this case is the archbishop of Canterbury, Berhtwald. Here, perhaps, is an indication of the degree to which the ecclesiastical nobility of Northumbria was allied to the 'Roman' Church.

Once again at the beginning of a reign there is evidence that it was not enough for the king just to make decisions. Without the acceptance of the other monastic groups, including Aelfflaed's, these decisions had little authority. Moreover, despite the fact that Wearmouth-Jarrow does not seem to be represented at this Synod, it is still possible that Ceolfrid played a role. Bede, in his metrical *Life of Saint Cuthbert*, welcomed Osred as a new Josiah, implying the acceptance of this monastery too (if not the textual legitimization of a king, who like his father came to power through the defeat of his immediate successor, Eadwulf).[100] Pertinently, Ceolfrid gained land from Osred during his reign, exchanging the land donated by Aldfrith for twenty hides nearer the monastery, again showing the maintenance of connections between the king and this royal foundation.[101]

Essentially, Aldfrith and Osred's (possibly even Eadwulf's) authority on accession depended upon the acceptance of the great monastic houses that, in their turn, played a role in legitimizing the position of the king. These monastic houses did not only represent individuals who wished to remove themselves from the secular world, they were also intricately related to secular aristocratic kin groups. Consequently, assuring their acceptance at the outset of a new reign was important. Whilst the historical record is noticeably bare concerning Osred's immediate successors, Cenred and Osric, this association with the monastic power groupings is the context in which Bede's gift of the *EH* to Ceolwulf should be seen. In 731, following his deposition and return to power, it is more than plausible that Ceolwulf looked to Wearmouth-Jarrow for such support. The support was made tangible in the form of a gift exchange, the highly symbolic action of giving the gift of a book to an individual, one that in its preface publicly acknowledged Ceolwulf as king. In this sense the text itself need not have been produced for a king but became the most appropriate gift to give. This, of course, explains the gift of the product itself but not the initiation or contents of the *EH*.

THE DESIRE FOR MONASTIC SUPERIORITY AS A STIMULATOR OF CULT DEVELOPMENT AND HAGIOGRAPHICAL WRITINGS

It is clear that the narratives of texts such as the anonymous *Life of St Cuthbert* and the *Historia Ecclesiastica* do contain evidence for political, social and economic relationships that existed outside the monastery. It is harder to state that the texts themselves played a role outside the monasteries, other than a predominantly symbolic one. However, hagiographies clearly did play a role in augmenting their monastery's own status within the ecclesiastical community and arguably the inter-monastic rivalry established through the existence of several royal-affiliated centres resulted in an attempt to claim ultimate superiority. In this sense, the Anglo-Saxon Northumbrian monastic *vitae* and *historiae* are evidence for a well-established textual community in which different types of information were being passed between monastic houses in texts produced ostensibly for spiritual purposes. Arguably, this inter-monastic rivalry, established by Ecgfrith and continued in the reigns of his successors, is the immediate context in which the sources were produced. The main method of achieving superiority was for a monastery to indicate that it had the closest associations with Rome, either directly or through Canterbury, in the body of its writings.

The author of the anonymous *Life of St Cuthbert* could only identify Cuthbert with the Roman Church by giving him a Petrine tonsure. The anonymous hagiographer at Whitby, however, could link her monastery directly with the earliest Roman evangelization under Paulinus. Professor Goffart has suggested that the Whitby *Life of St Gregory* was produced in response to claims made by Wilfrid at the Synod of Austerfield contained within Stephanus' *Life of St Wilfrid*.[102] However, the chronology of these two texts cannot be fixed, and whilst the first recension of the *Life of St Wilfrid* may have been written soon after Wilfrid's death, it is equally feasible that the *Life of St Gregory* was produced before 710.[103] Indeed, given the obvious power that Aelfflaed had at the 706 Synod of Nidd, and given also that the early years of Osred represented a minority it is plausible that this period (706–709) would have been the best time for a monastery to produce a text which involved the king of a rival royal family, that is Edwin. As was noted earlier it is inconceivable that a monastery would be able to elevate a royal saint without the permission of the current king unless, of course, that king were a child. It is perhaps also unlikely that augmenting the status of a royal saint in textual form could occur without the king's permission. Possibly, in c. 706, Aelfflaed had enough influence politically to circumvent the approval of the boy-king. Indeed, if Alan Thacker is right concerning Hexham's interest in Oswald being as late as c.700, the *Life of St Gregory*'s image of its own most Christian king could have been stimulated by this rather than any response to the claims of Wilfrid as written in the *Life of St Wilfrid*.[104] Arguably, then, the *Life of St Gregory* came before the *Life of St Wilfrid*, meaning that Wilfrid's claims need to be seen as a response to Whitby rather than the other way round.

Moreover, the appropriation of elements of the anonymous *Life of St Cuthbert* for use in the *Life of St Wilfrid* can be seen as representing a deliberate act of rivalry toward Lindisfarne.[105] Indeed, Goffart went so far as to say that Lindisfarne felt their original *Vita* to have been 'soiled and devalued' through Stephanus' actions.[106] However, the Wilfridian confederation did not settle for merely usurping Lindisfarne and Whitby in terms of association with Rome and the Rule of Benedict; it also appears to have refreshed its interest in a royal cult all of its own, that of St Oswald.[107] By returning its attention to this saint it responded textually to Whitby's assertions of the sanctity of St Edwin (which may, as has been stated, have been instigated in response to Hexham's initial interest in Oswald c.700) and it also claimed ownership of a saint with relics associated with Lindisfarne – effectively cutting Lindisfarne out of this potential status raiser. The point is that one cannot prove conclusively whether or not the Whitby Life responded to an earlier initiative on the part of Hexham concerning Oswald or whether Hexham adopted Oswald in response to Whitby. What is clear is that inter-monastic rivalry did occur and focussed both on the ownership of cults and on the production of texts.

In fact, Wilfrid's claims at Austerfield do not appear merely to have provoked a textual reaction from Whitby. The anonymous *Life of St Ceolfrith* also needs to be seen in this context. Firstly, it is worth being reminded of Wilfrid's claims in chapter 47 of the *Life of St Wilfrid*. He argued that he was the first (after the elders of St Gregory) to have converted all Northumbria to the true Easter and the Petrine tonsure.[108] He also stated that he instructed the Northumbrians in the appropriate choral rite.[109] And, finally, he pointed out that he was responsible for arranging the life of the monks according to the Rule of Benedict, something which no one had previously introduced.[110]

The anonymous writer of the *Life of St Ceolfrith* was not in a position to counteract these claims: Ceolfrid had not been the originator of Roman practices in Northumbria. Yet, as Ian Wood has noticed, there may have been considerable rivalry between Biscop's foundations and Wilfrid's over who was more accurately Benedictine.[111] Indeed, what the anonymous author could and did do was make Ceolfrid seem to be an even more effective proponent of the monastic life than Wilfrid. Thus the *Life of St Ceolfrith* established Ceolfrid as the man who, in Northumbria, had been more knowledgeable than anyone else in matters monastic. For example, Ceolfrid is shown as travelling to Kent to satisfy his desire for the fullest possible understanding of the rules of monastic life.[112] Following his return from Kent and East Anglia to Ripon it is noted that there was no one of that day more learned in either the ecclesiastic or monastic rule, by inference not even Wilfrid.[113] The anonymous author then follows this statement with what looks like a slight on those who do not remain humble in their knowledge or nobility of name.[114] One cannot help thinking that this is a direct reference to what could be viewed as Wilfrid's lack of humility as demonstrated in his speech at the Synod of Austerfield. Immediately after this statement the *Life of St Ceolfrith* reiterates the extent to which Ceolfrid endeavoured to observe the monastic rule.[115]

Benedict Biscop, too, is portrayed as being second to none in his knowledge of monastic rules.[116] Yet even though he was most learned in matters of monastic discipline he called on Ceolfrid to strengthen further the observance at his monastery of Wearmouth.[117] The inference of their superiority is impossible to miss, for even though Wilfrid is mentioned in the early chapters of the *Life of St Ceolfrith*, it at no times ascribes to him such a depth of knowledge concerning monastic life. The *Life of St Ceolfrith* continues to emphasize the extent of the regularity of Ceolfrid's monastic observance, noting that it was so strict that the monks at Wearmouth could not bear it.[118] He is also noted for his own observance of the monastic rule and the encouragement of others to do the same at Jarrow.[119] Furthermore, the *Life of St Ceolfrith* makes it clear that Ceolfrid's appointment as abbot over both monasteries was made in accordance with the Rule of Benedict (at least in terms of appointing an individual for his abilities rather than because he was a relative).[120] The importance of Ceolfrid's regular observance is therefore a recurrent theme in the text and should be viewed as a direct response to Wilfrid's claims concerning the Rule of Benedict at the Synod of Austerfield.

The anonymous author also made attempts to elucidate the Roman aspects of life at Wearmouth-Jarrow, such as Biscop's trips to Rome, the introduction of chant and the papal privileges (chapters 9, 10, 15, 20), but until Ceolfrid's final journey to Rome the overriding impression of the *Life of St Ceolfrith* is that it was produced to augment the status of monastic observance at Wearmouth-Jarrow at the expense of Wilfrid's confederation.

For Walter Goffart the production of Bede's prose *Life of St Cuthbert* also occurred as a hostile reaction to the *Life of St Wilfrid*.[121] Indeed, given Stancliffe's observations concerning Bede's reworking of the earlier text it does appear that Bede was trying to make Cuthbert a much more 'Roman' saint than the previous anonymous author had achieved. Thus, as Stancliffe notes, Bede depicted his Cuthbert by drawing upon images found in Augustine and Gregory, essentially viewing Cuthbert as a mix of active and contemplative in a manner associated more with the Roman monastic model than the Martinian one.[122] Arguably, Bede was much more successful in Romanizing Cuthbert than his anonymous predecessor and it is because of this that the author of the later *Vita Alcuini* could falsely assert that Cuthbert was a man who formed a link in the chain of tradition that passed from Pope Gregory, through Augustine and Benedict.[123]

It is questionable to what extent this text raised Lindisfarne's status as much as it did Wearmouth-Jarrow's. For Professor Goffart, Lindisfarne's request to Bede and the subsequent production of the *Vita* represents a reorienting of priorities in terms of ecclesiastical affinities for Wearmouth-Jarrow. However, one needs to remember that throughout the 720s Bede continued to produce biblical commentaries for Acca, suggesting that any orientation towards Lindisfarne was far from being mutually exclusive. In fact, Lindisfarne's request to Wearmouth-Jarrow should perhaps be seen as a reorientation of its ecclesiastical priorities. Firstly, one needs to remember that the status of Wearmouth-Jarrow would have increased dramatically following the association of Ceolfrith with Nechtan, king of the Picts and the subsequent conversion of the Picts to Roman traditions. Secondly, this monastery's status may have gained even greater heights because of Wearmouth-Jarrow's increasingly close relationship to Canterbury. Evidence suggests, for example, that Bede was receiving materials from Canterbury, if not Rome, during the late 710s and the 720s and that Nothelm's first visit (surely an honour) took place in 716–25.[124] Thirdly, David Kirby has alluded to the possibility that the episcopal succession at Lindisfarne following the death of Eadfrith was problematic.[125] This, plus Bede's own reputation, may have led to Wearmouth-Jarrow being viewed as an important ally by Lindisfarne.[126] In this sense, the gift of a representation of their own saint, Romanized by the esteemed Bede, produced in a monastery with unequivocal Roman credentials and a direct link to the bishop of Hexham, was a highly symbolic act, indicating Lindisfarne's movement towards Wearmouth-Jarrow rather than Wearmouth-Jarrow's inclination towards Lindisfarne.[127]

Wearmouth-Jarrow's textual responses to Stephanus' claims concerning Wilfrid in the *Life of St Wilfrid* were not limited to the rewriting of the *Life of St Cuthbert*, however. The focus on Roman and regular monastic observance in Bede's *History of the Abbots* needs to be included in the list of texts aimed at raising the status of its monastery higher than those of the Wilfridian confederation. Whilst the *Life of St Ceolfrith* focused on Ceolfrid's regular observance, Bede's text brought to life the extent to which Benedict Biscop was an unadulterated Roman and Wearmouth-Jarrow an incontestable Roman foundation. Indeed, within the *History of the Abbots* Bede linked his monastery to Rome so conclusively that the reader would be left in no doubt of its orthodoxy. Therefore, he showed it to be founded by an individual with no apparent links to Iona whatsoever. In chapter 2 Bede recorded that Biscop (unlike Wilfrid) went straight to Rome in search of his spiritual learning, a trip that became a relatively regular feature of his life.[128] In chapter 3, Biscop was associated directly with the Rome-chosen Archbishop, Theodore, having been placed by the Pope himself to act as a guide and, also, becoming abbot of the monastery of St Peter at Canterbury.[129] In chapter 5 Biscop was recorded as having built a stone church in the Roman fashion at Wearmouth.[130] In chapter 6 he was shown returning from one of his sojourns to Rome accompanied by both the cantor John and a letter of monastic privileges from Pope Agatho.[131] From the outside Biscop and Wearmouth-Jarrow are seen to be affiliated to Rome. Indeed, the extent of this narrated connection led Patrick Wormald to conclude that Bede's version of Biscop's horizons was considerably limited and overly stressed the perspective that it was only really Rome that counted in his making.[132] This was a deliberate attempt to edify his institution within an environment where a relationship with orthodoxy was viewed as highly meritorious. However, this preference on Bede's part should not be viewed in the context of the monasteries outside his own alone. Ian Wood has noted that in his *History of the Abbots* Bede subtly changed the emphasis of the *Life of St Ceolfrith* to present Biscop's Wearmouth in an even more favourable light than Ceolfrid's Jarrow, implying perhaps that the issue of monastic superiority, in textual form at least, extended into the relationship between Wearmouth and its sister house.[133]

In the hagiographical texts produced in eighth-century Northumbria, there appears to be a common theme of association with Rome, with each monastery claiming a closer connection than the previous one. Essentially, an affinity with Rome either directly through travel or indirectly in the form of links to the first evangelists, regular monastic observance or portrayals using textual allusions to Roman-identified sources increased the standing of a particular monastery in the ecclesiastical community. Interestingly, this process of competition appears not to have been instigated primarily by the production of the *Life of St Wilfrid*, as Professor Goffart believes, but may have had its origins in the founding of Wearmouth-Jarrow by Ecgfrith and the elevation of Edwin by Whitby. The subsequent initiatives taken by Adomnan and Eadfrith to make Aldfrith, Columba and Lindisfarne acceptable to the Northumbrian aristocracy (as reorientated by Ecgfrith) provided the first textual responses to Ecgfrith's activities. In their turn, these responses led to a production of hagiography, the extent of which was not witnessed elsewhere in eighth-century Anglo-Saxon England, as each respective monastery attempted to maintain its profile and raise its status in the ecclesiastical hierarchy.

Chapter 3
Bede's Agenda Revisited:
Monastic Superiority in the
Ecclesiastical History

THE PREVIOUS CHAPTER ATTEMPTED TO INDICATE THE REASON why so many cults and related texts were developed in the late seventh and eighth centuries. As was seen, the desire for augmented status did not just manifest itself in the interactions between the kings and their monasteries, it is also evident in the internal construct of the narratives of the texts that were produced. This chapter aims to examine Bede's desire to enhance the status of Wearmouth-Jarrow in the text of the *EH* through a sophisticated method of textual manipulation, omission, and apparent 'discretion'. To do this it will look at Bede's depictions of the monastic foundations and founders of Northumbria, particularly Iona/Lindisfarne – Columba and Aidan; Whitby – Hilda and Aelfflead; Ripon, Hexham, and York – Wilfrid.

Alan Thacker argued that in his *EH* Bede portrayed the Ionan Irish evangelists to Northumbria in an essentially positive light, but that their error concerning Easter observance needed to be accounted for.[1] To do this, Thacker stated that Bede played down this error and stressed how similar their methods in general were to that of the orthodox Roman approaches. Thacker concludes that Bede's images of the Ionan missionaries and Iona itself were essentially defensive but favourable. Goffart too has suggested that Bede was pro-Irish in order to side against the power of Wilfrid.[2] The text of the *EH*, however, indicates that these arguments are not as firmly founded as the authors have suggested. The first significant mention of Irish Christian practice occurs in Book II:4 and the chapter itself places the Irish firmly within the context of a transgression from orthodoxy. Thus Bede notes that Archbishop Laurence 'came to realize that in Ireland…the life and profession of the people was not in accordance with church practice especially concerning Easter.[3] Moreover, in this chapter Bede chooses to include Laurence's letter to the Irish bishops and abbots, making it unequivocal that the Irish were no better than the British in their observances. Such a comparison hardly suggests that Bede was predisposed towards the Irish.

From the outset of his description of the Irish, then, Bede makes it quite clear that they were in error and chose to remain so. After all it is clear from subsequent episodes that Laurence's letter fell on deaf ears. He continues this theme in chapter 19 of Book II, this time in the context of the epistles from Pope Honorius and Pope-elect John. Thacker argues that Bede makes it clear that the Irish were not Quartodecimans and views this qualification and limiting of the heresy amongst the Irish as Bede playing down the error.[4] Goffart takes this slightly further, commenting that Bede refuted the charge that the Irish were Quartodeciman schismatics in order to correct Stephanus' accusation.[5] To deal with this latter point first, it is not necessary that Bede was reacting to the portrayal in the *Life of St Wilfrid* in an attempt to abase the cult of Wilfrid in this chapter. Rather it could well be that Bede required his audience to have accurate information for its own sake. Secondly, whilst qualifying that the Irish were not Quartodecimans, his own text ensured that the Irish unorthodoxy was an indelible part of their ecclesiastical history and, furthermore, that when faced with the 'true practice' 'some of the Irish' resolutely refused to change. It is conspicuous that Bede does not leave his accusation crudely inaccurate (unlike his counterpart at Ripon) but by including these letters he left the reader in no doubt that those Irish who continued to follow a different Easter did so knowing that they were in error. As Cowdrey notes, these issues 'carried deep and grave implications ... a deliberate refusal amounted to a withholding of obedience that was due from all Christians to St Peter'.[6]

However, it is perhaps Bede's subsequent apparently controlled approach to St Columba that should alert us to his agenda. Thacker has stated that Bede's treatment of Iona was 'defensive'. Nevertheless, there is a clear tension in Bede's discussion in Book III:4. Firstly, although Bede opens by stressing Columba's monastic vocation, he gives him no superlative epithet and swiftly changes the focus from Columba to St Ninian and the southern Picts.[7] In this passage Bede is at pains to emphasize Ninian's orthodoxy. This emphasis, given Bede's predilection for stressing British inactivity on the missionary front, hardly indicates that he was overwhelmed with respect for Columba. Rather, it suggests that by thoughtful and deliberate placing of his reference to Ninian in the vignette of St Columba, Bede was subtly illustrating the contrast between the orthodox man of Whithorn and the unorthodoxy of Columba, Iona, and the northern Picts.

Moreover, if one examines closely the epithets Bede uses to describe Columba there is a conspicuous absence of the usual superlatives that he gives to saints and a noticeable reticence on his part to give the impression of a saintly individual who lived a holy life. Thus, he writes of him as a 'priest and abbot' and a monk 'in life no less than habit' [*presbyter et abbas habitu et uita monachi insignis*] and as the 'first teacher of the Faith to the Picts' [*primus doctor fidei Christianae transmontanis Pictis*].[8] It could be argued that this is evidence of Bede's lack of knowledge concerning Columba. However, Bede fails to bestow upon Columba the more usual superlative epithets he normally reserves for his saints whether he includes details of their lives in the text of the *EH* or not. For example, of the other two saints he mentions in the context of this chapter on Columba, Bede calls Ninian, 'that most reverend and holy man' [*reuerentissimo et sanctissimo uiro*] and of Egbert he says, 'that most reverend and holy father' [*reuerentissimo et sanctissimo patre*] and that he was 'most learned in the Scriptures' [*doctissimus in scripturis*].[9] Nor is the absence of eulogistic epithets determined by Columba being Irish, for Bede is quick to note that St Fursa was a 'holy man', 'renowned in word and deed'.[10] Consequently one must question how likely it was that Bede knew so little about Columba that he failed even to designate his sanctity through such simple laudatory phrases. It is true Bede himself seems to imply that his knowledge concerning Columba was limited: 'Some written records of his life and teachings are said to have been preserved by his disciples. Whatever he was himself...'.[11] Indeed, Wallace-Hadrill has interpreted this as Bede stating that though he had heard of written records of Columba's life kept by Iona he had not seen them.[12] Colgrave also assumed that Bede did not know of Adomnan's *Vita*.[13] One could infer from this that Bede really was unaware of information on Columba. Nevertheless, one needs to remember that Bede was not dependent on Adomnan alone; after all, any earlier copy of Columba's *Vita* may have been held at either Melrose or Lindisfarne upon which he could have drawn had he wanted.[14] Moreover, Bede's sources of information were not just literary and, given Adomnan's visit to Jarrow in 689, the appointment of bishops to the see of Lindisfarne from Iona, and the other links between Northumbria and Iona, it is rather hard to believe that Bede's knowledge of Columba was so limited, unless he specifically chose to remain ignorant (a fact which in itself would indicate Bede's prejudice). Furthermore, the sentence that begins: '*Uerum qualiscumque fuerit ipse*' [Whatever he himself ...], in the context of this paragraph, could easily be interpreted as a disdainful comment on Columba's authority. Thus Bede was insinuating that 'despite what Columba was' (i.e. a monk in error) his successors did maintain and were distinguished in their monastic life. He does, of course, go on to reiterate that they too persisted in an irregular observance of Easter.

In Bede's account of Columba, it is argued that there is an implicit but nonetheless perceptible lack of customary enthusiasm for his saintly attributes that seems to be less connected to Columba's Irishness, as to Columba himself. If this is so, one needs to bear it in mind when analysing the passage on Columba, for it implies that Bede intended (if not expected) a more negative reading of this episode than either Goffart or Thacker have intimated. Thus, it is possible that Bede's reasons for mentioning the unusual constitution of Iona were not entirely positive ones. He states:

> 'This island always has an abbot for its ruler who is a priest, to whose authority the whole kingdom, including even bishops, have to be subject. This unusual arrangement follows the example of their first teacher...'[15]

It would seem that Bede included this information to throw further into relief the point that Columba and Iona stood outside the universal church and, that, for Bede, this needed to be emphasized. Certainly, in this case, even Thacker has to concede that evidence from Adomnan's *Vita Columbae*, 'prompts the suspicion that the constitution of Iona may have been less odd than Bede thought' (or perhaps more accurately, 'would like his readers to believe').[16] Again, given the inter-monastic contacts, it is hard to maintain the thought that Bede was unaware of his over-exaggeration of the situation.[17]

From this, then, there appears to be a sub-textual dissonance within the depiction of Columba and the constitution of Iona, and it seems to be caused by Bede's disapproval of this saint. As Campbell noted, in his *Commentary on Samuel*, Bede made it explicit that it is wrong publicly to denounce priests (even evil ones).[18] Yet he also knew that any post-Theodorian studying his text would see the clear contradiction between Ionan practice and the Theodorian diocesan arrangements. In this case, Bede did not make an overt criticism but given his stance on denouncing clerics one would hardly expect him to. Nevertheless, the expression in writing of such an irregularity was a tacit recognition of an unfavourable judgement – which rather than doing 'the best' for Iona, actually merely enhanced the sense of Ionan error.

Bede qualifies this point in his depiction of events at the Synod of Whitby. When examining this episode, Goffart has argued that Bede removed all trace of condescension on the part of Oswiu towards Columba, which, he argues, Stephanus intimated in the *Life of St Wilfrid*.[19] He stresses that Bede shifted the focus of the condescension from Oswiu to Wilfrid, thereby emphasizing Wilfrid's insolence rather than being a comment of direct disapproval of Columba. However, the above interpretation of Bede's portrayal of Columba and Iona hints that Bede's intention was actually to undermine Columba's authority rather than just to abase Wilfrid. Thus Bede has Wilfrid assert that the Lord would deny knowing Columba and his followers if they chose to remain in error. Also, he has Wilfrid say:

> 'do you think that a handful of people in one corner of the remotest of islands is to be preferred to the universal Church of Christ which is spread throughout the world? And even *if* that Columba of yours – yes, and ours too, *if* he belonged to Christ was a holy man of mighty works...'20

The 'ifs' have been deliberately italicized to denote that they should be read with the implication that there was some question as to whether Columba actually belonged to Christ and from this, whether or not he was universally accepted as a saint. The contempt in these words is Bede's. Basically, he used Wilfrid in this instance as an agent to air his own views on the subject. By moving the focus from the lips of Oswiu to those of a saintly bishop (however much personal dislike for him Bede felt) the words gained authority – for the words of a saint carried far more spiritual weight than the words of a king. The words that Bede placed in Wilfrid's mouth epitomized his own scorn for the Ionans. In fact, in comparison, Stephanus' account is far less condescending concerning Iona and Columba than the consistent slights that seem to pervade Bede's narrative.

Throughout his discussion of Columba and Ionan religious practice there is an incongruence. He could not omit an individual and a monastery that played so crucial a role in the establishment of Northumbrian Christianity, nor could he encourage his readers to imitate Columba and Iona's unorthodoxy. But nor could he openly criticize a monk-priest-saint. What the reader is left with, upon closer inspection of the material, is a sense that within the limits of Bede's own 'discretion' he deliberately set out to undermine the spiritual authority of Iona.

Such an undermining of spiritual authority through a direct association with irregular practice can also be seen in Bede's portrayal of Aidan and his successors. Immediately following the chapter on St Columba, Bede opens the next narrative episode with the words:

'Such was the island, such the community, from which Aidan was sent to the English people.'[21]

Standing alone one could read these words as an implication of the greatness of Iona. However, when taken in the context of the paragraphs that precede it (i.e. that an unorthodox reckoning of Easter persisted amongst the community of Iona for 150 years and was only relinquished in 715), this seemingly innocuous connective phrase appears to be much less innocent. The emphasis is surely not 'what a great monastery' Aidan came from, but rather that the community from which Aidan came was in error and stood outside the universal church. Essentially, this sentence continued to establish that Aidan was attached to a monastic background of dissension.

In actuality Bede goes to considerable lengths to ensure that his audience cannot forget this fact. Thus, though Bede introduces Aidan as 'a man of outstanding gentleness, piety and moderation' [*summae mansuetudinis et pietatis ac moderaminis*], he hastily qualifies the point by noting that Aidan's zeal for God was not entirely according to knowledge [*quamuis non plene secundum scientiam*].[22] This sentence is then followed by a clarification that the issue of his fault was, of course, the celebration of Easter. Indeed, here Bede persists in expressing the inauspicious fact of apparent Ionan ignorance with the words: '*Quod an uerum sit, peritus quisque facillime cognoscit*'.[23] This sentence hardly reads as the words of an individual making excuses for a particular circumstance. Rather, given Bede's oft-noted distinction for discretion, one cannot help concluding that this was the nearest to an insult that he could get.

Throughout the sections of the text where Bede elaborates about Aidan he constantly reminds the reader of his error. Accordingly, after four chapters on Aidan's miracles (Book III: 14, 15, 16, 17) the observer is again faced with exposition on Aidan's Easter custom. Indeed, here one cannot help thinking that Bede, having spent so much time on attributes worth imitating, felt it was absolutely imperative that his audience did not forget Aidan's irregularity, emphasizing with some force that it was something he heartily detested: '*immo hoc multum detestans*'.[24] Again in Book III:25 Aidan is mentioned in the context of the Easter issue, and whilst Bede makes it clear that this particular unorthodoxy was 'patiently tolerated' during Aidan's lifetime, he makes it equally obvious that it was intolerable after his death.[25]

Nevertheless, where Aidan is concerned, there does appear to be a discernible tension in the text because it is hard not to infer that despite this issue Bede respected him. Yet, when examining the text one should remember that Bede's construction of the positives in regard to Aidan are inherently safe images, attainable to his readers, qualities worth imitating.[26]

Inasmuch as Bede appears subjectively biased towards Aidan, it should not be overlooked that his characterizations are textual constructs and, in fact, it is only after Bede has thoroughly established his point concerning Ionan religious observance that he chose to move onto this fairly innocuous narrative portrayal of Aidan. Such descriptions are not necessarily paradoxical. Rather, they cover two different aims of Bede's writing. When dealing with the Easter controversy Bede sought to guarantee that it was remembered that an unacceptable transgression of practice was persistently maintained at Iona and then, consequently, at Lindisfarne, thereby undermining the spiritual authority of the Ionan confederation. However, he also desired to provide his audience with appropriate models of behaviour to which it was worth aspiring. As a result of Aidan's closeness to the Northumbrian ruling house and his local status as a saint, Bede would have found it difficult to omit any mention of him. Once he had secured his initial point (which he had done so effectively in Book III: 3,4,5) there was no reason for him to avoid returning to the task he had established for himself in the Preface. At the same time Bede's fairly constant reiteration served to maintain the link between Iona and Aidan and may have been intended to remind readers that the early community at Lindisfarne, though in some ways propitious, did not have the same orthodox authority as monasteries without the connection (especially perhaps Wearmouth-Jarrow).

It may be true that where Aidan was concerned Bede offered a positive image and even attempted to explain Aidan's obvious error, but such acceptance is not present when he discusses Aidan's successors. For example, it was noted earlier that in his portrayal of Aidan in III:25, it is clear that 'patient toleration' of Aidan's practice was acceptable whilst he lived because he was a saint. However, the implication of this statement could well be that it was unacceptable in his successors who were not saints. Error could and had to be tolerated in those already known for their sanctity but this was not the same for those who followed them. In this sense it was not Aidan who was held accountable by Bede but individuals such as Finan and Colman who chose to maintain the error in full knowledge that they were doing so. Consequently, in his comments on Finan he notes how controversy arose over Finan's intransigence when confronted by Ronan.[27] Of Colman's actions at the Synod of Whitby too, Bede notes that he refused to be persuaded by the arguments of the orthodox Wilfrid.[28] Aidan had avoided such controversy but his successors, when faced with disputation, refused to concede that they were in the wrong. When reading of Iona (and its confederate house of Lindisfarne before the Synod of Whitby) it appears that Bede was intentionally attempting to weaken its authority in terms of its historical past.

In fact, on closer inspection of the *EH* it is clear that the Ionan confederation were not the only monastic sites that Bede subtly undermined. In one sense, by so conclusively establishing the depths of the Ionan error Bede managed to taint any of the monasteries subsequently founded before the Synod of Whitby using personnel either from Iona or, in the Northumbrian context, Lindisfarne. Indeed, Bede is at pains to remind the reader of these contacts, noting, for example, that in instituting his monastery at Lastingham, Cedd introduced religious observances according to the usage of Lindisfarne where he had been educated.[29] Given that Bede had clarified in no uncertain terms that these customs were questionable, the implication of this statement is obvious. Again, however, Bede tempers his inherent criticism by showing Cedd to be an upright, holy and wise man, '*uirum sanctum et sapientem probumque moribus*', who chose for his monastery a remote site, and who had intercessionary powers after his death.[30] From a cursory reading of this chapter, Cedd's spiritual authority and that of his monastery seems to be in no doubt. The reader, however, is not to forget the association with Lindisfarne and by implication what that entails. A similar conclusion can perhaps be drawn of Gilling (cf. III:24) and any of the other Northumbrian monasteries founded by drawing upon Lindisfarne before 664. Of course, given Lindisfarne's monopoly before Ecgfrith, Bede was not in a position to do otherwise than record the links ,but the way he does this ensures that the observer knows just how unorthodox some of the religious observances of the Ionan confederation were.

It is apparent from the narrative concerning Fursa that Bede's treatment of the Irish before 664 is not entirely uniform. In his portrayal of St Fursa Bede offers an indisputably favourable image of an Irish missionary who, having come to East Anglia in the 630s, must still have been practising customs in error of the Roman tradition. Nonetheless, Bede does not hint at this. Rather he focuses his vignette on noticing Fursa's virtues and his missionary activities,[31] on Fursa's learning ('*modicam lectionibus sacris simul et monasticis exhibebat disciplinis*') and on his vision of the angels showing him the fires of falsehood, covetousness, discord, and injustice, which consume the world.[32] He appears equally to praise Fursa's monastery at Cnobheresburg, noting that it was pleasantly situated on land given to him by the saintly King Sigeberht and subsequently endowed with even finer buildings and gifts by Anna and his nobles.[33] The absence of any insinuation of Fursa's possible Irish unorthodoxy is particularly well illustrated if one compares him with Bede's image of Aidan. Aidan, like Fursa, was an Irish missionary given land by a king on which to build a monastery and from which to evangelize. However, as has already been shown, from the outset Aidan is introduced within the context of his error and the reader is consistently reminded of it. (This contradicts Alan Thacker's image of Aidan and Fursa as models of orthodox holiness.[34] Aidan may well be holy, his virtues inculcated by the Church fathers, but his is a sanctity not without its unorthodoxy. The picture of Fursa, on the other hand, is noticeable for its lack of any irregularities.)

One could argue that because Bede had shown the existence of this unorthodoxy he relied on his audience transferring through association such non-conformity to Fursa. He certainly appears to have engineered such an inference when discussing other houses linked to Lindisfarne. However, as Fursa's monastery was an independent foundation without any stated Columban connection, one cannot help thinking that Bede would not have left his point implicit and, had he wanted his audience to know of unorthodoxy, he would have reiterated Irish irregularities. His omission in this case, then, could well be deliberate. This notwithstanding one could also suggest that as Bede's source for Fursa, the *Life of Saint Fursa*, did not dwell upon any unorthodoxies he was just following his evidence.[35] Bede, however, having outlined Archbishop Laurence's concerns about Irish practice, cannot have failed to notice that by implication it was likely that Fursa followed Irish customs and that at least some of these customs were contrary to Rome.

Perhaps the key to understanding this inconsistency is the geographical location of the saints and monasteries in question. Iona and, more particularly, Lindisfarne were competitors for the patronage of the Northumbrian kings. Cnobheresburg in East Anglia was not. In the *EH* Bede made a concerted attempt to remind his audience that the initial foundations of both Iona and Lindisfarne, rivals to his own monastery at Wearmouth in terms of patronage and spiritual authority in Northumbria, were fundamentally unorthodox (despite the apparent sanctity of their founders). This is in stark contrast to Bede's portrayal elsewhere of his own monastery, as shall be shown later, which he portrays as conspicuously orthodox in all regards. Beyond the geographical proximity of the Northumbrian kingdom Bede could afford to praise other monasteries and their saints more, so Fursa is glossed over as a model of holiness, his monastery (for as long as it existed) a model of a royal foundation. The implication of this argument is, of course, that in the text of the *EH* Bede appears to be motivated by monastic rivalry, subtly debasing the Ionan confederation as part of a broader attempt to increase the superiority of his own monastery.

One of Bede's underlying agendas, therefore, may have been the desire to play down the status of other Northumbrian monasteries whilst, as an ecclesiastical historian, being bound to include their saints and some of their traditions. This is important when one considers attempts to elucidate the hidden agenda in Bede's *EH*. Goffart has argued that the *EH* was essentially a piece of ecclesiastical rhetoric produced as a direct response to Stephanus' *Life of St Wilfrid*, relating in particular to the metropolitan status of York.[36] Kirby, on the other hand, places the initiation of the production of the *EH* far more amidst the aims of Albinus and Canterbury rather than Wilfrid and York.[37] What both have in common is a focus on episcopal rather than monastic authority. Though one cannot deny the extent of the influence of episcopal politics within Anglo-Saxon Northumbria, one needs to remember that the rise in the cult of the saints and the consequent textual production that accompanied it was predominantly a monastic affair and, as was shown in the previous chapter, had far more to do with the relationship between the monasteries and their respective royal patrons than just with episcopal needs. A hidden monastic agenda in Bede's *historiae* texts is therefore more than likely.

If this is so, one would expect to find such an undermining of other monastic houses in Northumbria in the *EH*. In the preceding chapter it was suggested that Whitby in the late 670s and early 680s was being established, under the direction of Ecgfrith, as a monastic royal centre with a conscious shift taking place towards a more 'Roman' image. The increasingly close relationship between Ecgfrith, Theodore, and Hilda as evidenced by Ecgfrith's choice of Bosa as bishop of York in Wilfrid's place in 678, the emphasis in the hagiographical material of Hilda's relationship to Edwin and baptism by Paulinus, the revelation and subsequent translation of Edwin's relics under the auspices of Aelfflaed, and the later production of a *vita* concerning Gregory the Great, all intimate that Whitby's identification with the Ionan faction in 664 had been de-emphasized and Whitby's loyalties reoriented. Nonetheless, in Bede's portrayal of Hilda and Whitby there are a number of inconsistencies that suggest Bede might have deliberately been leaving the reader with a sense of ambiguity concerning this change.

In his portrayal of Hilda, Bede clearly creates a tension for the reader. Firstly, before one even reads the vignette of Hilda's life, Bede has identified her with the anti-Wilfridian, pro-Ionan faction of the Synod held in her monastery in 664: '*Hilda abbatissa cum suis in parte Scottorum*'.[38] Secondly, in his sketch of Hilda's abbatial role at Hartlepool he makes an incontrovertible association between her and Aidan. Thus, it was Bishop Aidan who called her from East Anglia ('*Deinde ab Aidano episcopo patriam reuocata*'), initially to a site on the Wear and then to Hartlepool.[39] Moreover, the rule she set about establishing there was in all respects like that which she had been taught by many learned men, particularly Aidan ('*mox hoc regulari uita per omnia, prout a doctis uiris discere poterat ordinare curabat. Nam et episcopus Aidan...*').[40] Bede also records that the rule Hilda subsequently established at Whitby was the same as at Hartlepool – by implication associating it with the Ionan/Lindisfarne tradition. Here again would seem to be Bede's insinuation of unorthodoxy in the foundation of the way of life at Whitby with, one assumes, the attendant undermining of its status. Yet at the same time links with Edwin and Paulinus are recorded at the beginning of this chapter, as is Hilda's desire to pursue her vocation in Frankia, and (as with Aidan) she is a model of virtue. The apparent ambiguities of loyalty in Bede's portrayal of Hilda led Wallace-Hadrill to conclude that this account was not consciously pro-Celtic.[41] At one level he was correct in this observation – the account is not pro-Celtic. Arguably the references to Hilda's connections with the Synod of Whitby and Aidan are, rather, a conscious effort on Bede's part to taint yet another great Northumbrian monastic house with a stigma he went to great lengths to show his own did not have.

In this context Bede's reticence to indicate the apparently close relations between Theodore and Hilda in the late 670s is also pertinent. In his narrative concerning Hilda one could only link Theodore indirectly to Hilda through the bishops her monastery produced. Thus Bede notes that Oftfor, in his desire to reach greater heights of scriptural learning, went to Kent to join Archbishop Theodore.[42] However, the implication of the *Life of St Wilfrid*'s chapter concerning Pope John's letter of judgement to Aethilred and Aldfrith concerning Wilfrid was that Hilda and Theodore had a more direct relationship.[43] If Bede had made more of this shift in Whitby's orientation towards Canterbury's desires, its 'orthodox connection' would have been more visible and its apparent Ionan/Lindisfarne taint diminished. Of course, one could argue that Bede was merely being discreet to protect his image of Theodore who, after all, was judged against by the Pope on this occasion. Alternatively, one could posit the theory that had Bede mentioned these events, it would have stressed rather than de-emphasized Hilda's pro-Ionan sympathies connecting her emissaries to Rome with a vendetta begun because 'her side' was defeated at the Synod by Wilfrid in 664. Nonetheless, it is more plausible that in 678 Hilda had the vested interest of her newly consecrated bishop, Bosa, at heart and was, in fact, supporting Theodore's aims of dividing large episcopal sees rather than attacking the pro-Roman Wilfrid. Essentially, by introducing apparent inconsistencies in terms of royal and episcopal connections into the description of Hilda, Bede, as he had done with Aidan, offered the reader an image of a virtuous saint with one small but important flaw. This flaw by association introduced an element of unorthodoxy into the history of the monastery that at the same time augmented the authority of any monastery that did not have it. Underneath Bede's models of virtuous behaviour lies a thinly-veiled theme of monastic hierarchies, with his own firmly placed at the top.[44]

Bede's treatment of Whitby as a monastic competitor whose status, if compared with his own, needed to be played down was not limited purely to Hilda and her pro-Ionan connections. The absence of any acknowledgement on Bede's part of a cult of the saint-king Edwin at Whitby is also part of his tendency to minimize Whitby's authority. This statement implies agreement with Goffart that Bede did know of the Whitby *Life of St Gregory* but chose, except for two stories contained within it, to ignore it.[45] It is arguable that anxieties concerning Bede's knowledge of this text, aroused by the omission of the English traditions surrounding Gregory the Great in the *EH* are easily calmed. Such omissions relate less to Bede's dearth of knowledge of the text and more to his desire to link his narrative concerning Gregory with the Roman sources at his command in the library of Wearmouth-Jarrow. In essence, the Whitby *Vita* lacked authority in terms of being a credible witness for Gregory, and credible, if not always accurate, witnesses were, as shall be shown in the next chapter, crucial to Bede's method of *historia* construction. Thus, rather than drawing on 'new' traditions about Gregory, Bede depended instead on the *Liber Pontificalis*, some of Gregory's own works, particularly his epistle to Leander of Seville which he prefixed to the *Moralia*, and also on the Prologue to Gregory's *Dialogues*.[46] However, whilst a Whitby author may not have seemed an authentic enough witness for Gregory, the same cannot be said of Edwin. This would suggest that Bede disregarded Edwin's sanctification for a reason.

To identify this reason one need only return to some of Goffart's observations concerning Edwin. As he commented, 'Edwin epitomized the earliest Roman evangelization of Northumbria'.[47] As such, his cult at Whitby, if fostered within the *EH*, would have overshadowed by priority not so much Wilfrid's acts (as Goffart thought) as the deeds of Biscop and the status of the monastery Bede wished to be viewed as 'Northumbria's most Roman' house. In this understanding of Bede's portrayal of the initial Northumbrian evangelists one can get a hint as to why James the Deacon's role in the Christianizing of Northumbria is understated in the *EH*. Goffart has intimated that James is of importance to Bede, who uses him to offer a 'gripping proof of continuity' of Roman practice in Northumbria.[48] In fact, there is nothing legendary about Bede's picture of James and Wallace-Hadrill was drawn to conclude that, for Bede, James merited no more than an affectionate reference.[49] Yet James had all the qualities of a potential hero for the *EH*. He was, according to Bede, a man of industry and nobility in Christ and the Church ('*uirum utique industrium ac nobilem in Christo et in ecclesia*'), a saintly evangelist who remained at York following Edwin's death and Paulinus' return to Kent and an individual who kept the true Easter and was, for Bede, on the 'right side' at the Synod of Whitby.[50] Yet except for a few platitudes the reader is left knowing very little of James, and on the one occasion where Bede could have elaborated on James's influence in Northumbria he actually understates it. Therefore in Book II:20 Bede does not emphasize that James was the inaugural singing master to bring the Roman form of church music to Northumbria, preferring instead to seem to give this honour to Aeddi, the man invited to Northumbria by Wilfrid. Indeed, in IV:2 James is portrayed as an exception, with Aeddi clearly being singled out as the first singing master: '*primusque, excepto Iacobo de quo supra diximus, cantandi magister Nordanhymbrorum ecclesiis Aeddi cognomento Stephanus fuit*.[51] In the *EH* James is an understated, almost incidental feature. One can perhaps say that he remained in relative obscurity because it did not suit Bede's purpose to give him prominence. For Bede, it was better to focus on Paulinus, the individual who did not stay in Northumbria following Edwin's death, and whose authority, consequently, posed no threat to Bede's attempt to emphasize the greatness of his own monastic foundation.

It would appear that where Whitby was concerned Bede further minimized the reader's knowledge of the extent of its authority by omitting any allusions in the *EH* to the influence of Aelfflaed following Hilda's death. Stephanie Hollis has suggested that Bede's omissions in regard to Aelfflaed are evidence of his considerable hostility to her, particularly because he perceived her as not fitting into his rigidly orthodox view of women religious.[52] However, a modification of this argument provides an equally plausible hypothesis. It is clear that Stephanus does seem to give a more substantial glimpse of Aelfflaed's role in Northumbrian politics than does Bede. In chapter 43 he indicates that in 686–7 she was of enough importance to merit Theodore urging her to make peace with Wilfrid.[53] Stephanus also implies that she was present at Aldfrith's deathbed, bearing witness to his desire for his successor to be at peace with Wilfrid.[54] What is of importance here is less the image of Aelfflaed as a witness, which (as shall be shown later) could be a rhetorical device, as the fact that she is being associated with the court. This is further emphasized in his subsequent portrayal of her at the Synod of Nidd in 706. Here he depicts her as '*semper totius prouinciae consolatrix optimaque consiliatrix*', and has her give a speech witnessing Aldfrith's final wishes.[55] He further shows her as acting as counsel to the bishops at this Synod.[56] It is clear from this evidence, as Thacker has observed, that after Hilda's death Whitby still played a role in the career of Wilfrid and that Aelfflaed had a powerful role in Northumbrian ecclesiastical events.[57] It is also clear, from the anonymous *Life of St Cuthbert* and also Bede's, that Aelfflaed had sufficient autonomy to turn to Cuthbert rather than York in the 680s to dedicate her church at Osingdun.[58] From the hagiographical evidence the picture of Aelfflaed one gets is of an autonomous, royal abbess with a role outside the confines of her monastery. In this it is apparent that the monastery of Whitby in the c.680s–710 was authoritative and closely linked with the royal family. Indeed, Thacker has even gone so far as to suggest that Whitby more than York seemed to be the focus of the diocese during this period.[59]

If one depended purely on Bede's *EH*, however, it would be hard not to assume that apart from the production of Bishops Bosa and Wilfrid II, following Hilda's death, the monastery settled into a much less public role. Aelfflaed is mentioned only twice in the *EH*. In Book III:24, Bede relates her consecration as a nun and entrance into Hilda's monastery at Hartlepool and then Whitby.[60] And, in Book IV:26, he notes that she and her mother presided over Whitby when Trumwine was forced to retire there, following Ecgfrith's death at Nechtansmere.[61] This latter reference hints at the continued importance of Whitby but Bede appears to have deliberately chosen to suppress any implication of Whitby's greatness during the abbatial rule of Aelfflaed. She certainly is not mentioned in connection with either Wilfrid or Aldfrith, and even the association with Cuthbert that Bede described in his *Life of St Cuthbert* is absent. Nonetheless, I am inclined to disagree with Hollis that this was due to 'hostility' as much as a desire to ensure that the audience's memory of Whitby was manipulated in such a way that it did not seem to have the same status as Wearmouth-Jarrow. By utilizing Hilda as a model, with the initial stigma from 664 attached to her, Bede kept the record of Whitby firmly in the period before it fully embraced a more 'Roman' image, connecting itself to Edwin, producing literature of Gregory the Great and housing Eanflaed (one of the Roman protagonists in the conflict of 664) as its joint president alongside Aelfflaed. Bede's portrayal then appears to be affected as much by the desire to augment his own monastery's status as out of a pseudo anti-feminist reaction to a powerful woman.

If elevating the status of Wearmouth-Jarrow through a sophisticated manipulation of discretion, omission, and insinuation on the one hand, and the exploitation of specific praise of his own monastery on the other, was a feature of the *EH*, one would expect to find that Bede did not only limit his machinations to those individuals with the obvious stigma of unorthodox practice. One would expect to find that, in comparison with Biscop and Wearmouth-Jarrow, even other 'Roman' identified saints and monasteries were subject to this treatment. James the Deacon is a perfect example of this, as apparently are Aelfflaed and the post-Hilda Whitby. Wilfrid, and his foundations at Hexham, Ripon and his restoration at York, can also be viewed in a similar light.

In the narrative of the *EH* the reader gains very little insight into the extent of status of Wilfrid's monasteries at Ripon and Hexham, either in their relation to royalty or as focal points for the cult of Wilfrid. The first mention of Ripon occurs within the chapter concerning the Synod of Whitby and here Bede is content to note that Alhfrith gave Wilfrid forty hides of land that he had previously donated to monks following the Ionan tradition.[62] In his later, brief *vita* of Wilfrid in V:19 Bede is more specific about this grant, noting that Alhfrith gave Wilfrid ten hides at Stamford and thirty at Ripon.[63] Bede also, incidentally, records that Cuthbert's successor to the solitary life on the Farne, Oethilwald, was initially a monk at Ripon.[64] Yet, pertinently, in this chapter, though Bede commented on Oethilwald's worthy deeds whilst he was a monk at Ripon, he fails to elaborate on these deeds, choosing instead to focus on the miraculous powers Oethilwald exhibited on the Farne.[65] Moreover, when it comes to mentioning Wilfrid's death and subsequent burial at Ripon Bede passes swiftly over it. Firstly, he notes that he was carried from Oundle and buried at Ripon with the honour befitting so great a bishop and, secondly, he repeats this brief notice later in the same chapter only this time adding Wilfrid's epitaph.[66] In Bede's notice there is no mention, as there is in the *Life of St Wilfrid*, of the miracles associated with Wilfrid's relics, nor of the white arc in the sky that started from the place of Wilfrid's burial.[67] Indeed, in Bede's account of Wilfrid the thaumaturgical features are manifestly absent.

A similar restraint can be viewed in Bede's references to Hexham. If one was to depend on the *EH* for information concerning Hexham during Wilfrid's lifetime, all one would glean would be that the Hexham monks annually held a vigil for Oswald's soul at Heavenfield, that one of their number, Bothelm, had been cured through the intercession of Oswald, and that the episcopal see based there changed hands frequently.[68] Without the *Life of St Wilfrid* the observer would be completely unaware of the fact that Hexham was founded on land donated by Bede's epitome of virginal sainthood, Aethelthryth, and that the estate was extensive.[69] Indeed, as with the omission of the secular founder of Whitby, one cannot help wondering if this was an act of deliberate literary suppression on Bede's part in order to underplay the initial status of Hexham.[70] Arguably, of course, one could suggest that if this were the impression Bede wanted to create he would have been more consistent, omitting the details of Ripon's and Selsey's endowments. However, it is clear that Bede had access to the *Life of St Wilfrid* and, therefore, would have known about Aethelthryth's gift.[71] Even so, in the passage where he specifically links Wilfrid with Aethelthryth's veiling there is no hint of any practical reciprocity of the friendship on her part.[72] To understand Bede's silence here one needs to consider the geographical placing of Hexham. In many respects the main Bernician monastic foundation other than Lindisfarne and Wearmouth, it was a definite contender for the king's patronage and, as such, as much a competitor of Wearmouth-Jarrow as the other monasteries Bede had so carefully described. Acknowledging that it was initially endowed by so esteemed a saint would have guaranteed a social standing Bede perhaps did not want to emphasize. The author of the *Life of St Wilfrid*, on the other hand, most certainly wanted it remembered. The grant of Ripon from Alhfrith also had its own status, although as a sub-king his gifts would not have carried as much weight as that of a royal saint. The endowment of Selsey by King Aethelwealh, moreover, was geographically distant enough not to be a cause of concern for Bede.

This point endorses the observation that in the *EH* Wilfrid's actions are only unequivocally positive when he is discussed in relation to Sussex. In other words, when Wilfrid's authority outside Northumbria was being examined it was acceptable to Bede to enhance it. In Northumbria, however, despite appearing repetitively in the pages of the *EH*, Bede does understate Wilfrid's power – especially any related to sanctity – and by so doing minimizes the role of Ripon and Hexham. This is of importance for it is clear that Bede recognized the extent of Wilfrid's influence purely in quantitative terms. It is interesting that Wilfrid is mentioned far more than Cuthbert. Bede was well aware that Bishop Wilfrid had been an eminent prelate but he appears not to have accorded him any image of saintliness. Bede's extract of Cuthbert's *Life* in *EH* reads more like hagiography, whereas his obituary of Wilfrid is exactly that – an obituary – and reads merely like a catalogue of the major events in Wilfrid's life. Apart from one vision, he is accredited with no miracles, nor is he spoken of in the same terms of reverence as, for example, Cuthbert. Thus, if one compares the terminology Bede uses for Wilfrid with that for Cuthbert, the contrast is stark. Of Wilfrid, Bede uses terminology such as 'the most reverend Bishop Wilfrid (*reuerentissimum*); 'the venerable Bishop Wilfrid' (*uenerabilis*); 'Bishop Wilfrid of blessed memory' (*beatae memoriae*), or just plain 'Bishop Wilfrid'.[73] Of Cuthbert, Bede's terminology is much more personal. In the preface he refers to him as 'the most holy father Bishop Cuthbert' (*sanctissimo patre et antistite Cudbercto*); and also, 'Bishop of Lindisfarne the holy and venerable Cuthbert' (*uirum sanctum et uenerabilem*); Cuthbert the 'venerable servant of the Lord' (*uenerabilis Domini famulus*); 'the man of God' (*uiri Dei*); 'blessed Cuthbert' (*beato*); 'most reverend Father' (*pater reuerentissimus*) and 'blessed Father Cuthbert' (*benedicti patris*).[74] Bede attributes the title 'Father' only once to Wilfrid.[75] In Bede's depiction of Cuthbert there is no doubt of Cuthbert's sanctity; he is portrayed as holy, as are his actions ('As bishop he followed the example of the blessed Apostles and enhanced his dignity by his holy actions …').[76] Wilfrid is not seen in such lofty terms – he may have been recognized as an eminent prelate by Bede but his portrayal does not convey any emphasis on his sanctity. In this sense it is not so much that he escapes any suspicion of greatness, than that any hint of saintliness eludes him. Had Cuthbert been present with the South Saxons during the drought and famine noted by Bede in the context of Wilfrid's evangelization, one cannot help thinking that a miracle rather than practical measures would have brought abundance!

Bede's portrayal of Wilfrid plays down his sanctity, and his description of Hexham and Ripon during Wilfrid's lifetime is deliberately brief. From the *EH* the observer would not get a sense of the wealth or authority of Ripon or Hexham in the late seventh century. In this context it is also poignant that in Book V:19 Bede disregarded any recognition of Wilfrid's restoration programme at York, being content instead to record that Oswald finished building the church there.[77] Just as Bede debases the Ionan-connected monasteries by association with unorthodox practice, just as he omits critical information concerning the extent of Whitby's influence, so he finds a way to ensure that, for his audience at least, the written memory of the foundations of Wilfrid was limited, his sanctity minimized.

Iona, Lindisfarne, Whitby, Hexham, Ripon, York, and possibly

Lastingham all play a role in Bede's *EH* but their authority is subtly noted to be deficient in some regard. All of these monasteries can be viewed as competitors in the desire for royal patronage and the spiritual authority of Wearmouth. However, before this chapter proceeds to examine how Bede characterized his own monastery as 'best of the best', one must acknowledge the exceptions to the rule. There are three Northumbrian bishops associated with monasteries where it is difficult to see Bede's negative manipulations at work. The first of these is, of course, Cuthbert. Bede's portrayal of Cuthbert in the *EH*, although limited, is unhesitatingly favourable. Indeed, in this context it is interesting that in the *EH* Bede omits mention of Cuthbert's period at Ripon. As he had made it clear elsewhere that Ripon was initially a house founded on Ionan principles and that the monks, rather than amend their ways, had been forced to leave, pre-Wilfridian Ripon was a source of stigma, obviously one Bede, at least in his portrayal of Cuthbert in the *EH*, did not want emphasized. As Wallace-Hadrill commented, in his *EH* image Bede's Cuthbert was a Romanized product of the Ionan discipline.[78] The allusion to Sulpicius Severus's *Life of St Martin* and the setting of Lindisfarne in a Gregorian context created an image of orthodoxy at Lindisfarne which Bede had previously eschewed.[79] One can postulate that, having already ensured that Lindisfarne's earliest foundations would be remembered for their irregular practice, Bede no longer felt it necessary to continue to imply its non-conformity. It is also worth considering that in the case of Cuthbert, however, his sanctity transcended even monastic competitiveness. Cuthbert's uncorrupt status testified that his virtues were worthy of sanctity and on this occasion Cuthbert's life was too impressive even to hint at unorthodoxy.

The same can perhaps be said of the second of Bede's exceptions, John of Beverley, bishop of Hexham. In Book V:2–7, Bede offered another image of unequivocal sanctity. John was noted as a *uir sanctus* with miraculous powers of healing: helping a dumb youth speak; saving the nun, Cwenburh, at Watton from illness; curing both the wife of the *comes*, Puch, and the servant of the *comes* Addi as well as helping one of his clergy recover from an accident.[80] In his description of John, Bede brought status to Beverley in a form that he did not use unhesitatingly with other Northumbrian houses, and again one is faced with the possibility that his miraculous powers were just too great to be ignored.

(Of course, it is also pertinent that having been bishop of Hexham until 721, memories of John were comparatively recent.)

The third individual whom Bede avoided associating with stigma or debasing was Acca. Thus he is shown as a companion of St Willibrord, as a source of information, and as a confidant of Wilfrid.[81] However, it is in Book V:20 that one can see the extent to which Bede admired Acca. This chapter reads like a chapter from Bede's *History of the Abbots*. Acca is credited with enriching the fabric of the church at Hexham with all kinds of decoration and works of art ('*aedificium multifario decore ac mirificis*'), with gathering relics of the blessed apostles and martyrs ('*adquisitis undecumque reliquiis beatorum apostolorum et martyrum*') and establishing chapels.[82] He also, like Benedict Biscop in the *HA*, is commended for building up a large and noble library of histories of the martyrs as well as other ecclesiastical books ('*Sed et historias passiones eorum, una cum ceteris ecclesiasticis uoluminibus, summa industria congregans, amplissimam ibi ac nobilissimam bibliothecam fecit*').[83] He, again like Biscop, is acknowledged by Bede for zealously providing sacred vessels, lamps and other objects of the same kind of adornment of the house of God ('*necnon et uasa sancta et luminaria aliaque huiusmodi, quae ad ornatum domus Dei pertinent, studiossime parauit*').[84] Moreover, similarly to Biscop once more, he is noted for bringing a Gregorian chanter to Hexham and for going to Rome.[85] As will be shown later the recording of the acquisitions gained by an abbot or bishop for their church was an exploitation of their resources in order to augment the status of that church. In the case of the *EH* Bede's depictions, whilst at times commenting on the building materials of a particular church, refrain from elaborating on the ecclesiastical fabric in the manner he does with Acca in this chapter or in the *HA*. This association with the material wealth of Hexham does not underplay its authority; rather it emphasizes it and is in this sense atypical when compared with Bede's illustrations of Iona, Lindisfarne, Whitby, York, Ripon, and Hexham during Wilfrid's episcopacy.

The reason for this difference is perhaps simple. Acca was Bede's bishop, patron, and contemporary and, consequently, not an appropriate individual for any minimization. However, Bede perhaps gives a hint of why he favours Acca in the text of this chapter. Bede makes it clear that Acca was a learned theologian, as Colgrave says, untainted (most pure) in his confession of the Catholic faith and thoroughly familiar with the rules of ecclesiastical custom (*'Quomodo etiam in litteris sanctis doctissimus et in catholicae fidei confessione castissimus, in ecclesiasticae quoque institutiones regulis sollertissimus extiterat'*).[86] Acca's purity of Catholicism surely refers to the fact that he had no direct Lindisfarne/Iona connections (which, after all, even Wilfrid had, having spent his noviciate at Lindisfarne whilst its Easter practices would still have been in place). Bede elucidates that Acca was brought up by the Whitby 'product' Bosa at York (*'utpote qui a pueritia in clero sanctissimi ac Deo dilecti Bosa Eboracensis episcopi nutritus atque eruditus est'*), not, therefore, under the initial tutelage of the Irish or even Wilfrid.[87] Acca, like Biscop, is an unadulterated, orthodox clergyman and as such Bede has nothing but respect for him. Wallace-Hadrill commented that it was remarkable how closely Acca's achievements at Hexham seem to parallel those of Wilfrid.[88] In fact, what is remarkable, firstly, is that in terms of the depiction of Hexham in the *EH* at least, Acca's achievements seem greater than Wilfrid's (after all, if the reader was dependent on Bede alone one would have no idea of Wilfrid's relic collecting and church embellishment). Secondly, that Bede creates an image of Acca that actually corresponds closely with that of the founder of his own monastery.

Nevertheless, in the Northumbrian sections of the *EH* the depictions used in these three cases are exceptional in their unlimitedly positive portrayal. It is only when one turns to Bede's portrayal of Biscop, Ceolfrith, and Wearmouth-Jarrow in the *EH* that the cause of his literary manipulations becomes evident. Whilst the pages of the *EH* are not overflowing with information concerning Wearmouth-Jarrow one needs to take two points into consideration. Firstly, having already completed the *History of the Abbots* c.716, Bede did not need to reiterate what he had already established in text form elsewhere. Secondly, a key theme in the *EH* appears to be the orthodoxy of the Anglo-Saxons, especially in terms of religious observances in Northumbria. Whilst Bede was clearly at pains to record the peculiar customs of the Ionan tradition in the *EH*, he went to equal lengths to show his own monastery as a champion of Roman monasteries. His main reference to Biscop, for example, came in the context of those individuals who attended Theodore's Synod at

Hatfield (itself a record of the freedom of the taint of heresy in the English church). Thus, having noted the presence of the aforementioned Roman cantor, John, Bede elaborated that he had come to Britain at the command of the Pope and under the guidance of Biscop.[89] The connotation of closeness between Biscop and Pope Agatho is noticeable. Moreover, by staying at Wearmouth, John made this alliance physically visible. The effect of this and John's reputation as a cantor in terms of the monastery's standing in the Northumbrian ecclesiastical community should not be understated. Bede, furthermore, enlarged this link between Biscop and the Pope by reiterating that the monastery had gained privileges from him [the Pope?]. This part of the *EH*, however, is derived mainly from the *HA*, therefore restating what his audience could find in the earlier text. Nonetheless, Bede does add to the *HA* material in this chapter of the *EH*, informing his reader that John was not just sent to instruct in singing, but also to inquire into the beliefs of the English Church.[90] The point was that the Pope had seen fit to place his inquisitor not under the guidance of Wilfrid, nor Hilda, but to give the honour to the untainted Catholic, Biscop, and his monastery.

Through his portrayal of Biscop in the *History of the Abbots* and in the *Ecclesiastical History*, then, Bede augmented his monastery's standing by stressing its orthodox affiliations. Where the *EH* is concerned the same can be said of the information surrounding Ceolfrith. In the *EH* Bede's depiction of Ceolfrith's response to King Nechtan's request for assistance concerning both the Easter and tonsure issues acts like a continuation of the *HA*. In Book V:21 Bede picks up a theme he began in his narrative of Biscop's orthodoxy and shows how Ceolfrith took it to new heights. In V:21 the inclusion of Ceolfrith's letter provides evidence for the influence of Wearmouth-Jarrow in enabling the Picts under Nechtan fully to accept the Roman customs.[91] It also indicates that Wearmouth-Jarrow supplied builders to construct an ecclesiastical edifice in the Roman manner, of stone.[92] Moreover, it shows the role Ceolfrith played in persuading Adomnan to follow Roman practices.[93] By incorporating this letter into the *EH* Bede categorically illustrated that his monastery, rather than any other Northumbrian foundation, had successfully taken orthodoxy to the Picts and even to an abbot of Iona. By implication Bede's Ceolfrith had removed the Picts from the influence of Iona and brought them to submit not only to St Peter in Rome but also to St Peter's at Wearmouth. The triumphalism in this chapter is unmistakable.

In the text of the *EH*, therefore, it is evident that Bede employed methods of narrative construction that deliberately favoured his own monastic institution at the expense of others in Northumbria. To return briefly to the possible presence of classical rhetorical assumptions, one could say that Bede was employing a rhetorical technique akin to that which is indicated in Cicero's *De Inventione* as *insinuatio* (present also in the *Rhetorica ad Herrenium*).[94] To use Cicero's phrasing, at first glance Bede does appear to be applying dissimulation and indirection to steal unobtrusively into the mind of his readers.[95] This need not, of course, be proof that Bede had access to *De Inventione*, rather that he had a point to prove and that what we think of now as insinuation was the most effective way of doing it to an audience that might have a variety of views. The trouble with considering concepts seemingly derived from Ciceronian or pseudo-Ciceronian works on rhetoric is, of course, that they are based on apparently common-sense communicative strategies. What else could Bede have done in this situation? That he used insinuation is not *de facto* proof that he learned the technique from studying Cicero. Arguably, Bede reflected his own sense of Wearmouth's monastic superiority, utilizing material in a manner that would guarantee his audience would remember some points in Anglo-Saxon history more than others. This should perhaps not surprise the modern reader. Such a technique of memory manipulation was not something new to Bede. It is patent from his information concerning the apostate kings, Osric and Eanfrith, that there was already an established tradition of omission to ensure the abolition of the memory of individuals.[96] As far as it is possible to tell, Bede just took this to rather more sophisticated heights than before.

Bede's desire to augment his own monastery in the text of the *EH* could in the first instance have been merely to meet the needs of his own community in terms of his audience. As was shown in chapter 1, the gift of the manuscript itself would have augmented Jarrow's status and the content may actually have been less important to secular recipients than to ecclesiastical ones. It could have also played its part in a long-running attempt by the monasteries in Northumbria to augment their status by implying that they were more orthodox than any of the others. In his compilation of the *EH* it is clear that Bede brought his own monastery into closer association with Canterbury, and, as Kirby has noted, this relationship more than any other could have inspired the first 'edition' of the *EH*.[97]

However, the desire to impress an external influence after the initial 'publication' should not be ruled out. This refers to the second edition of the *EH*, represented by the c-group of manuscripts and possibly produced in 734.[98] It is plausible that this second recension should be seen as a text directly linked to the wishes upon which Bede elaborated in his letter to Egbert, bishop of York. The first chapters of this book attempt to argue that the cult of saints and the literature that developed from it in Northumbria related in part to the augmentation of a monastery's status. In terms of orthodoxy and lack of conflict, Wearmouth could ostensibly show a standing second to none. It was not linked with the Ionan schismatics, nor were its abbots remembered for their turbulent relationship with the ruling family. It had an outstanding library, possibly the largest ever assembled in Anglo-Saxon England.[99] The one office of prestige that Wearmouth-Jarrow did not have, however, was that of a bishop. As noted in chapter 2 at the Synod of Nidd the inference one seems to get from the *Life of St Wilfrid* is that only abbeys with bishops attended, except of course for Whitby, which was represented by the daughter of a previous king.[100] There is no record of Ceolfrid being present and it is hard not to conclude that on this occasion Wearmouth-Jarrow's lack of a directly associated bishop may have led to their exclusion. This is obviously a highly speculative point, but given Bede's attachment to the creation of new bishoprics in his letter to Egbert, is it inconceivable that the production of a subsequent edition of the *EH*, with its focus on an orthodoxy Theodore would have been proud of, was actually designed to raise Wearmouth-Jarrow's profile to the extent that if a new diocese were to be created its focal point would be this monastery? This would certainly make sense of Bede's comments in chapter 9 of his letter to Egbert in which he argued that the church of Northumbria would be put into better condition with the consecration of new bishops.[101] This was not just a Gregorian or Theodoran desire being expressed, it was possibly also the wish of Bede's community. This is perhaps emphasized by Bede's subsequent proposal that the new see should be based at a monastery and that the monastery should be able to elect one of their own number to be bishop, who in turn would exercise episcopal authority over both the monastery and the locality.[102] Bede's assurance to Egbert that this would bring him metropolitan status should be read, therefore, less as a sign of any difficulty in Egbert's gaining of the pallium than as a subtle verbal incentive to encourage the bishop to undertake the aspirations of Bede's community.

Chapter 4
Bede's Approach to the Genre of *Historia*

THE PRECEDING CHAPTERS HAVE ESTABLISHED INTERPRETATIONS of the *historiae* of late seventh- and early eighth-century Northumbria in frames of reference common to modern empirical history. One chapter uses evidence from the texts to recreate the overall historical context within which the writings were produced; the third chapter puts forward the possible political agenda that specifically motivated Bede as indicated by the rhetorical strategies evident in the *Ecclesiastical History*. This chapter aims to examine Bede's comprehension of genre in terms of how he classified historia, and consequently, within what generic boundaries and traditions he worked. To do this, the chapter will explore the extent to which Bede deliberately chose to cite his historiae texts in traditions established by patristic forefathers; the specificity Bede exhibits concerning genre boundaries and the insights this can offer on his material; and the implications Bede's apparent approach might have on the expectations of historia of both his audience and ourselves.

The influence of previous writings on a text is a critical factor in the understanding of its nature. Thus writings of the early medieval period should not be viewed in isolation, but rather should be seen in the light of preceding texts (especially Late Antique ones). In fact, from the apparent similarities of a chronological series of historiographical texts it has been possible for historians to comment on the definition and development of specific genres within this area of narrative.[1] Although the definition of the genre of history is not new (as is seen in Isidore of Seville's *Etymologiae*)[2], it is important to note from the outset that such a mapping of generic development as found in *Typologie des Sources* is a modern approach. Bede, for example, did not directly discuss the pattern of a particular textual tradition in which he wrote nor did he explicitly define *historia* as had Isidore. Nonetheless, despite the absence in his writings of a specific definition of the genre of *historia* it is clear that the concept of genre was of interest to him. As Arthur Holder has commented, Bede listed the products of his prodigious literary endeavours at the close of the *EH*, not in the order in which they were written, but by genre: firstly, exegesis, then history, then poetry, and finally chronological and literary studies.[3] Moreover, his interest in the concept of genre is particularly visible in relation to his biblical exegesis. Thus, as Ray has observed, in *De Arte Metrica*, Bede used genre to explain the *historia* of the Book of Job.[4] Understanding generic boundaries was of relevance to Bede as it could be applied to reading the Bible. Furthermore, although Bede made no attempt to classify generic boundaries of history, on occasion the observer can make inferences about such boundaries in terms of both the concept of *historia* and the generic relationship between one text and another.

To rely on such inferences is obviously problematic as one is faced with the possibility of categorising boundaries unintended by the author. Nevertheless, whilst acknowledging that mapping generic boundaries (and development) may have all the usual problems of classifying texts, many of Bede's writings have implied and, at times, obvious boundaries and links with particular generic traditions. The significance of this is two-fold. Firstly, by looking at a text's links with its generic tradition the historian may be able to comprehend certain limitations of such texts. For example, by choosing to place a text in a specific generic tradition the content, tone, and form of this text may be restricted to remain in that genre.[5] If one translates this to Bede's works, one immediately becomes aware of the need to understand textual restrictions and apparent omissions in the light of previous generically similar texts. Secondly, by observing generic boundaries between the actual texts produced by Bede, the observer may come to a better understanding of Bede's methods as an historian and his perception of history. After all, remaining dependent on a personal definition of *historia* will colour expectations of his texts, creating unnecessary unease when a text does not conform to expectations.[6] Of course, whether it is possible ever to detach fully from received concepts of what Bede meant by *historia* is the great conundrum for post-modern historians.

Walter Goffart centred his researches on the political bias of a text, often viewing any discussion of the influence of a particular generic tradition in which the text exists as secondary to the apparent political motivations of an author.[7] Nevertheless, it should be remembered that the explicit or implicit choice by an author to place a text in a specific genre may introduce a whole series of prescriptions, restrictions, and expectations to the text.[8] Moreover, by placing a work in a particular type of source tradition, the author may be communicating (consciously or unconsciously) information to an audience concerning how they should approach the text.[9] Through the title, the preface, or generic signals throughout the text the author may seek to influence an audience's reception of the text.

The generic boundaries of Bede's *historia* are not just his creation but are also the result of the preceding generic tradition in which his texts are cited. For example, one can seemingly quite confidently state that the *EH* follows a generic tradition established by Eusebius.[10] Markus has firmly argued that, like Eusebius, in the *EH* Bede included extensive documentation, enumerated on many of the common themes found in Eusebius, and aimed to write a history of his Church from its beginnings.[11]

Wallace-Hadrill, however, was not entirely satisfied with this identification and instead has also indicated that Bede's *EH*, despite its title, belongs far more to the historiographical genre of the so-called 'vulgar historians' such as Cassiodorus, Jordanes, Gregory of Tours, Isidore, and the later Paul the Deacon.[12] This association is not perhaps surprising when one looks at the features which the texts by these writers have in common. Firstly, their obvious commitment to Christianity is all-pervasive. (However, only Bede focuses his information on ecclesiastical history.) Secondly, they attempt to narrate a history of a particular people or 'nation'.[13] It is this second link that seems to have been most influential in the subsequent compilation of monastic catalogues in the twelfth century. Walter Goffart has noticed that one particular catalogue, describing an eleventh-century manuscript containing Jordanes, Bede, and Paul the Deacon's history texts, lists these and other texts as 'the histories of the English, Trojans, Romans, Lombards and the Goths'.[14] For the medieval compiler, as for Wallace-Hadrill perhaps, *gentes* were the defining feature of this historiographical genre. Nonetheless, this fails to take into account that Bede's *EH* is not an unqualified examination of the history of the Anglo-Saxons. His was a history that described ecclesiastical developments first and foremost.

Whilst secular information is included, on the whole it relates to establishment and growth of the Church among the Anglo-Saxons rather than just offering a narrative of the Anglo-Saxons *per se*. This distinction, though lost on the subsequent compilers, was important to Bede as it definitively influenced the focus of his text.

One perhaps needs to note here that Wallace-Hadrill was identifying a generic tradition from *historia* texts both preceding and subsequent to that of Bede. For the purposes of genre this chapter attempts to show how Bede's *EH* fits into a series of previously established texts. Obviously, this excludes the writings of Paul the Deacon, reducing Wallace-Hadrill's list to the three antecedents of Bede he mentions.

If one takes just one or two of these 'vulgar' historians and compares their *historia* with that of Bede, the differences in primary aim and focus are clear. Cassiodorus, for example, aimed to make Gothic history 'Roman'.[15] His focus is far from being the development of the Church among that people. An examination of Isidore's *History of the Kings of the Goths* shows a similar distinction between his work and that of Bede.[16] One can see from its title and its contents that its purpose was not either primarily or even, perhaps, secondarily ecclesiastical history. Out of seventy chapters only eight deal specifically with ecclesiastical issues: chapter 6, Athanaric's persecution of the Christians; chapter 7, Athanaric's adoption of the Arian heresy; chapter 8, Bishop Ulfilas and the Arian beliefs; chapter 45, the attack by Agila on the tomb of St Acisclus; chapter 50, Leovigild's persecution of the orthodox Catholics; chapters 52–53, Reccared's conversion and convocation of a Synod of bishops; and chapter 60, Sisebut's forced conversion of the Jews. On the whole Isidore plays down ecclesiastical input into the rise of the Goths to their current status until he reaches the orthodox Reccared. This, of course, makes perfect sense; Isidore was not interested in increasing knowledge about Arianism. Nonetheless, it is perhaps noticeable that he allows the political focus of this text to cause him to avoid examining Hermangild's career. Hermangild had been marked out as a martyr saint in Gregory the Great's *Dialogues* and is also listed as such by Bede in his *Greater Chronicle*.[17] All Isidore says of him, however, is that Hermangild was defeated by his father whilst being in rebellion against him (chapter 49).[18] If Isidore was aware of Hermangild's saintly status, he ignored it in this text. Essentially, Isidore does not divert from his task of portraying the kings of the Goths – any information concerning the Church is incidental in this context, it is there only to supply material relevant to the task.

Moreover, Isidore's history does not focus on a narration of personal action in Bede's manner as presented in his *historia*, rather it generally reads more like a chronological sequence of events similar to a series of annals. It certainly does not function convincingly as a text offering models of individuals who are worth imitating for the greater good of the reader's soul. Instead, it reads like a catalogue of plundering and slaughter, with only a few brief pauses to indicate that on occasion their savagery could be restrained.[19]

In fact, it is in the chapters including these pauses that Isidore's focus seems to change, albeit briefly, to resemble Bede's. Chapter 16, for example, indicates that during the 447 attack on Rome one particular plundering Goth (unnamed) came across a consecrated virgin and advised her in 'a decent manner' that if she had any gold or silver she should hand it over. As the virgin handed him the sacred objects she warned him that they belonged to the sanctuary of the Apostle St Peter. Upon hearing the Apostle's name, the Goth, in terror, reported what had occurred to his king through a messenger who in turn immediately ordered everything be returned as he was waging war against the Romans not the Apostles.[20] It is hard, in the light of Bede's approach to *historia*, not to read this as an example of Isidore using this well-bred Goth as a model to show would-be plunderers that they should think first before taking ecclesiastical plunder (however politely they might do so).

Additionally, and perhaps more pertinently, Isidore's portrayal of Reccared in chapters 52–56 provides an image that might not be out of place in Bede's understanding of *historia*. Thus one is told of Reccared's piety: '*hic fide pius et pace praeclarus*';[21] his ability to preserve peace, administer with fairness, and rule with moderation: 'The provinces which his father conquered in war, Reccared preserved in peace, administered with equity, and ruled with moderation';[22] his character traits: 'He was kindly and mild, of remarkable goodness, and he had such a graceful demeanour and so benevolent a heart, that, influencing the minds of everyone, he brought even bad men to desire his love (ch.55);[23] his generosity: 'He was so generous that he restored by his own authority the wealth of private citizens and the treasures of the churches which his father had shamefully appropriated to the fisc' (ch.55) and, 'Reccared enriched many with gifts and elevated even more with honours' (ch.56);[24] and Isidore gives him the epithet 'most religious prince' *'religiossimus princeps'* (ch.53).[25] For Isidore, Reccared seems to be a 'most Christian king', reminiscent of Bede's Oswald in all but the miraculous element. [26] King Sisebut also receives more than just the cursory annalistic narrative of the first two-thirds of Isidore's text (ch.60). Whilst Isidore is not unequivocal in his picture (challenging Sisebut's forced conversion of the Jews), he notes that Sisebut was, nonetheless, 'eloquent in speech, informed in his opinions, and imbued with some knowledge of letters'.[27]

Arguably, Isidore's departure from his annalistic style in this passage relates to an expansion of his general purpose. This text provided him with an instrument with which he could not only show how the Gothic kings rose to a position of power, but at the same time emphasize that the real authority came only with their conversion from Arianism to orthodox Christianity. Thus, of Reccared Isidore records that with the help of the Faith he achieved a victory greater than any of the Goths in Spain: *'nulla umquam in Spaniis Gotharum uictoria uel maior similis extitit'.* (ch.54).[28] Of interest here though is that once again there is a difference between Isidore and Bede, albeit a subtle one. It was mentioned earlier that Reccared is reminiscent of Bede's Oswald. This is a fair comment. One should note, however, that as Oswald followed the Ionan tradition and, therefore, observed an irregular Easter practice, Bede's most Christian king can hardly be viewed as Bede's most orthodox king.

If one returns to the story of the well-bred Goth and the consecrated virgin one can see that Isidore's general purpose did in fact affect his use of his sources, at least in this tale. Comparing Isidore's text with that of his source, Orosius, one can see how the subsequent conversion of the Goths to orthodox Christianity required Isidore to change Orosius' original story. For Orosius, viewing Alaric as acting as an instrument of God in his attack on Rome, there is no mention of Alaric being a heretic. Of Alaric, Orosius states in a complementary way that he was a Christian and more like a Roman: *'quorum unus Christianus propiorque Romano'.*[29] To Isidore, however, Alaric, though a Christian in name, was a heretic in profession and needed to be remembered as such: *'nomine quidem Christianus, sed professione haereticus'* (ch.15).[30] Both are agreed that Alaric was restrained in his attack on Rome but again the difference of hindsight allows Isidore to omit some of Orosius' information. In his narrative describing the well-bred Goth, Orosius notes not only his breeding but also the fact that he was a Christian. Isidore, on the other hand focuses his information on the fact that the man was of powerful status, omitting completely Orosius' statement concerning his Christianity. Essentially, in this story one can see that despite making truthfulness a central requirement of *historia* in his *Etymologiae*, Isidore was prepared to manipulate the facts to serve his purpose.[31]

These examples are exceptions in Isidore's text, however, and Isidore, of course, had made it quite clear in his *Etymologiae* that his view of *historia* was different from Bede's. One should not be surprised, therefore, to find that these two authors' works do not comfortably fit into the same genre. Isidore's task and his own concept of *historia* supplied him with different genre boundaries from those of Bede. This is all the more important when one considers Goffart's attempt to revise Levison's article: 'Bede as Historian'.[32] Goffart has argued that Levison was quite wrong to view Bede's historiography as being created in an arid landscape. He suggests that the works of Cassiodorus, Jordanes, and Isidore, as well as that of an unnamed Italian show that Bede 'follows upon more than a century of self-assured activity'.[33] Surely the point is, however, that Bede chose to do something different from previous Late Antique and early medieval historiographers and, thus, in this case can still be viewed as fairly unique. (Moreover, such self-assured activity is only really relevant if Bede was aware of it: as Levison notes, and Goffart does not contradict, there is no evidence to suggest that Bede knew of the histories of Cassiodorus, Jordanes, or Isidore.)[34] Cassiodorus, Jordanes, and Isidore were all producing *historiae* about the Gothic *gens*, not about the church history of the Gothic *gens*. Both in aim and in focus their 'vulgar' histories differed from Bede. Perhaps the only link these texts have in terms of a historiographical genre is that unlike Eusebius's *EH* they included secular affairs. One should be wary, then, of viewing them as part of one tradition.

In fact, one is perhaps forced to return to a qualified agreement with Markus: Bede wanted his *EH* to be viewed as part of the tradition established by Eusebius. It was important for him not to stand alone in his written work but rather to be seen as directly linked with the fathers of the Church. In a sense, by describing his text as an ecclesiastical history and by using some of Eusebius' techniques and themes he gave his text an authority, particularly within the monastic and ecclesiastical communities for whom he wrote. Having said this, however, it is clear that Bede's *EH* is a unique text, produced in circumstances quite different from those of Eusebius, integrating both the Church and secular past in a way Eusebius did not. Essentially, Bede had established his own generic boundaries of *historia*: the title *Ecclesiastical History* gave these boundaries some legitimacy.[35]

It was stated at the beginning of this chapter that the study of genre boundaries can help observers understand apparent limitations of a text and enable them consequently to adapt their own expectations. The classification of a text in a genre could determine the type of information selected for the narrative and the way that material was expressed in the narrative. It is to the issue of Bede's own understanding of the genre of *historia* that this book now turns. The main evidence that Bede clearly differentiated between his *historiae* can be found in the autobiographical note in his *EH*, where *historia* is divided into three separate sub-groups, or sub-genres: *historiae sanctorum*, *historia abbatum*, and *historia eccelesiastica*.[36] In this division he shows a specificity of categorization not made, for example, by Gregory of Tours who merely listed them by title.[37] Such explicitness on the part of Bede is significant. By noting these three historiographical groups Bede, quite consciously, was classifying these texts by type. This has two main obvious implications: firstly, that Bede perceived that each of these categories contained distinctions important enough to warrant differentiation (to which this chapter will return later): and secondly, that Bede was using the term '*historia*' to note a common element in the three groups.

One common element is, of course, that Christian '*historia*' should be the record of a community and its path to salvation.[38] One needs, however, to take Bede's understanding of *historia* further than this. Unfortunately, as has been commented, Bede did not offer a definition of *historia*, rather the observer is forced to rely on inferences drawn from statements made in works that are considered to be essentially historiographical. The Preface to the *EH*, indeed, has been studied on many an occasion with this in mind.[39] In the opening paragraph of this Preface Bede's focus is on the idea that history should record the deeds of good men rather than that it should offer an analysis of events, a focus that is critical to Bede's comprehension of the term *historia*.[40] In the actual text of the *EH* Bede further emphasizes this in his discussion of Aidan:

> 'as a truthful historian, I have described in a simple manner those
> things which were done by him or through him, praising such of
> his qualities as are worthy of praise and preserving their memory
> for the benefit of my readers.'[41]

By implication this is Bede's clearest statement of the historian's task: to record and preserve for memory the actions of particular individuals, in order that the audience might be influenced by them.[42] (In this sense *historia* can be placed firmly in the remit of rhetorical exposition.)

The reason for such a focus is, at least from Bede's point of view, relatively straightforward. The individuals singled out in Christian *historia* function as ideals, offering Bede instruments with which he could illuminate those personal attributes most likely to lead to salvation.[43] This reasoning is not particular to Bede. Diana Greenway has noted that there was a tradition dating back to Gregory the Great of using historical persons and their vices and virtues as resources of moral examples in the rhetoric of sermons.[44]

One of Bede's own sources, Gildas, in his *The Ruin of Britain*, portrayed his country's past as a series of moral models, a fact that cannot have escaped Bede's attention.[45] The core of *The Ruin of Britain*, as Neil Wright notes, consists of direct attacks on the corruption of the kings and the clergy.[46] Gildas elaborately spells out the 'vices' of the first five tyrants: Constantine (parricide and adultery); Aurelius Caninus (parricide, fornication, adultery, and hatred of peace); Vortipor (incest); Cuneglasus (hatred of peace and adultery); and Maglocunus (murder and broken vows). He then stresses the potential punishments for their sins as indicated in the Old Testament, only briefly touching, at the end of this section, on those virtues a king should have. Even here though, his focus is more on the absence of these virtues than on creating a model for imitation. Gildas is slightly less harsh in his treatment of the British clergy yet his underlying approach remains the same.[47]

Unlike Gildas, though, Bede ensured that positive models were given more prominence than those with deplorable vices. This can be seen if one compares Gildas and Bede on the period from Roman times up to the arrival of the Saxons in Briton. Gildas opens his historical narrative with the statement: 'Ever since it was first inhabited, Britain has been ungratefully rebelling, stiff-necked and haughty, now against God, now against its own countrymen, sometimes even against kings from abroad and their subjects.'[48] The bulk of the subsequent narrative concerning Roman Britain appears to prove this point, drawing on the proverb that the British were viewed as cowards in war and faithless in peace ('*ita ut in prouerbium et derisum longe lateque efferretur quod Britanni nec in bello fortes sint nec in pace fideles.*')[49] The inclusion of St Alban provides some contrast to this, but such positive images do not form the basis of Gildas' record.[50] Bede omits his sweepingly negative statements, maintaining what seems to be a factual account in his opening chapters, as he narrates the Roman period of British history. Indeed, rather than drawing on Gildas, Bede turned to Orosius' *History Against the Pagans* for less ambiguous chronological information concerning Roman Britain.[51] Thus, Gildas' text may not fall into the genre of *historia*. A comparison with the *EH* does, however, assist the elucidation of Bede's emphases. Firstly, it is perhaps worth noting that Bede chose to depart from Gildas' record concerning St Alban, instead using material from the *Passion of St Alban*.[52] Consequently, Bede offers a much more elaborate narrative about this saint. He mentions not only the story of Alban's exchange of clothes with the cleric to whom he was giving hospitality and his arrest, but also describes Alban's confrontation with the judge, his torture, and his execution. In essence, Bede gives more weight to the story of Alban than did Gildas. Though he does refer to the Britons up to this point it seems more 'in passing' than as any concerted effort to say what they were like. His initial chapters are more interested in Roman influences in Britain than they are with the British *per se*.

Moreover, Bede seems to soften some of Gildas's judgements concerning the British. Thus in Book I, chapter 4, of the *EH*, Bede mentions Lucius' request to become a Christian, stating that: 'His pious request was quickly granted and the Britons preserved the faith which they had received, inviolate and entire, in peace and quiet, until the time of the Emperor Diocletian.'[53] Gildas, however, is less equivocal about this

particular conversion, noting a lack of enthusiasm on the part of the
Britons: 'Christ's precepts were received by the inhabitants without
enthusiasm; but they remained more or less pure, right up until the nine
year persecution by the tyrant Diocletian...'[54] Bede does not, it is true,
ignore all of Gildas' comments concerning the Britons and Book I
chapters, 12, 14, 15 and 22 draw almost exclusively from *The Ruin of
Britain*. Nonetheless, there are other examples of Bede's modification of
Gildas' tirades. Firstly, when dealing with Aurelianus Bede omits Gildas'
statement concerning the inferiority of his current descendants.[55]
Secondly, Bede introduces into the British narrative five chapters
concerning St Germanus of Auxerre.[56] In this case Bede not only moves
the central theme of the narrative away from British vices to saintly
virtues, but he also plays down any failings on the part of the Britons.
Hence he indicates that the British resisted the perverse teaching of
Pelagius, not wanting to blaspheme the grace of Christ, calling instead on
the wisdom of the Gaulish bishops to help them uphold the Faith.[57] His
image of the Britons here, though implying a degree of ignorance on their
part, does not read as an insult, but rather suggests the Britons made a
wise decision. In chapter 21 Bede again indicates that the British clergy
took their responsibility to prevent the spread of the Pelagian heresy by
calling on St Germanus.

Walter Goffart has also noticed that Bede changed Gildas' emphasis
concerning the building of the vallum from the incompetence of a
'leaderless British mob' to admiration for the building work that had
been undertaken.[58] In these chapters concerning Germanus Bede presents
an image of the Britons that is different from that of Gildas. This is not
to say that Bede ignored all their failings. In chapter 22 he returns to
Gildas (26) and seems to tell his readers that more information
concerning the unspeakable crimes of the British can be found in his
source's writings.[59] However, by only alluding to these crimes, Bede again
modified Gildas, forcing his source's narrative to take second place
behind the issue that Bede felt was key in terms of the British relationship
with the Anglo-Saxons: that 'they never preached the faith to the Saxons
or Angles who inhabited Britain with them' (*ut numquam genti Saxonum
siue Anglorum, secem Brittaniam incolenti, uerbum fidei praedicando
committerent*).[60] However, in Book I Bede even plays this crime down,
implying that God did not desert the British but instead had appointed

worthier heralds to bring the Faith to the Anglo-Saxons. Bede's picture of
the British in Book I is far from being totally negative and, as Wallace-
Hadrill eloquently put it, Bede shows them as having 'had their ups and
downs, and for all their moral turpitude, they remained Christian and
had responded positively to the threat of heresy'.[61]

Walter Goffart has argued that Bede's text actually produces a far
greater indictment of the British than does that of Gildas.[62] Agreeing
with Hanning, he notes that by deliberately placing the narrative
concerning Germanus near the end of the order of British events, Bede
was making a point.[63] Basically, he suggests that by doing this, Bede
made a stark contrast between Germanus' willingness to answer the
Britons' call for help and the British refusal to evangelize the Saxons.
This may well be true – although if it is, it is hard not to question why
Bede appears to have played down their lack of preaching in his
narrative. It is perhaps pertinent that his statement noting that God was
to send worthier heralds was immediately followed by the chapter
introducing Augustine.[64] Perhaps Bede's intention here is quite simple:
Augustine was orthodox and the British were not. In one sense the British
refusal did the Saxons a favour, for it meant that their first conversion
had a degree of spiritual superiority. Perhaps for Bede everything was as
God intended, for had the British converted the Anglo-Saxons, their
initial conversion would have been to a heresy not to an orthodoxy. After
all it certainly appears to be their heresy that Bede sees as the cause of
God's vengeance in Book II:2, rather than just their refusal to
evangelize.[65] In fact, perhaps what the reader is viewing is a tension in the
text. On the one hand Bede believed that God had chosen worthier
missionaries than the British to convert the Anglo-Saxons, thereby at
some level making British reticence understandable (if not acceptable).
On the other, however, their refusal to accept orthodoxy was not
understandable, acceptable, or perhaps forgivable. The point is of course
that in Book I it is clear that Bede changes the emphasis of Gildas' text
towards one that seems to offer a more balanced appraisal of events and
greater concern with presenting human virtue. The British are important
to Bede, but of more significance are the deeds of good men; thus Alban,
Germanus, and Augustine are offered as models worthy of imitation. In
some respects the British provide a useful context in which to highlight
their excellence. It is clear that Bede's additions to and omissions from

Gildas' text served a critical role, for on the whole they acted to reverse the absence from *The Ruin of Britain* of role models. Whilst not ignoring vice completely (nor the punishment of God it incurred), Bede's primary interest was in those individuals who illustrated those virtues most worthy of aspiring to rather than those vices most likely to invoke God's wrath. In this it is perhaps possible to suggest that in his use of *historia* Bede's aim was to inspire through example rather than teach purely by threat or fear.[66] This orientation differed significantly to that of Gildas.

Thus Bede not only distanced himself from the writing of Gildas; he also moved away from the emphasis of the narrative of another of his sources, Orosius.[67] In his *History Against the Pagans*, Orosius made it quite clear that a key theme of his *historia* was to show the *iusta punitio* of God when men misused the freedom He had given them. In his first chapter he notes that man's changeable nature needs to be reproved with justice.[68] In his final chapter he comments further that he has written about the desires and punishments of sinful men, the struggles of the world and the judgements of God from the beginning of the world until the present day.[69] Even a cursory glance at Orosius' seven books shows the reader the extent of his focus on God's just judgement (*iusto iudicio Dei*). Book VII, which provided Bede with some of his information for Book I of his *EH*, is no exception to this rule. Thus with some relish Orosius tells the reader that the emperor Licinius' insides rotted away because of God's anger at his behaviour;[70] concerning Valens (an emperor Bede himself mentions) Orosius makes it clear that his death in a burning house after being shot by an arrow whilst in battle was divine retribution (*iusto iudicio Dei*) for having sent an Arian bishop to convert the Goths (Bk VII: 33).[71] In the chapter concerning Mascezel, brother of Count Gildo, Orosius elaborates on this theme by indicating how God's judgement is ever vigilant to the actions of an individual. Thus, while Mascezel had followed God he had been assisted but when he desecrated a church, God brought about his death: '*ad utrumque semper diuinum uigilare iudicium, quando et, cum sperauit, adiutus et, cum contempsit, occisus est*'.[72] Time and time again Orosius repeats his message of divine judgement, in essence backing up Gildas' prophecies concerning the corruption of the British kings and clergy.

In his concept of *historia* Bede does not seem to give this theme such importance – it certainly is not all-pervasive in the text as it is with

Orosius. It is perhaps interesting to note that when he mentions Valens he omits the comments on the retributive nature of his death. In the context of his Book I they are unnecessary and can thus be left out. This is not to argue that Bede never used the judgement of God to make a point in his *EH*; after all in his own preface he stated the importance of recording the evil deeds of wicked men.[73] Additionally, those parts of his text which examine the destruction of the Britons (Bk I: 15; Bk II: 2), the apostate Eadbald's afflictions (Bk. II: 5), the deaths of the two Northumbrian apostates, Eanfrith and Osric, at the hands of Cadwalla (Bk. III: 1), and the destruction of Coldingham Abbey (Bk. IV: 25) make it very clear that Bede does not ignore the role of God's 'justice'. Nonetheless, unlike Orosius, Bede did not use just any apparently appropriate incident to restate the explicit power of God's judgement. This can perhaps be particularly clearly seen in his treatment of Cadwalla's death at the hands of Oswald and Penda's death at the Battle of Winwaed.[74] Arguably, both present excellent opportunities for commenting on how their behaviour brought about their deaths. However, Bede, far more sophisticated stylistically than Orosius, either did not want to repeat himself, as in the case of Cadwalla (he had already made his point concerning God's judgement in his discussion of the apostate kings), or shifted the focal point away from Penda's death to Oswiu's oath.

The subtlety of Bede's use of this theme can also be seen in his description of Cynegisl's son, Cenwealh, king of the West Saxons.[75] At the beginning of his narrative concerning Cenwealh Bede states that he refused to receive the Faith and not long afterwards lost his kingdom. In exile he then accepted the true Faith and subsequently regained his kingdom. However, at this point Bede does not draw the obvious conclusion. Instead, for dramatic effect, he waits until he has described how Cenwealh latterly suffered losses again after he had offended Bishop Agilbert and expelled Bishop Wine from his kingdom. Only then does he show Cenwealh realizing that his unbelief had led to the loss of his kingdom and his conversion had led to his restoration. In doing this Bede allows Cenwealh to acknowledge that a kingdom without a bishop is deprived of divine protection without repeating his message of divine judgement more than once in the chapter. Nevertheless, even with Bede's stylistic subtleties the theme of retribution does not repetitively pervade his *historia* as it does Orosius' apologetic text. In essence, Bede was writing for a predominantly Christian audience and did not need to keep repeating the effect of God's justice. He perhaps could take for granted that his audience already knew this. In a sense, then, Bede's concept of *historia* is quite distinct from that of Gildas and Orosius. For Bede, the emphasis was not so much what to avoid doing as what *to* do. *Historia* should centre on the narration of the actions of individuals worthy of praise and imitation.

If one turns to the texts Bede classified as *historiae sanctorum*, one can see that a similar definition of *historia* can be inferred. Thus, for example, in the Preface of *Life of St Felix*, Bede notes how he is going to discuss the 'history of this holy confessor' (*sancti confessoris historiam*), thereby equating *historia* with the activities of Felix's life.[76] As one would expect, the *Life of St Cuthbert* too concentrates on Cuthbert's actions. Unfortunately, the *History of the Abbots (HA)* does not have a preface. Nevertheless, by his mere description of it as an *historia* and the narrative itself one can see that Bede is concentrating on the actions and acquisitions of the abbots of his monastery. The common link in Bede's designation *historia* then is that it should emphasize the role of individuals.

In essence *historia* should concern itself with the actions (both public and personal) of the individual rather than merely analysing the events that occurred on an impersonal level. Moreover, as shall be shown in subsequent chapters, these actions had a fundamentally conventional basis. If one accepts this, it is clear that Bede's perception of what 'history writing' is and should do is not only very different from that expected by historians today, but, as mentioned in the introduction, is also very different from the one definition of the genre of *historia* to which Bede had access: that to be found in Isidore of Seville's *Etymologiae*. Isidore's opening line concerning *historia* is: '*Historia est narratio rei gestae*'.[77] He goes on to note that history is quite different from argument and fable, relying on true events that really happened. Essentially, Isidore appears to be outlining a definition suitable to the modern concept of history but neither to Bede's method of construction of history nor to his understanding of its generic boundaries. (Of course, having said this, it is clear from the *History of the Goths* that Isidore's practice was not entirely confined to his own prescription.) For Bede the aim of Christian *historia* could clearly subordinate what a modern audience might consider a historical truth. Bede was not unique in this. As Giles Constable commented of the Middle Ages in general, Isidore's 'high flown sentiments' concerning *historia* were considered a *topos*.[78] The aim of *historia*, the method of selection and the presentation of facts in *historia* were as important as, if not more so than, the facts themselves.

The common generic link in Bede's three *historia* texts is, then, the narration of personal action. Having acknowledged this, however, one now needs to question why Bede chose to divide them into sub-genres. In fact, on a general level, this is fairly clear. The *EH* selectively focuses on those individuals and their relevant actions that led to the growth and establishment of the Christian church in the Anglo-Saxon kingdoms; the *Historiae sanctorum* concentrates on the deeds of individual saints from birth until after death, and the *Historia Abbatum* illuminates the activities of the abbots in the monastery (that is not a full life as in *historiae sanctorum*). If one accepts the interpretation with its emphasis on deeds rather than events, the use of hagiographical material in *historia* becomes more admissible. For instance, some historians of the past have found the miraculous element in Bede's *EH* unacceptable in relation to what they understand as history.[79] However, miracles, as well as exhibiting the posthumous power of a saint, are also merely the deeds of individuals after death and are, therefore, very much part of *historia*.[80] For Bede there was no tension or contradiction in including the miraculous element. In fact he no doubt thought that it played a vital role in *historia*.

The generic focus on the role of an individual (as opposed to an event) in *historia* becomes more evident when one compares these texts with other works by Bede that some historians are 'reclaiming' as historiographical. This is especially evident in Bede's chronicles, especially the *Greater Chronicle*, in his *De Temporum Ratione (DTR)*, written in 725,[81] a text which has been relatively ignored by historians, having only recently been translated with both the *Chronicle* and published alongside Bede's *EH*.[82] A universal chronicle that catalogues the Six Ages of the World, the *Greater Chronicle* forms Chapter 66 of the *DTR*. It is a composite text that draws from many of its generic predecessors, including the *Chronicle of Jerome-Eusebius*, the *Chronicle of Prosper*, and that of Isidore. It also selects from the *Book of the*

Pontiffs (Liber Pontificalis), Orosius' *History Against the Pagans* and Gildas' *Ruins of Britain*.[83] Jones has catalogued 245 manuscripts of this text, some of which have been copied as part of the *DTR* and some which stand alone.[84] Interestingly, Jones has also indicated that great care appears to have been taken concerning its reproduction.[85] Consequently, variations are slight among these texts and the observer may accept, without too much anxiety, that the manuscripts represent Bede's words and not those of a particular scribe.

The sections of this *Chronicle* concerned with events narrated in the *EH* are a valuable source of genre comparison and serve to illustrate the personal/individual bias of *historia*. As Hanning has already compared the British material found in the *Chronicle* and *EH*, this chapter concentrates on those entries that relate to events in the Anglo-Saxon kingdoms.[86] It is important to note from the outset that Anglo-Saxon events are not particularly emphasized, rather they fall into a general pattern of interest in events elsewhere in Western Christendom. If, however, one compares the entry for 596 in the *Chronicle* with its relevant counterpart in the *EH* (I:23), the generic differences become clear:

> 'He also sent to Britain Mellitus, Augustine, and John, and many other God-fearing monks with them, to convert the Angles to Christ. And when Aethelberht was soon converted to the grace of Christ, together with the people of the Cantuarii over whom he ruled, together with those of neighbouring kingdoms, he gave him Augustine to become his bishop and teacher, as well as other holy priests to become bishops. However, the people of the Angles north of the river Humber, under kings Aelle and Aethelfrith, did not hear the word of life at this time.'[87]

Primarily, the tone and focus of the texts are different. In the *Chronicle* the tone is matter of fact. The focus concerns the point that this was the year the Anglo-Saxons in Kent converted and a bishopric was established (and that the people north of the Humber had not yet heard the Word of Life). Essentially, the event of conversion is of more importance to this text than the participants. In the *EH*, however, Bede focuses on Gregory's divine inspiration, the missionaries' obedience and terror, and Gregory's encouragement.[88] It then goes on to give a significant narrative of how these individuals established the Church. [89] In the *EH* Bede is not only concentrating on the event but on the emotions and interactions of those involved.

Moreover, in the *Chronicle* Bede makes no effort to separate the missions of Augustine and Mellitus even though in the *EH* he himself clearly demonstrates that they arrived on two dates. Blair has suggested that this may be evidence to suggest that in 725 Bede did not actually know that there were two missions.[90] Although this is possible, it is interesting that if one compares Bede's entry in the *Chronicle* with the source from which he was drawing, the *Book of Pontiffs*, it is clear that he had changed the order of the names. The *Book of Pontiffs* states:

'Then the holy man of God sent God's servants Mellitus, Augustine and John...' ('*Eodem tempore beatissimus Gregorius misit seruos Dei Mellitum, Augustinum et Iohannum*').[91]

The *Book of Pontiffs* lists Mellitus first. Bede places him after Augustine. This does seem significant. By placing Augustine first Bede may well have been correcting his source to suit the actual events. In other words, as Augustine arrived first, Bede felt that he should be cited first. Another interpretation is of course that as Augustine became archbishop, Bede considered that he should have pre-eminence in the list.

Nevertheless, if one observes Blair's argument for Bede's ignorance of the mission events the former of the explanations rather than the latter seems more plausible. Blair notes that Bede was able to correct a previous chronological error that he had made concerning the conversion of the Saxons in *DTR* because of new information he received after writing it.[92] This material included the *Libellus Responsionum*, Gregory's response to Augustine's questions. It has been accepted that Bede had access to this by 721 when he used it in his prose *Life of St Cuthbert* (four years before he wrote the *Greater Chronicle*).[93] If he had acquired this it is more than likely that he also had Gregory's letter to Mellitus. This certainly seems evident in the Preface to the *EH*, where he implies that he received the letters of St Gregory and other popes together.[94] The letter to Mellitus clearly indicates that he followed on after Augustine.[95] From this evidence it would seem probable that Bede altered the order of the information in the *Book of Pontiffs* deliberately to follow the chronological sequence of events. One can only suggest that he chose not to tamper with the material further because he was directly quoting from a work held in esteem. Perhaps, as he had already been accused of heresy in *DTR* on computational grounds, he felt it was prudent not to be seen questioning the authority of this document by amending it.[96] This suggestion, that the change was deliberate, is made stronger when one realizes that to justify and prove such changes Bede might have been forced to quote the 'personal' material not relevant in the genre of Chronicles.

The generic variations between the *Greater Chronicle* and the *EH* become even more stark when one observes the *Chronicle's* comment on the conversion of Northumbria.[97] Here the focus is obviously different. Unlike the *EH's* account, this entry concentrates only on relating to the reader that this was the year that Edwin and his people heard the Word of Salvation from Paulinus and that a bishopric was established at York. The *Chronicle* makes no attempt to discuss Edwin's decision to convert, nor does it offer details of those individuals who did convert.[98] Indeed, it does not mention anything about Edwin and Paulinus other than their titles and names. For Bede, chronicles focused on events, *historia* on the people in the events.

Chronicles, then, place episodes in time and concentrate on offering the observer brief factual information. Indeed, because Bede's *Greater Chronicle* does centre on events in time it might be easy to feel it is of more historiographical relevance than *historia*. Nevertheless, in this text Bede is his usual highly selective self! The impression that one gets is that the Anglo-Saxon material included is only there by virtue of the fact that it exemplifies themes which run through the work, themes which themselves determine those events Bede chose to cover. It is significant, for example, that Bede mentions the conversions by Augustine and Paulinus, and the sending of Theodore, Hadrian, and Vitalianus, whilst studiously avoiding any mention of the British and Gallic influence.[99] This fits in with an overall theme of the Sixth Age, that is the conversion and establishment of Roman Catholic orthodox Christianity. This can be seen in another of Bede's Anglo-Saxon entries into the chronicle concerning Egbert. Once again the emphasis is on the fact that Egbert converted the Irish from their aberration of non-canonical Easter

observance by preaching.[100] Nothing else is mentioned of his life. This
conversion is merely placed in time. The importance of conversion to
orthodoxy is further stressed if one looks at other entries unrelated to the
Anglo-Saxons. For instance, in his discussion of Hermangild and
Reccared, Bede's focus is on Hermangild's orthodoxy and martyrdom
and Reccared's conversion to the Catholic (*catholicam conuertit ad
fidem*), as opposed to Arian, faith.[101] Though clearly influenced by
Gregory the Great's *Dialogues* here, Bede does not waste time detailing
Leuvigild's actual attempts to persuade Hermangild to apostasize.[102] The
events to be placed in time were the martyrdom and the conversion. Bede
is even more selective here than he is in the *EH*.

His selectivity, however, is surely a consequence of the purpose of a
universal chronicle. Such a chronicle is essentially eschatological.[103]
Indeed, the last five chapters of *DTR* are devoted to these eschatological
ideas. The interest in placing the conversions and martyrdom in time
basically relates to what will follow the Sixth Age. For Bede conversion
and martyrdom were critical to the Second Coming and the Day of
Judgement: the Eighth Age. Bede himself shows this when, in the chapter
concerning the time of the Anti-Christ, he notes that God at this time
'will crown firstly those who have the love of the faith implanted already
in their minds with the virtue of martyrdom, thereafter snatching up the
rest of the faithful, making them either glorious martyrs or damned
apostates'.[104] Ultimately, Bede was showing the importance of conversion
and martyrdom in the Sixth Age. Such events concerned the salvation and
judgement of mankind.

Indeed, the eschatological bias of the *Greater Chronicle* should not
be underestimated. Fundamentally, the last six chapters of *DTR* are a
single unit which follow a sequential route. The *Chronicle* should not be
observed out of the context of the Seventh and Eighth Ages, for it is these
ages that determine the choice of themes. This is excellently shown if one
regards the other Anglo-Saxon events Bede has recorded. These concern
Aethelthryth and Cuthbert. In the case of Aethelthryth, Bede concentrates
on noting who her father was, her marriage to Ecgfrith, her perpetual
virginity, the construction of the monastery at Ely, and her
incorruptibility.[105] Her personal interactions are not noted and neither
are the miracles. Of Cuthbert, Bede merely makes brief comments on the
fact that Cuthbert was at Lindisfarne, that he, Bede, had written a prose

and verse life, and that Cuthbert remained incorrupt after death.[106]

The ultimate question is, of course, why are they included? If the entries concerning the Anglo-Saxons focus on the establishment of a Roman Church in England, why is that great champion of Romanism, Wilfrid, unmentioned? Walter Goffart might be tempted to suggest that once again Bede was illustrating his political prejudice with this omission. However, if one regards this chronicle as merely part of the discussion of eight ages and not just six, the political bias may not have been a main factor.

In fact, one needs to examine the one element that both Aethelthryth and Cuthbert had in common to understand Bede's choice. Ultimately, they are included whilst others are not, for a specific reason: the incorruptibility of their bodies. In the Eighth Age, the age always to be loved and hoped for, Bede states that, 'Christ will lead their souls [the faithful], gifted with *incorruptible bodies*, to the gathering of the heavenly kingdom, and the contemplation of His divine majesty'.[107] Cuthbert and Aethelthryth are mentioned because their incorruptibility already assures them a place in the heavenly kingdom. To Bede this was an event very worthy of being placed in time.

In the context of this chapter these two entries are also interesting for their lack of miracle information. It was stated earlier that miracles were perfectly acceptable in *historia* because they concerned themselves with the actions of individuals, albeit dead ones. If this were so one would not expect to find them in a chronicle which, it has been said, is less interested in the individual than the citing of an event in the scheme of God's time. This is certainly reinforced by the *Chronicle*, which is notably lacking in miracle material.[108] In fact, Bede does not discuss either Aethelthryth or Cuthbert's miracles here. This is remarkable when one considered the descriptions in the *EH*. Essentially, Bede has made no attempt to add the 'personal' information so prevalent in his *historiae* to the *Chronica*. In this sense, he did not cross genre boundaries.

In Bede's writing of *historia*, particularly the *EH*, he worked within an understanding of history that focused on the actions of individuals worthy of imitation. To do this he significantly shifted the emphasis of *historia* away from that of some of his predecessors, moving from those acts one should not undertake to those that one should. As will be shown in subsequent chapters, to elaborate on these actions Bede drew heavily on non-contemporary, biblical and Late Antique images. However, his interest in the patristic authors was not limited to the models of deeds they could provide. This chapter has attempted to show that the study of generic boundaries and traditions can add valuable insights to the study of Bede's *historia* texts. In essence, Bede's generic boundaries were Roman ones. He chose to place his writings amongst traditions established by such authors as Eusebius and Jerome. Significantly he was not greatly interested in British, Irish, or Gallic texts – perhaps he did not feel that they were of enough worth. By siting his works in genres instituted by Roman authors Bede confirmed his orthodoxy and his reverence for all things Roman. He also provided signposts to his own textual community as to how to read his text. What is perhaps of interest here, particularly in terms of the 'literacy' of his audience, is that whilst he may have intended that the *EH*, in particular, should be read as part of the Eusebian historiographical tradition, it is clear that this did not always happen.

Chapter 5
A Case of Generic Discomfort:
Bede's *History of the Abbots*

THE PREVIOUS CHAPTER ILLUSTRATED THAT THE *ECCLESIASTICAL History* clearly fits within a particular genre of writing. However, it was also stated that if a text did not fit into a particular generic tradition it became a source of unease. This certainly seems to be the case with Bede's *History of the Abbots (HA)*.[1] This text is an anomaly to which surprisingly little attention has been given. Both Patrick Wormald and Alan Thacker (in greater detail) have offered evidence as to the sources that have influenced this text but very little has been done to discuss it in its wider context.[2] Even a superficial glance at the *HA* reveals elements of hagiography, history, and biography which together make it a fairly complex book – and one that is especially difficult to categorize as its function is not immediately clear. The main objectives of this chapter are to assess the nature of the *HA* as a text and thereby suggest a possible motive for its production; to question certain comments made about its hagiographical content by authors such as Alan Thacker; to show that the predominantly influential sources of this text were not necessarily only the Lerins texts which have been emphasized; and, finally, to suggest that what Bede is attempting do becomes clearer if a comparison is made with the Carolingian *Deeds of the Abbots (Gesta Abbatum)* texts.[3]

The first object of this analysis is, then, to look at the nature of the *HA* as a text. The observer of the *HA* is faced with an immediate problem when attempting to do this for this text has no preface and, therefore, no dedication to a patron; nor, more importantly for this study, any statement of intent. As was noted earlier, Halporn has shown that often a preface invites the reader to consider and read a text in a particular way.[4] Consequently, one has certain expectations of the text and can normally categorize it as, for example, a piece of hagiography, or a history, or a biography. With the *HA*, expectations are determined merely by the title and knowledge of other contemporary texts.

It is perhaps as a consequence of this that much of the academic discussion concerning the *HA* has concentrated on trying to explain it in the context of hagiography.[5] Indeed, if one looks for information on the *HA* it is clear that it is the hagiographical elements that have sparked the most debate. Thus *HA* is usually spoken of in the context of other *Lives*, especially the *Life of Ceolfrid*. In doing this historians have assembled a set of assumptions about the text which relate less to it and more to saints' Lives.

It is clear even from a cursory glance at this text that it is not a *vita*. Nevertheless, historians such as Wormald have attempted to explain the apparent lack of hagiographical material in terms of the sources used in the production of the text.[6] Both Thacker and Wormald focus on the influence of writings from Lerins, especially the *Life of Honoratus* (founder of Lerins) by Hilary, bishop of Arles, emphasizing that these sources focused less on biographical information than other *Lives* and showed sanctity to be confirmed less by signs and wonders than by personal virtues and affecting deathbed scenes.[7] Certainly if one looks at chapters 12–14 of the *HA* this does appear to be true. However, even with such information historians are still ill at ease with the hagiographical aspect of the *HA*. For example, five years after Wormald and Thacker's pieces Donald Bullough stated quite clearly that the *HA* 'is not hagiography in the normal sense of the word'.[8]

The dilemma of the text then comes from two clear areas: firstly, the unfortunate lack of prologue, and secondly, the text itself does not conform to the general discussion of the genre of hagiography.[9] This is, of course, understandable, for our criteria of what constitutes 'hagiography' come from the study of *vitae*; but, as has been made clear, this text is not a *vita*, it is in fact *historia*. Consequently, even acknowledging the possible sources, one would not perhaps expect to find the same kinds of general hagiographical details evident in a text such as the *Life of St Wilfrid*, or the *Life of St Cuthbert* or even the *Life of St Ceolfrith*. As Thacker himself noted, 'Bede treated the lives of his abbots very selectively. He made no attempt to show each of his subjects in the characteristic situations of a monastic saint'.[10] Thacker continues that Bede selected events from the subjects' lives to illustrate the chosen themes and that he deliberately designated the text a *historia* rather than a *vita*. He concludes that, as *historia*, the text was in the genre of the Christian history as established by Eusebius and continued by

Gregory of Tours, and as such was a record of a community and its path to salvation.

However, this idea in some ways contradicts the reason Thacker gives for the absence of the miraculous element in the text (an element which is visible at the end of the *Life of St Ceolfrith* but is not in the *HA*). Thacker notes that miracles are omitted from the *HA* because they were irrelevant to Bede's purpose.[11] Yet, if this is *historia* in the same genre as Eusebius' *History* and that of Gregory of Tours, the direct intervention of God in the life of the community in the form of miracles (which is, after all, so prevalent in Bede's *EH*) would surely have been an integral part of the text. If one looks at Bede's own biographical information at the end of his *EH*, it is clear that he himself distinguishes between the 'Histories of the Saints', which are essentially *vitae*, the *EH*, which seems more in the style of authors such as Eusebius, and the *HA*, which seems to be in a category of its own. It would appear that contemporary definitions of history were more varied than just the Eusebian model.

In attempting to understand the nature of the *HA* one should perhaps concentrate on Bede's descriptions of the work. It could be inferred from Bede's own entitling of the book as *Historia Abbatum Monasterii* that the text was to show exactly what the abbots did for the monastery in which it was Bede's joy to serve God. This suggests, therefore, that Bede's concentration was not on the abbot's lives *per se* but rather on what they brought to the monastery (either spiritually or materially). Book 1 opens not with a narration of Biscop's life (as one might expect from a *vita*) but with a direct statement concerning his foundation of the monastery of Wearmouth.[12] Thence with narrative details of certain events, the text shows how Biscop brought knowledge, books, stone masons, ornaments, a monastic privilege, pictures and images of saints and land to the monastery at Wearmouth-Jarrow.[13] In short, Book 1 indicates the substantial material wealth Biscop gained or purchased for his monastery: as Bede notes in chapter 6, Biscop was 'tireless in providing for his church' [*..aecclesiae suae prouisor inpiger..*].[14] This theme is continued in Book II's discussion of Ceolfrith. In chapter 15 Bede is keen to emphasize what Ceolfrith had brought to the monastery. Thus he records that Ceolfrith built several oratories, increased the number of vessels of the church and altar, and augmented the number of vestments of every kind and the library of both monasteries, adding three complete editions of the new translations of the Bible, one of which was the great *Codex Amiatinus* (derived possibly from the *Codex Grandior*).[15]

Also in this chapter Bede comments on the land acquired by the monastery during Ceolfrith's abbacy.[16] Moreover, if one observes the (albeit brief) notice on Hwaertberht's abbacy, the text centres on privileges and translations.[17] It would be fair to say that essentially the *HA* shows less of the lives of Bede's abbots and more of the establishment of Wearmouth-Jarrow and its growth into a site of no little status.

Indeed, though it appears that one of the functions of this text is to show the abbot's contribution to the monastery's development, the discussion in the *HA* often actually seems more focused on the objects brought to the monastery than on the individual who brought them. Biographical information is minimal and in some cases only seems to be given to supply a narrative context to what, at times, reads like a monastic inventory. Thus, in chapter 2 Biscop's first visit to Rome forms the context to explain how Biscop amassed knowledge concerning the forms of Church life. In chapter 5 Bede's stress is not on Biscop's journey to Gaul (as it is in chapter 7 of the *Life of St Ceolfrith*, where the emphasis is more on Biscop's relationship with the abbot Torthelm) than on the masons themselves, and then on the glass-makers.[18] Biscop's journey in the *HA* provides an immediate context for his descriptions of what was brought to the monastery, whereas the anonymous *Life of St Ceolfrith* was more interested in recording Biscop's general biographical information. Chapters 6 and 9 also provide a context for Bede's extremely detailed accounts of objects gained by Biscop for the monastery. These chapters more than any other in the text appear to function primarily as narrated inventories.

The chapters relating to Ceolfrith and Hwaertberht exhibit a similar emphasis. Thus though chapter 15 begins with a characterization of Ceolfrith using established hagiographical *topoi*, it is kept noticeably short and Bede immediately follows by commenting in considerable detail on the assets Ceolfrith gained during his abbacy.[19] This is also evident in Bede's description of Hwaertberth's term of office. In chapter 18 he gives only scant details with regard to Hwaertberth's life and in chapter 20, summarizing his abbacy, Bede is only interested in the privileges he recovered, and in particular the translations of the relics of Abbots Eosterwine and Sigfrid.[20]

As Jones noted, 'this emphasis on material fact is so exaggerated as to be the noteworthy characteristic of the work'.[21] Indeed, if one compares this text with both the Lerins and other contemporary sources it soon becomes clear that Bede's descriptions were not typical either in the extent of the detail or in the immediate context of the description. For example, if one looks at two of the texts which have been seen as having influence on the *HA*, the *Life of St Honoratus* by St Hilary and the *Life of Augustine* by Possidius, it is quite clear that there is actually little overall comparison.[22] These texts function as hagiography, following through the lives of individual saints until their death. The *Life of St Honoratus* discusses Honoratus' childhood, baptism, his *peregrinatio*, and his pastoral role and care. Essentially this text and the *Life of St Augustine* are testimonies of the faith and sanctity in their lives.

It would be wrong to dismiss these texts as having no influence on the *HA*. It is, for instance, interesting that Possidius notes, in the context of Augustine's death, that he 'always ordered [that] the Church's library, with all the books, [was] to be carefully preserved for posterity', a parallel too close to Bede's note concerning Biscop's final wishes to be ignored: 'The noble and extensive library... he ordered should be carefully preserved as a single collection and not allowed to decay through neglect or be split up'.[23] However, in general these texts actually bear less comparison with the *HA* in terms of the focus of the text than has perhaps been suggested. This is made especially clear if one compares St Hilary's description of the foundation of the church at Lerins by Honoratus with that of Biscop's foundation at Wearmouth. St Hilary merely notes that because of Honoratus' 'industry a church was built there [Lerins] sufficient for the elect of the Church of God; shelters arose, fit dwellings for the monks..'.[24] Indeed, rather than being interested in the fabric and furnishings of this church (as Bede so clearly is with Wearmouth), Hilary concentrates on an allegorical discussion of Honoratus as a temple of Christ: 'Whoever yearned for Christ sought Honoratus, and whoever sought Honoratus found Christ fully. For Christ reigned there supreme and dwelt in the heart of Honoratus as in a lofty citadel and a shining temple'.[25] When discussing Biscop's foundation at Wearmouth Bede is more interested in relating actual details of the building programme, noting that Biscop's zeal meant that within a year of the foundations having been laid the 'gable ends of the

Church were in place'.[26] Bede continues to describe the glaziers and other furnishings.[27] As has been seen, such an interest in the actual material evidence of the church, as opposed to the individuals founding the churches, can also be seen in his description of Ceolfrith's additions to the monastery. Bede makes no attempt to allegorize his subjects as 'temples of Christ'. In the *HA* he is concerned with describing real objects, not abstract concepts relating to them.

This emphasis on a description of land, buildings, and furnishings of the monastery for their own sake becomes even clearer if one compares the *HA* with two contemporary *vitae*, the *Life of St Wilfrid* by Stephanus and the anonymous *Life of St Ceolfrith*. For example, Stephanus' discussion of the gift of land by Alhfrith to Wilfrid and his dedication of the monastery at Ripon clearly differ from Bede; firstly, when Stephanus narrates the donation of the monastery at Ripon by Alhfrith, he places it firmly in a Biblical context and the attention is on Wilfrid rather than the monastery itself:

> 'he [Alhfrith] granted him [Wilfred] the monastery at Ripon together with thirty hides of land, and he was ordained abbot. And now, even as the door of this world was being opened wide by the Lord and the holy Apostle Peter, so ever more widely opened the door for the giving of alms in the Lord's name....[28]

However, when Bede describes such donations they read like charters and are not placed in any biblical-related context.[29] Moreover, although the *Life of St Wilfrid* does give some details concerning the buildings of the churches of Ripon and Hexham, Stephanus places much more emphasis on describing them allegorically:

> 'For as Moses built an earthly tabernacle made with hands, of diverse varied colours according to the pattern shown by God in the mount, to stir up the faith of the people of Israel for the worship of God, so the blessed Bishop Wilfrid wondrously adorned the bridal chamber of the true Bridegroom and Bride with gold and silver and varied purples...[30]

Also, even where Stephanus comments on the adornment provided by Wilfrid for the house of God, all of these objects are placed in the context of being a witness to his blessed memory.[31] The objects are not mentioned so much for the their own sake, as directly concerned with Wilfrid's piety. Such depictions do not read like the narrated inventory that the *HA* offers, rather they form an integral part of and are directly related to eulogising Wilfrid. In terms of depth of detail, sources such as the anonymous Life of St Ceolfrith are not meticulous in their reports, but instead prefer to offer general comments. Thus chapters 9–10 of the anonymous Life of St Ceolfrith are content merely to record in unspecific terms the objects Biscop brought back from Rome on his fourth trip. Indeed, this source concentrates more on the bringing back to Britain of the arch-chanter of the Roman Church (John), than on the other objects. Moreover, unlike the comprehensive list in the corresponding chapter of the HA, the Life of St Ceolfrith omits some of the items recorded by Bede, including the papal privilege. If one looks at other contemporary Continental vitae, such as the Life of St Gertrude, one can see that though it is noted that sacred books were brought to Nivelles from Rome and elsewhere by Gertrude's mother, Itta, there is no in-depth account, and the objects are directly related in terms of Itta's holy life.32

The fact that the detailed accounts found in the *HA* are unique is further emphasized by a comparison with Bede's other works. For example, Bede's homily to Benedict Biscop depicts, perhaps more typically, Biscop's life around his 'pilgrimage for Christ' and concentrates ultimately on placing the context of his life in that particular day's biblical reading, Matthew 19: 27–29. As Wormald has noted, this is essentially a '*peregrinatio* text' concerning the abandonment or renunciation of one's kin group, social standing, and gender expectations.[33] Though the text mentions the large library, the relics of the blessed martyrs, and the church fabric, these are secondary to relating his spiritual life and the description is considerably briefer than that in the *HA*.[34] Essentially, in the homily the material evidence is there only to augment the primary theme of Biscop's religious life, whereas in the *HA* it appears to exist in its own right.

A similar statement could be made of Bede's biblical commentaries. Benedicta Ward has shown Bede's interest in the actual building material and furnishings of the church in his commentaries, such as *Libri Quatuor in Principium Genesis, In Cantica Canticorum Allegorica*

Expositio, In Ezram et Neemiam, De Tabernaculo, and *De Templo*.[35] However, as with the other evidence cited here, these texts relate their information more in terms of the allegorical exegesis of the Bible than mere details of the fabric and furnishings of a particular church, and in this sense do not compare with the *HA*. Thus when considering the building and furnishing of Solomon's Temple, as detailed in 1 Kings 6:1–38 and 1 Kings 7:13–51, Bede's main interest lies in emphasizing the allegorical relationship of the house of God in Jerusalem as an image of the holy universal Church, which from its first election to its end is being built up by the grace of Christ's peace which is redemption.[36] For Bede the description of the Temple as given in the first book of Kings should be seen in the light of Christian truth. In this treatise his interest in the specific fabric and furnishings of the Temple is a purely allegorical one.[37]

In terms of the extent of detail, one needs to turn to the other works Bede classed as *historia* for a comparison. For example, although in his other *vitae*, such as the *Life of St Felix*, the rebuilding and furnishing of St Felix's church is commented on, it is only a brief notice, lacking in any great detail.[38] Predominantly the text is concerned with Felix's attributes as a saint. Moreover, the information on church foundations and their growth in the *EH* are similarly undetailed notices. Thus, concerning the church of SS Peter and Paul at Canterbury, Bede does comment that it was endowed with various gifts, but unlike the *HA* he does not go on to detail them; this is a pattern generally followed throughout the *EH*.[39] To summarize, two main points can be drawn for the comparisons offered here. Firstly, although some texts do show an interest in the 'material culture' of their church, this is not often described to the extent that it is found in the *HA* and, secondly, where contemporary texts do concentrate on describing the actual fabric they place it either in the context of the actual holiness of an individual or in allegorical expositions. Essentially Bede's focus on the objects in the *HA* seems unique when placed amongst other contemporary works.

If it is accepted that neither traditional hagiographical nor historical works were the over-riding influence on the focus of the content of Bede's *HA*, then the model he used needs to be identified. To find a possible answer one needs to turn away from the hagiographical material of Lerins and the insular contemporary works of Northumbria to Bede's beloved Rome. The *Book of Pontiffs* provided Bede with his model for concentrating on the material wealth of a church. The *Book of Pontiffs* also gives biographical information second place to what the individual brought to the monastery.[40] Indeed, the most recent translator has commented on what he calls the text's 'endowment catalogues'.[41] Judith Herrin too has noted that, 'the notices of the *Liber Pontificalis* [*Book of Pontiffs*] usually record in great details the buildings and rich decorations endowed by Roman bishops, often to the exclusion of initiatives in other fields'.[42]

Two chapters of the *Book of Pontiffs* exemplify the many parallels in emphasis between it and the *HA*. These are the chapters on Pope Silvester (314–335) and Gregory the Great (590–604).[43] First, there is no allegorical or biblical contextualization of the material culture. Secondly, the general construction of the chapters follows the pattern of very briefly describing biographical details of the relevant individuals and then going into long, detailed endowment catalogues, decrees made, and councils called. Thus with Silvester it is noted that he was born in Rome, son of Rufinus, and that he held the see twenty-three years, ten months and eleven days. It then goes on to note when he was bishop, giving a brief historical context before turning to the extensive list of his church endowments and their ornamentation.[44] Following a notice on his decrees it further concentrates on church foundations and ornamentation, but this time the text is concerned with Emperor Constantine's gifts during Silvester's pontificate.[45]

Likewise, the chapter on Gregory the Great accentuates what Gregory did for the fabric of the church. The chapter follows the pattern of birth, parentage, and the length of time that he held the see.[46] Thence it goes straight into discussing the works he produced, the canopy he built for the altar at St Peter's, the purple-dyed cloth (decorated in gold) to go above the Apostle's body and finally his church dedications and death.[47] In both of these examples, biographical information is kept to the minimum, whilst the fabric of the church is comprehensively described.

Although the *HA* does not follow exactly the same pattern (it does for example generally give more narrative details about the characteristics of an individual) there are some clear similarities. Primarily, there is the focus on the material fact evident in Bede's text and the lack of allegorical contextualisation of the church fabric. Indeed, chapters 6 and 15 could be 'endowment catalogues' from the *Book of Pontiffs* in narrative form. Also, in chapter 20 one can see quite clearly the concentration on 'objects' gained for the church during an individual abbacy. The chapter that relates Hwaertberht's abbacy is, as has been said, devoid of comment on his 'spiritual' life and is merely recorded in terms of the restoration of privileges and the translations of relics.

It is not suggested that Bede constructed the *HA* by copying directly from the *Book of Pontiffs* – although it is interesting to note the correspondence in the fabric and ornamentation that is mentioned – but rather it provided him with a precedent from which to develop his own endowment catalogue. If this is accepted there is still a problem with the narrative elements of the text, which are more hagiographical. Perhaps Bede realized that long lists did not make for enjoyable reading and thus he placed his inventory in the context of a narrative using standard (if brief) hagiographical forms. Alternatively, perhaps he felt that the only way to ensure that this text was viewed as having legitimacy was to place it in the genre of Christian *historia*. By alluding to a hagiographical framework he effectively linked his text to orthodox predecessors. The point is that the hagiographical material was of secondary importance to the actual physical evidence of the church in this work. In fact, Bede's concentration on the wealth of objects makes one wonder if Bede was primarily attempting to portray the status of the monastery rather than the lives of its abbots. (Indeed, such a relationship was to be found not only in the *Book of Pontiffs*. One need only look to the autobiographical information concerning Gregory of Tours in his *Histories* to see a connection between the man and the fabric of the church.)[48]

As Thacker has noticed, the holy men of Wearmouth-Jarrow were neither royal warriors nor outstanding ascetics.[49] Is it possible that in the face of not having an outstanding saint with which to augment the position of the monastery Bede was forced to acclaim the status of the monastery through its great collection of sacred objects, art and great knowledge? If one looks at the other monasteries, such as Whitby, Ely, Lindisfarne, Iona, and Whithorn, it is easy to see how they augmented their positions through the development of successful saints' cults.

A fundamental aspect of the success of such a cult was the saint's *vita*. For example, there are fifty-nine known manuscripts of the Cuthbertine lives; in this sense one is looking at a successful *vita*.[50] There were only two of the *Life of St Ceolfrith* – this was not a successful text. If one accepts that the anonymous Ceolfrith *vita* came first and that it was not a success, is it not just possible that the status of the monastery could be increased by stressing the wealth of other relics and holy objects that it had?[51] Brown has noted that *De Gloria Martyrum* by Gregory of Tours is a book about the tapping of the new resources, in this case, relics.[52] It is the contention of this author that Bede's *HA* is also about the tapping of new resources, but Bede was not restricted to relics alone. He focused on knowledge, relics, endowments from a king, religious ornaments and paintings, a papal privilege, and the fact that whilst the monastery may not have had a great ascetic or royal saint, its first five abbots were all sanctified. Essentially, the *HA* is a text that is not so much a witness to the status of a monastery's saintly abbots, as a record of the status of the saintly abbots' monastery.

Having acknowledged this point, one way for the modern researcher to overcome the problems of expectations concerning the *HA* would be to suggest that we consider it by a different title. Bede himself singled it out as a separate or sub-genre of *historia*. He, too, appears to have been aware that it did not sit comfortably within the boundaries of either *historia ecclesiastica* nor *historiae sanctorum*. So, the question must be, what title should we now give this text?

The *HA* was not the only early medieval text to have the *Book of Pontiffs* as a fundamental source. It has been noted that the *Book of Pontiffs* also had great influence on texts which are designated *Gesta*.[53] It is the contention of this author that the title *Gesta Abbatum* may well be more fitting for Bede's *HA* than either *historia* or *vita*. Generically speaking *Gesta* was the title given by editors to narrative texts that were constituted of a series of notices concerning successive abbots of a particular monastery.[54] Moreover, this particular genre placed the emphasis on achievements and events rather than just on biographical details.[55] Such an outline could be a general reference to Bede's *HA*, where, it has been shown, biographical information does appear secondary to the achievements and objects brought to Wearmouth-Jarrow by its successive abbots. Indeed, Bede may have had his own dilemma in entitling and thus classifying this work for though it does touch on personal details, as *historia* should, it does not give them the same emphasis as his other *historia* texts.

If one compares Bede's *HA* with the ninth-century *Gesta Abbatum Fontanellensium (GAF)*, one can see striking affinities.[56] Although the *GAF* is a composite text (composed of four parts, compiled and revised according to particular circumstances over a period of time) the similarities concerning focus of content strongly suggest that Bede's *HA* was at least as influential as the *Book of Pontiffs* in its construction.[57] Firstly, both texts have a preponderance of information concerning the acquisition of books and the consequent development of a monastic library. Thus, in the *HA* the collection of books is mentioned in chapters 4, 6, 9, and 15, with explicit statements being made about which books were being collected in Ceolfrid's abbacy (chapter 15).[58] The *GAF's* authors also place an importance on the accumulation of books. Indeed, they appear to have taken far more delight even than Bede in cataloguing the additions to their library. For example, the chapter concerning the abbacy of Wando contains a specific list of the numerous books received by the monastery during his tenure. These included expositions on the three evangelists, John, Matthew, and Luke, Rufinus's *Ecclesiastical History*, the *Life and Passion of Felix of Nola*, the *Rule of St Augustine*, *Letters from Augustine*, Jordanes' *History of the Goths*, the rules of St Benedict and Columbanus, to name but a few.[59] In the chapter concerning Gervold one finds another of these catalogues, albeit shorter.[60] This is followed by a more extensive list of books associated with the priest Harduin, including books by Gregory the Great, Augustine and, perhaps more pertinently, Bede's *De Naturis Rerum ac Temporibus*.[61] Such an extensive catalogue is again present in the chapter concerning Ansigisus.[62]

However, these texts do not just list the books; both the *HA* and the *GAF* place a focus on the degree of learning of their abbots. The *HA*, therefore, makes it quite clear that Biscop amassed a great deal of knowledge.[63] Abbot Sigfrid was well versed in scriptural knowledge.[64] Hwaertberht, too, was notable for his studies, having gone to Rome during the pontificate of Sergius to learn.[65] Not only this, but a direct link was said to have been made between the collection of books and the improvement of Christian education by Biscop on his deathbed.[66] As

Wood intimated, the premium placed on learning can also be seen in the *GAF*.[67] Thus, St Hugo is noted for his knowledge of the Scriptures and St Gervold for his zest for teaching.[68] Indeed, the *GAF* attributes the foundation of a school to improve literacy at Fontanelle to St Gervold.[69] Whilst it is clear from the *GAF's* booklists that the Fontanelle authors supplied more in-depth information concerning library acquisitions and learning than Bede, the focus on the accumulation of knowledge is the same, and to a certain extent the significance of this focus is the same. The acquisition of knowledge, particularly in the tangible form of books, as well as the allusion to Christian learning associated with it, brought the monastery status.

Also, both texts emphasize the building up of the fabric of the church in terms of donations and purchases of land, as well as the actual construction of the respective monasteries. Thus, Bede notes in detail Ecgfrith's donations of land to Biscop on which to found the two monasteries, Ceolfrith's purchases of land from Aldfrith, and also the gift of land received from Witmar at his consecration to the monastery of St Peter.[70] Wood has observed a similar preoccupation with the details of land-holdings in the *GAF*, noting that it was an important repository of charter evidence for the abbey.[71] Like Bede, therefore, it mentions the initial grant of land given through the largesse of Echinoald.[72] It then continues to list further gifts as well as restorations of previous gifts taken away from the monastery.[73] (A notable example of this latter occurrence is to be found in the abbacy of St Gervold, where Charlemagne restored all the estates taken unjustly from the abbey or which had been conferred on the king's followers.)[74]

The accruing of the fabric in terms of sacred objects and ornaments is another area of parity found in both texts. Bede is at pains to note that Biscop collected not only books but relics, ornaments, pictures, and everything necessary for the service of the church and altar: *Sed et cuncta quae ad altaris et aecclesiae ministerium competebant.*[75] Moreover, whilst he might not have elaborated on the titles of the books Biscop collected, Bede did specify the pictures and where they were placed in the church.[76] The authors of the *GAF* also list the appropriation of ecclesiastical and other articles. Such lists can be found, for example, in the records of Hugo.[77] They are also evident in the chapters concerning the abbots Wido and Gervold.[78]

Nonetheless, these are not the only similarities of focus to be found in the two texts. The *HA* and the *GAF* additionally seem equally uninterested in any miraculous element concerning their respective abbots.[79] Both texts record the translations of previous abbots. Hence, just as Hwaertberht is remembered (and revered perhaps) for having translated the relics of Eosterwine and Sigfrid, so Abbot Bainus is noted as having translated the relics of Wandregisil, Ansbert, and Wulfram.[80] Both texts also comment on the monastic immunities their respective communities gained.[81]

There are a few discrepancies between these texts that need, however, to be recognized. Firstly, as noted earlier, the *GAF* appears to be a composite text, reworked by different authors. The *HA,* on the other hand, appears only to have had one author. The *GAF* appears more interested in the particulars of family connections, often recording the actual parentage of its abbots, whereas Bede appears content merely to record the 'nobility' of the abbots without elaborating on who their parents were.[82] And, of course, the bibliographic lists in the *GAF* are far more explicit than they are in the *HA*. Nevertheless, even these differences are relatively minor and the two texts are clearly similar in overall content and focus. Arguably, whilst the *GAF's* authors' penchant for detail may have come from their reading of the *Book of Pontiffs,* the structure and content-focus of the work appears to have been heavily influence by Bede's *HA*. Essentially, the two texts illustrate how the status of the monastery was bound up in both the stature of its abbots and in the possessions accumulated for the fabric of the church during their abbacies.

In his *HA* Bede achieved a text which not only conformed to his understanding of *historia* (narration of personal actions often with the aim of inspiring imitation) – after all his abbots provide excellent examples of model abbatial behaviour – but also extended *historia's* boundary to take into consideration that the abbot's life was inextricably linked to the fabric of the church. The reason for such a text is perhaps simple: not only the memory of the abbots but also the fabric of their churches were commodities of status worth exploiting.[83] If one considers the text from this viewpoint, seeing it more as a *gesta abbatum* than a *historia* much of the unease concerning its generic placing is dissipated. Bede's *HA* is a prototype *GA* and one can only question whether he chose to call it *historia*, rather than anything else to ensure that his text was viewed as having legitimacy amid a community where this was a critical issue.[84]

Chapter 6
A Case of Innovation within
Generic Boundaries: Bede's *Martyrology*

THROUGHOUT THE PREVIOUS DISCUSSION OF BEDE'S UNDERSTANDING of *historia* it has been stressed that the narration of personal actions performed a central role. Moreover, it has been noted that for reasons of authority and legitimacy many of Bede's *historiae* have obvious generic links with patristic and Rome-associated predecessors. At the same time they included deviations from these texts, thereby making Bede's writings unique within the genre in which they are normally classified. Within this framework Bede's *Martyrology* is another of his works that deserves to be admitted, at least as a sub-genre, to the corpus of his history writings. Although Bede did not himself identify it as a *historia*, he did place it directly after his histories in the bibliographic note at the end of the *EH* and the importance of this text as the first of the 'historical' martyrologies has been noticed by Hippolyte Delehaye, Wilhelm Levison, and Jacques Dubois.[1]

Despite the undoubted originality of Bede's approach to his *Martyrology* the text has been little considered by academics.[2] Quentin, Dubois, and Renaud are the only authors to have really attempted any significant research and the results of their studies have remained largely confined to the writings of a handful of Bedan scholars.[3] Indeed, there is no critical edition of the *Martyrology* and for the purposes of this chapter the 'practical' edition drawn up by Dubois and Renaud has been used.

This chapter aims to look at the innovations Bede introduced that led to his *Martyrology* being called a 'historical martyrology'. However, whilst attempting to do this, one needs to be well aware that the source itself is problematic. At present it is difficult to determine the exact date for the production of this text by Bede, though Colgrave suggested that it was written sometime between 725 and 731.[4] Furthermore, although Quentin listed the entries that appear to have comprised the original text, these entries were derived from fifteen manuscripts of the *Martyrology* and there are obvious variations. Thus, the earliest surviving manuscript is a ninth-century manuscript of the Bibliothèque de Saint-Gall (no. 451) which, is as Quentin notes, unfortunately incomplete.[5] Moreover, many of the manuscripts, such as Vatican MS Pal. Lat. 833, have later additions that appear to bear no relationship to Bede's original *Martyrology*.[6]

Nonetheless, this is a text that merits observation. For example, it has been stated that Bede drew predominantly from patristic and 'Rome'-related sources. Never is this more evident than in the entries found in his *Martyrology*. Quentin's work shows nearly all of the entries to have been compiled from non-literary hagiographic sources such as the *Martyrologium Hieronymianum Epternacensis* [MHE] (similar to the early eighth-century manuscript: Codex Epternacensis lat. 10837), *Book of Pontiffs*, and hagiographical literary texts such as the *Vitae* written by Jerome and Augustine.[7] The only exceptions to this rule come from the entries that relate directly to the few Anglo-Saxon saints mentioned, Aethelthryth and the Hewalds. Noticeably, no martyrs or confessors associated with the Irish tradition are elaborated and it is not possible to state if the short notices, which include Cuthbert for 20th March, were original to Bede. Missing also are other important local Northumbrian Anglo-Saxon saints, such as Oswald. Essentially, Bede focused his extended notices on 'Roman orthodox' texts, once again exhibiting his deep respect for all things 'Roman'.

It was suggested earlier that many of Bede's texts have an obvious generic link with patristic and Roman-associated sources. The *Martyrology* is no exception to this rule. As has been noted by Dubois, Lapidge, and Goffart, Bede's *Martyrology* appears to have been based on an existing martyrology ascribed to Jerome.[8] Indeed, Bede appears to have relied heavily on this text: if Bede's sources offered several dates for an individual, he gave preference to the date in the *MHE*.[9] Nevertheless, despite this generic connection there are certain innovations introduced by Bede, which led to his *Martyrology* (rather than *MHE*) becoming the generic prototype for later martyrologies. The first, most obvious distinction is the level of information that Bede offers. Bede noted in his *EH* that he had written 'A Martyrology of the feast days of the holy martyrs: in which I have diligently tried to record all that I could find about them, not only on what day, but also by what kind of combat and under what judge they overcame the world'.[10] As McCulloh commented, the form of Bede's notices often parallel this description closely.[11] Usually he began by stating a place and name, adding also the name of the reigning emperor and persecuting judge and then finishing with a variety of gruesome tortures. This stands in stark contrast to the majority of the entries of the *MHE*. As Lapidge stated 'the *MHE*, on the whole, offers the observer only skeletal, telegraphic information'.[12] Normally, only a name and place is included. Bede's decision to extend the material, therefore, does not seem to relate to his reading of the *MHE*.

Nevertheless this generalism is not without its notable exceptions. For example, the first notice of Bede's *Martyrology* (for KL IAN, 1st January) is that of St Almachius. In this case Bede drew heavily on the *MHE*, which appears to have offered all the material Bede required.[13] Bede's entry is almost a verbatim copy of the *MHE*. The same can be said of the listings for Macedonis (III ID MAR, 13th March) and Montanus (VII KL. APR, 26th March).[14] Perhaps these fuller notices from the *MHE* actually formed the basis for Bede's idea of an extended narrative. The innovation in Bede's work was essentially that he introduced fuller comments for most of the notices. It is not difficult to suggest from this that by building from certain examples that he found in the *MHE*, Bede maintained a direct contact with the generic predecessor and thereby maintained the legitimacy of his text.

Bede's innovative approach is further exhibited in his preoccupation with the tortures that the martyrs suffered. This is clearly seen, for example, in the entry for Pope Alexander, and the two priests Eventius and Theodulus (3rd May). In this passage Bede focuses immediately on their imprisonment and tortures, and continues by noting their burning and Alexander's beheading. Only once this has been done does Bede note the 'judge' under whom they died:

> 'At Rome, [the commemorative festival] of Sts Alexander, pope, and Eventius and Theodulus, priests: the first of whom was slain, after chains and prisons, the rack, claws and fires, by means of punctures repeated throughout all his limbs: and the following ones, themselves after the long endurance of prison, were tested by fires and at last beheaded under the judge Aurelianus, in the time of Prince Trajan'.[15]

Bede's seemingly morbid fascination with extreme torture is not restricted
to this one entry, however, but is, in varying degrees of detail, a feature of
nearly all of his notations on the martyrs of the persecutions. Even in
those cases where Bede comments on confessors rather than martyrs he
is inclined to focus (although admittedly not always) on material which
exhibited a torment that they were prepared to undergo. Thus, when
dealing with the feast-day of St Felix of Nola (14th January), Bede centres
the entry on the episode where Felix is thrown into prison and tortured
rather than on his asceticism or posthumous miracles:

> 'In Campania, the commemorative festival of St Felix, priest and
> confessor: about whom Bishop Paulinus wrote, among other
> things, that when he was placed in prison by persecutors and was
> lying, chained up, upon snail shells and small potsherds, he was
> released and let out at night by an angel.'[16]

This interest in detailing the macabre events leading to the eventual
martyrdom of an individual or group of people is not found in the *MHE*.
Indeed, when discussing Bede's *Martyrology* Plummer was prepared to
imply that this preoccupation was a later addition to a much more sedate
work: 'The *Martyrology* as we have it has been so added to, that it is
impossible to tell what part, if any, is really due to Bede. And there is
much in it that one would willingly believe not to be Bede's – too much
ecclesiastical gloating over the physical horrors of martyrdom, and
legends of the purely silly kind.'[17]

Nevertheless, to find a parallel for such an interest one need look no
further than a text referred to by Bede in the *Martyrology*, Eusebius'
Ecclesiastical History. Delehaye himself indicated the influence of
Eusebius' writings about various martyrs on texts such as the *MHE*.[18]
These works had a direct impact on Bede's *Martyrology*. If, for instance,
one reads Book 8 of Eusebius' *HE* one quickly sees how Eusebius also
appears to have taken an inordinate delight in concentrating on the
actual physical torments facing people who professed Christianity.
Thus, when discussing the results of the third edict of Diocletian's
persecution, Eusebius notes how people endured various forms of torture
(scourged, racked, and burnt*): flagris alii discerpebantur, alii ungulis
fodiebantur, alii ignitis lamminis urebantur...'.*[19] Moreover, when

detailing the martyrs of Egypt in chapter 8 the focus is almost entirely on the tortures endured:

> 'Some of them were committed to the flames after being torn and racked and grievously scourged, and suffering other manifold torments terrible to hear, while some were engulfed in the sea, others with a good courage stretched forth their heads to them that cut them off, or died in the midst of their tortures, or perished of hunger; and others again were crucified, some as malefactors usually are, and some, even more brutally, were nailed in the opposite manner, head downwards and kept alive until they should perish of hunger on the gibbet... .'[20]

Essentially, from chapters 3 to 13 Eusebius recounts with great relish the trials endured by the martyrs. In fact, Plummer was ignoring the fact that standardized, stereotypical texts concerning the martyrs that focused on the tortures undergone by individuals were a popular part of the Cult of Martyrs from the third century.[21] As Roberts has noted, a principle of these texts is that the glory of a martyr is proportionate to the cruelty of his suffering.[22] From reading Eusebius' text it is not difficult to suggest that Eusebius' interest influenced Bede's selection of material from the sources that he had at his disposal.

Eusebius was not necessarily the only source of influence on Bede's interest in detailing torture. Jerome's *Letter to Innocentius* concerning the adulterous woman struck with seven swords is particularly ghoulish. He notes how the woman showed a courage superior to her sex as her body was stretched on a rack, and her hands, blackened by prison filth, were bound with cords, before she was executed.[23] David Scourfield has suggested that this particular letter should be seen in the light of Late Antique rhetoric and that the narration of torture had its origins in the classical tradition of declamation.[24] (This opens up interesting possibilities for examining the extent to which the literature of the Cult of Martyrs was influenced by the rhetorical training provided by the practice of declamation.) He then argues that Quintilian might have been the source for Jerome in this case. Applying an examination for the possible presence of classical rhetorical assumptions, it is tempting to suggest that Bede drew his descriptions in this case not from a knowledge of Jerome but from the actual source of Jerome's knowledge of declamation. However, it is more likely that Rufinus-Eusebius and Jerome's *Letter to Innocentius* were the sources for his framework. As Augustine himself noted, 'those with acute and eager minds more readily learn eloquence by reading and hearing the eloquent than by following the rules of eloquence'.[25] Bede did not need access to the original textbooks of classical rhetoric; he was fed by intermediaries, which by their very nature were passing on the rhetorical tradition from antiquity.

Bede's study of poetry may also have influenced his development of the *Martyrology*. Both the *Liber Peristaphanon* by Prudentius and Aldhelm's *Carmen de Virginitate* (itself influenced by Prudentius) contain lurid descriptions of the torture of martyrs.[26] However, having acknowledged this, it is interesting to note that Bede did not opt for a poetic martyrology. Even a brief comparison between the corresponding entries in the *Liber Peristaphanon* and Bede's *Martyrology* (Agnes and Cassian) shows that Bede concisely summarizes information, and, as Lifshitz has commented, uses an extraordinarily compressed style.[27] Where he was drawing on the poetry of Prudentius for his information with regard to torture, he stripped the text of any poetic aspects, and tempered the eulogistic rhetoric associated with the narratives of the martyrs. Poetry may have provided specific information but it does not seem to be a source of his overall framework.

Another distinction which makes Bede's *Martyrology* stand out from the *MHE* and the historical martyrologies which were the successors of his text is the fact that it follows the Julian calendar, beginning with the kalends of January, rather than the ecclesiastic calendar.[28] This anomaly is problematic for it represents a significant break from the generic predecessor. As a liturgical text one might understandably expect to find such a martyrology following the ecclesiastical year (i.e. beginning on 25th December). Indeed, it would appear that this is the assumption that Goffart is making when he incorrectly states that Bede's *Martyrology*, like its Hieronymian predecessor, did start on the 25th December. Thus he continues, it is unlike 'the annalistic framework normally used for chronicles'.[29] In fact, by beginning his text on 1st January, Bede made it far more like an annal than what one might understand as a liturgical martyrology. It is not clear, however, why Bede chose to do this.

One possible solution to the problem of why Bede chose the Julian calendar may be found in his *De Temporum Ratione* (*DTR*). Bede himself implies that a Julian calendar accompanied *DTR* in its codex.[30] The editor, C.W. Jones, has established that such essentially computistic calendars gave rise to the martyrologium of the calendar (i.e. the entries beside the Julian date of the names of the saints of local cult).[31] Further to this, he has shown how the commentator of the *DTR* describes this calendar as a martyrologium.[32] Nevertheless, Jones differentiates between this martyrology or calendar and Bede's historical *Martyrology*. The former, he believes, was designed for computistical requirements, the latter for reference and meditation. Although Jones concedes that the historical martyrology may have been a consequence of *kalendarium* , he adamantly stresses their differences and emphasizes that the manuscript tradition of the two is 'wholly separate'.[33] In fact, whilst Jones may be right to differentiate between the two, Bede's decision to use the Julian rather than the ecclesiastical calendar could have been influenced by the computistical martyrology that was an appendage to the *DTR*. If this is so, it surely implies a closer link between the two texts than Jones has been prepared to accept.

There is another link between the *Martyrology* and the *DTR*. As has already been commented, in the *Greater Chronicle (Chronica Maiora)* Bede makes the importance of the martyrs of the Sixth Age very clear. In the *Greater Chronicle*, however, he is selective with those martyrs he singles out. The genre of the martyrology allows him much greater scope to convey details on the martyrs. Indeed, some of the martyrs he mentions in the *Greater Chronicle* also occur in the *Martyrology*. Common to both texts are entries on Polycarp, Perpetua and Felicitas, Pope Alexander, Fabian, Cyprian, Pope Gaius, Pope Marcellinus, Alban, Gervase and Protase, Anastasius and Aethelthryth. A comparison of these entries confirms that in the *Greater Chronicle* Bede concentrated the material on brief, matter-of-fact notations that placed an episode in time. This is clearly shown, for example, if one views the respective accounts for Perpetua and Felicitas:

Greater Chronicle
   Perpetua and Felicitas were thrown to the beasts for Christ in the
   arena at Carthage in Africa on 7 March.

Mart.

> At Carthage, [the commemorative festival] of Perpetua and
> Felicitas, who were condemned to the beasts, under Prince
> Severus: and since Felicitas was pregnant in prison, it was
> procured by the prayers of all the soldiers [of Christ] who were
> likewise suffering that she would give birth in the eighth month.[34]

In the *Greater Chronicle* the entry is a mere listing of when (in terms of
chronology and day of death) and where they were martyred. In the
Martyrology this information is extended to note, as Bede himself
indicated, not only where, but also the judge and the extent of their
persecution. This is even more obvious if one compares the entries for
Pope Alexander, Polycarp, and Alban.

Essentially, the primary focus of the *Martyrology* is on the
person represented rather than locating the event within a specified
chronology. Thus, in the case of Pope Alexander as listed in the *Greater
Chronicle*, Bede is interested in noting only when his beheading occurred
and where:

> 'Alexander the bishop of Rome was also crowned by
> martyrdom. He was buried on the Via Nomentana at the seventh
> milestone of the city, where he was beheaded.'[35]

In the *Martyrology* one sees Bede's emphasis on what Alexander and
his companions were prepared to endure and the notification of the
beheading only follows after Bede has detailed a variety of tortures.[36]
This difference in concentration is all the more evident with Alban. The
Greater Chronicle's entry is a mere sentence indicating when Alban
crossed the ocean to Britain and was killed with his associates:

> 'It even crossed the Channel to Britain, where Alban, Aaron, and
> Julius, together with many other men and women, were
> condemned to their happy fate.'[37]

The Martyrology has a far more expanded narrative, focusing on Alban's
torture and martyrdom:

'In Britain, [the commemorative festival] of St Alban, martyr: who, in the time of Diocletian, in the city of *Verulumium*, after lashings and bitter torments suffered capital punishment: but as he was falling on the ground, the eyes of the one who killed him likewise fell to the ground. One of the soldiers also suffered with him, because he was unwilling to strike him when ordered to do so: for he was completely terrified by a divine miracle, since he had seen the blessed martyr, as he was hastening to the crown of martyrdom, render the bed of an interposed river passable for himself through prayer.'[38]

To achieve this change in emphasis Bede selected information from different sources for each of these works. Thus, in the *Greater Chronicle* entry for Felicitas and Perpetua, Bede only used Prosper's *Chronicle*.[39] However, in his *Martyrology* he supplements this source with material drawn from the *Passio* of Felicitas and Perpetua.[40] In the *Greater Chronicle*'s entry for Alexander, Bede is content to rely on the relevant information from the *Book of Pontiffs*.[41] In the *Martyrology* his main source is the *Passio Sancti Alexandri*.[42] For Polycarp, his *Greater Chronicle* note comes from the *MHE*, whilst his *Martyrology*'s narrative is derived from St Jerome's *De Viris Illustribus*.[43] Finally, for St Alban's entry in the *Greater Chronicle*, Bede depended on Gildas whilst using the *Passio Albani* as his main source for the *Martyrology*.[44] In the context of the *Greater Chronicle* Bede was generally uninterested in the specifics of an individual's actions and could thus depend upon sources which offered only brief notices. However, his aim for the *Martyrology* was clearly different and by deriving his entries from a broader selection of hagiographical material he introduced an extended narrative into his *Martyrology* with elements that resemble his *historiae*.

In this sense the *Martyrology* is more akin to Bede's *historiae*, which focus on personal action, than the *Greater Chronicle*, which appears to attempt to place an event in a chronology. This is excellently illustrated by the information Bede offers the reader about St Marcellinus (26th April). In the *Martyrology* Bede specifically notes the pontificate of Marcellinus, his beheading, the people he was persecuted with, and where he was buried:

'The deposition of St. Marcellinus, pope, who when he had ruled
the church for nine years and four months, in the time of
Diocletian and Maximianus, had his head chopped off, for the
faith of Christ, along with Claudius and Cyrainus and Antoninus,
by that same Diocletian, and after thirty-five days he was buried in
a small chamber on the Salarian Way by the priest Marcellus and
by the deacons, with hymns on 26th April.' [45]

The *Greater Chronicle* listing for this persecution omits his name. In fact,
it does not single out any individual, aiming only to record when the
persecution occurred and how many were martyred:

'In the second year of the persecution [Diocletian &
Maximimian]....This persecution was so savage and cruel that in
the course of a single month it was found that seventeen thousand
had died as martyrs for Christ.'[46]

This example does appear to confirm the emphasis placed upon the event
in time's framework in the *Greater Chronicle* rather than the actions of
individuals.

Nevertheless, a comparison of the *Greater Chronicle* and the
Martyrology shows that Bede was not entirely consistent in his approach
to the *Chronica*. In at least two cases the opposite to what has been
shown above can be seen. For instance, in his *Greater Chronicle* Bede
writes more about Aethelthryth (23rd June) than he does in the
Martyrology. The *Martyrology* is essentially taken up with Aethelthryth's
incorrupt status:

'In Britain, [the commemorative festival] of St. Aethelthryth,
virgin and queen: whose body, which had been buried for sixteen
years, was found uncorrupted.'[47]

The *Greater Chronicle* does give more background detail:

'The holy and perpetual virgin of Christ Aethelthryth, daughter of
Anna king of the Angles, was given as wife firstly to one great
man and then to King Egfrid. After she had preserved the

marriage bed uncorrupted for twelve years, having taken the holy veil she was transformed from a queen into a consecrated virgin. Without delay she also became a mother of virgins and the pious nourisher of holy women, and received the place called Ely in order to build a monastery. Her merits while living were also testified to when her body and the clothes in which it had been wrapped were found uncorrupted sixteen years after her burial.'[48]

The lack of material on Aethelthryth in the *Martyrology* is perhaps understandable as she was not a martyr through persecution. Rather it was her perpetual virginity, the truth of which was proved by her incorruptibility, which made her a martyr. Perhaps Bede felt that nothing more needed to be said than that in the *Martyrology*.

What cannot be so easily explained away, however, is the anomalous case of St Anastasius. The relevant entry in the *Greater Chronicle* is a much more extended one that usual. The listing does, in fact, open by centring on placing the event of Anastasius' martyrdom in time.[49] However, it then proceeds into a more extended description that reads like a synopsis of Anastasius' life. Thus Bede talks of Anastasius' boyhood, his conversion and baptism, his entry into monastic life, his captivity and torture, his martyrdom, posthumous miracles, and the translation of his relics from his monastery to the monastery of Aquas Savias.[50] The information in the *Martyrology*, on the other hand, remains firmly within the parameters that Bede appears to have set for it. He merely mentions the place, tortures, martyrdom, and judge under which Anastasius' death occurred.[51] It is clear that in the *Martyrology* Bede does consciously and consistently stick to the boundaries which he indicated in his résumé of this text in the *EH*. When he does not do this it is often either because of a lack of sources or purely because it was unnecessary to do so (as in the cases of some non-martyr saints). What is not clear is why, when discussing Anastasius in the *Greater Chronicle*, Bede felt it necessary to break the generic limitations he appears to have otherwise generally followed when compiling this text. Nevertheless, this exception does not alter the overall pattern seen in these two texts.

Whilst acknowledging that the primary focus of these two texts is essentially different, the comparison of the *Greater Chronicle* and the *Martyrology* indicates that the variation of emphasis is very subtle. The extent of this subtlety becomes all the more apparent when one returns to comparing Bede's *Martyrology*, with the *MHE*. It has been shown that for Bede's *Martyrology* to have been seen merely in the tradition of the *MHE* it would only have comprised listings and that, for once, Bede was prepared to move away from generic boundaries established by 'Roman' predecessors. In fact, by extending the information he placed in his *Martyrology*. Bede significantly altered the nature of the martyrology, for its concentration was no longer purely to record the name, place, and day of the martyr. Bede, however, did not just introduce anecdotal material, he also instilled an implicit element of linear time. It is this that makes the difference between the *Greater Chronicle* and the *Martyrology* so subtle.

This suggested (though not specifically stated) element of time is illustrated in Bede's decision to note the judge under whom a martyr met his or her fate. In a *martyrology* such as the *MHE* time is essentially cyclical – revolving around events in one year, which are repeated *ad infinitum*. In this sense, time within a martyrology is only a year in extent, until with the New Year it begins again. In essence, the material recorded in a martyrology such as the *MHE* functions only within the time of the liturgical year. Usually any evidence that might suggest the chronology for a particular action is omitted. The absence of any chronological markers within the notations means that outwith this text the information is timeless. By introducing into his *Martyrology* notification of the judge or emperor under which the martyr perished, Bede, perhaps unconsciously, introduced an implied element of time, in a chronological sense, during which a martyrdom occurred. Thus, whilst the *MHE* only offers *'in sicilia ciuitate cateruas agathe uirginis'* for St Agatha, Bede notes that her torture and martyrdom happened under the consul Quintianus, at the time of Diocletian, *tempore Diocletiani*.[52] The same can be said of St Alexander. In the *MHE* the focus is on name and place. Bede, however adds 'the time' of the martyrdom – Alexander's beheading occurred under the judge Aurelianus, at the time of Trajan, *tempore Traiani*.[53] These are just two examples, but this insertion of an implied chronological time in the entries pervades many of the listings of the text and can be seen in the listings for: Theodota (under Count Leocadius, at the time of Diocletian); Anastasia (*tempore Diocletiani*); Benignus (*tempore Aureliani*); SS Speusippus, Eleusippus, and Melasippus (*tempore Aureliani imperatoris*); Caesarius and Julian (*tempore Claudii*);

Felix and Eusebius (*tempore Claudii imperatoris*); Euplus (*tempore Diocletiani et Maximiani*); SS Felix, January, Fortunatianus, and Septiminus (*tempore Diocletiani*); Sosius (*tempore Diocletiani imperatoris*); Juliana (*tempore Maximiani imperatoris*); Lupus (*tempore Attilae*); Papias and Maurus (*tempore Diocletiani*); Marius and Martha (*tempore Claudii principis*); Fabian (*tempore Decii*); and Alban (*tempore Diocletiani*).[54] In those entries where *tempus* is not specifically mentioned, the naming of an emperor alone will often imply the era when the torture and martyrdom occurred. By adding the judge Bede added an implied chronology. Basically, the time of the martyrs was a 'recurrent time'. By adding contextual information Bede introduced an element of linear time. Consequently he enabled the martyrs to exist not only in this recurrent time but also in linear time, which in eschatological terms ran from the Creation to the Day of Judgement.[55]

Bede's choice of information appears to have been influenced by his chronological work in the *Greater Chronicle*. In fact, if the *Martyrology* was used in conjunction with the *Greater Chronicle* the reader would easily be able to place the martyrs' death within the period it occurred in the Sixth Age. Another of Bede's innovations then was to introduce a wider temporal context for each of the martyrs mentioned, thereby changing the *Martyrology* from having only a cycle of 'annual time', to also having an implied chronology in the actual listings. It would be inaccurate to say, nevertheless, that this innovation meant that the *Martyrology* should be seen in terms of a 'chronicle of saints'.[56] The framework of time is only implied in the *Martyrology* and it is secondary to the details of the person noted. For it to be considered a chronicle this framework would need to be explicitly specified and of primary importance.

In compiling his *Martyrology* Bede showed ingenuity but even here he was not prepared to step out of the boundaries of the patristic influences so prevalent elsewhere in his works. Thus, working from the structure of the *MHE*, inspired by Eusebius' 'ecclesiastical gloating' on torture, and influenced by his work on chronology, Bede produced a text which became the generic prototype for succeeding martyrologies.

Chapter 7
Bede's Compositional Techniques in the Genre of *Ecclesiastical History*

Authenticity and Authority in Northumbrian Saints' Lives in the *Ecclesiastical History*

BEDE USED COMPOSITIONAL TECHNIQUES AND STRATEGIES IN THE *EH* to which historians have tended not to pay enough attention. Yet when approaching any historical analysis of the *EH* it is vital to be aware of how Bede constructed his models of saintly behaviour. It was shown in a previous chapter that Bede was not averse to the rhetorical strategy of insinuation. In fact he seemed to relish it. It has also been illustrated that Bede both used directly and alluded to patristic and Roman texts to imbue the overall framework of his works with a sense of authority. In so doing, most of his *historiae*, whilst unique in some aspect, can still be placed in genres which had gained their status through being products of the revered Fathers of the Church. However, it is clear that Bede's intertextual connections in the *EH* were not just limited to genre considerations.

If Bede intended to imbue the overall framework with a sense of authority by placing a text within an established genre, it should perhaps be no surprise to the reader that such a connection with authoritative texts would be more profoundly evident in the manner in which Bede constructed his characterizations. Their inter-textuality can be seen to function on three main levels. He clearly borrows and reframes verbatim passages from patristic texts. He uses variations on Christian literary themes and the reminiscences of biblical and Late Antique texts inherent in them. He also provides eyewitness accounts expressed through established literary frameworks. As an individual in the monastic milieu, Bede's writing was subject to the texts he and his community took as authoritative and, as a consequence, he borrowed from them extensively in one form or another. This should not lead us to call Bede a plagiarist, rather his method of textual construction represents the notion of a collective Christian scholarship, embedded in authoritative Roman texts, placing the individual writer within though subsumed by the collective.

Such an approach can only have implications for our considerations of authenticity. Arguably, for Bede, an account's authenticity was based first and foremost in authority and order from the literature in which he was steeped, not a factual representation of what happened. Authenticity came not from the mundane reporting of events in an individual's life as might be found in biography, but from the re-viewing of certain, apparently contemporary, situations through the sublime narratives of the Bible and patristic fathers. Having acknowledged this one need not consider Bede to be solely a prisoner of what he read and meditated upon; rather, he was a talented manipulator of rhetorical tools which he used to introduce textual models into the lives of the people he was portraying. Indeed, the dissemination of these often Late Antique, distinctly Roman, models in a form accessible to Anglo-Saxon society may have been a primary aim.

When Bede was dealing with individuals, then, he was above all creating inter-textual images and these images did not necessarily always relate to the experience of the individuals on which he focused. This is a challenge to which medievalists are only now really beginning to rise. After all, although Mayr-Harting repeatedly argued that Bede's world was essentially a textual one, we still search and hope for evidence of where he depicts reliable, factual accounts concerning individuals and places. Timothy Reuter has drawn to our attention the point that whilst we can discern literary elements in texts, we tend to take the incidental features as reliable because the 'authors must have been concerned to present a realistic or plausible story to their audience'. The crux of his point is not this, though; rather it is that our notions of plausibility are presentist and, therefore, not always reliable guides to the discerning of what did and did not occur.[1] I agree wholeheartedly with this and, in fact, would take it one step further to suggest that even incidental features which we have assumed are included for plausibility may themselves be textual allusions (an example of which will be indicated in this chapter) and that seeming textual plausibility may have been a greater consideration than the reflection of an actuality. Whilst this should not rule out the possibility that Bede does represent aspects of the historical record, caution should draw us to look for literary parallels first before concluding actuality. It cannot be denied that there may have been occasions when life really did seem to imitate literature or vice versa, but there is no certainty that this can always be determined.

To illuminate Bede's methodology in the *EH*, this chapter aims to re-examine his approaches to his 'native' informants with regard to his Northumbrian royal saints, as well as his exploitation of sources found within the monastic libraries at his disposal. It also aims to analyze the conventional compositional techniques Bede applied in the *EH*. In this, more prominence will be given to the issue of the inter-connectedness of Bede's textual authorities and narrative techniques in his *historiae*, stressing that Bede's methodology has profound implications for the portrayal of apparently historical events.

THE RESOURCES OF RHETORICAL AUTHORITY: NATIVE SOURCES

In 1965–66 David Kirby aimed to set out Bede's native sources for the *EH*.[2] In so doing Kirby noted the care with which Bede supplied the names of informants in both the Preface and text of the *EH*.[3] Essentially, Kirby assumed that at least to a certain degree Bede's seeming dependence on eyewitness and oral accounts represented his desire to provide his readers with the most accurate renditions of previous events. Kirby, like most historians (except perhaps Walter Goffart), optimistically assumed that Bede's method of source selection was determined by a similar wish for historical accuracy that modern historians claim to apply today. Such a supposition is not without criticism, however, and one should ask whether Bede really believed that historical accuracy as opposed to convincing representation and inter-textual allusion was all-important in the construction of his models.

It has already been noted that the Preface of the *EH* is highly stylized and rhetorically convention-based. This point can be extended further to argue that Bede's references to eyewitness and oral accounts are themselves rhetorical devices designed to encourage the reader to be convinced that what he stated had historical accuracy. The fact that Bede needed to offer some semblance of an authenticity familiar to the modern reader suggests a challenge to the earlier statement that authenticity came through the re-viewing of situations in the light of textual precedents. This suggestion is only valid, though, if there was a contemporary consensus of belief that Bede was not indulging in rhetorical acrobatics but was a historiographer in a manner similar to the modern concept of the discipline of History. His consistent naming of individuals who could plausibly have verified his narration gives the *EH* a feel of authenticity. It is this sense of authenticity with which the modern reader can identify – after all, if Bede is naming contemporaries he is hardly likely to falsify their statements, or so it seems if one believes that historical accuracy is his ultimate goal. Such a sense of authenticity, however, belies the level of convention and construction contained in the text.

Before examining Kirby's points concerning the use of oral information it is worth acknowledging the recent work that considers the use of memory and 'remembering' the past. Patrick Geary, in particular, has added much to this debate, noting that early medieval historiographers were operating in a situation in which the collective had some impact on what was to be remembered and what was not.[4] Indeed, Geary himself refers to an occasion where the hagiographer, Letaldus of Micy, appears to have circulated a draft of his *Miracula S. Maximini* among the older monks of his community, who reminded him of what had been omitted, and recalled to his memory many things including a miracle he went on to add to his text. He then, Geary notes, went on to revise his text in accordance with the collective advice of his elders.[5] Such an example seems to imply a close relationship between the author and his oral sources and would suggest that Bede's account of oral witnesses at least reflected some collective memories relating to actual events. However, in his analysis of remembrance Geary tends to avoid examining the use of such information as a rhetorical device. After all we only know of the procedure of correction that Letaldus of Micy used from his own text. Surely such a statement was designed to give greater weight to the miracle story he subsequently went on to narrate? Collective memory may have been drawn upon, but a stated reference to it in a text should arouse our suspicion as to the possible rhetorical nature of that particular reference. Essentially this discussion of Bede's oral sources attempts to provoke discomfort in the reader in order to make him or her question their own belief in the reliability of Bede as a source drawing upon other reliable sources. As indicated in the first chapter, it seems evident that Bede was writing for a 'textual community', and would, to some degree, have reflected the needs of that community. The needs of that community, however, were as much the dissemination of the biblical and Late Antique ideals in which they were submerged as an accurate rendition of individual lives from the Anglo-Saxon past. In this Bede acts as a transformer of the past, but he does this primarily by superimposing images from a different period on to that which he claims to be depicting. He is using some of the methods Geary identifies, such as selecting what he believed (and his textual community believed) to be worthy of remembering about individuals, but this value was predicated on the texts far more than it necessarily was on any lived reality.[6] The textual sources of monasticism provided a new interpretative structure within which to understand memories of the past but they also provided models with which the past could be recreated so that it reflected specifically Christian ideals.[7] This argument may seem one-sided but it seems clear that for too long we have, at some level, taken Bede's trustworthiness for granted. It is this sense of 'taking for granted' which this book wishes to dispel, challenging the reader to view Bede's *historiae* from the perspective of the Christian rhetorician rather than as the discerning recorder of oral tradition.

Kirby himself indicated three key problems with the oral accounts. Firstly, they were highly localized.[8] Secondly, some of the so-called eyewitness accounts related to periods long before Bede completed the *EH*.[9] Thus Bede implies that he has heard information from individuals who had known Aidan.[10] This seems to be similar to the type of collective memory to which Geary refers. Given that Aidan died in 652 such a claim should still raise some misgivings. It is true that Bede's informants in this case may have spoken to him about Aidan when they were old and he was young, but it is still hard not to question the accuracy of the transmission of such information from his sources to a text finalized nearly 80 years after the subject's death. As Kirby states, the scope for error was wide.[11] Moreover, one needs to question how often Bede referred to such sources in order to bring authority to his narrative. Another example can be found in Bede's description of relations between Ecgfrith and Aethelthryth. Here Bede claims to have spoken with Wilfrid himself – what greater proof of authenticity?[12] Yet again one must consider the effect of time on a conversation that would have occurred before Wilfrid's death in 710, about the period of the early 670s, and which was written down in its final form c730. What is perhaps implied by Bede's choice of individuals in these cases is that the names of his sources were more important than the verification of the material they supplied. Basically, the naming of sources provided a 'rhetorical' authority, making the information seem authentic. In the light of this proposal Bede's repeated efforts to note the trustworthiness of his sources read as a rhetorical device designed to persuade the reader of the validity of his narrative. Given our acceptance of the basic outline of seventh and eighth-century Anglo-Saxon history that Bede presents, he was evidently successful.

The third problem Kirby isolated was that Bede could make a story which was considered doubtful by its original author appear an unquestioned part of tradition.[13] To do this Bede merely removed any phraseology likely to imply caution concerning part of the narrative. This he does successfully, for example, with the tale of Edwin's vision whilst in exile in East Anglia. Thus, in the anonymous Whitby *Life of St Gregory*, the author notes that he is retelling the story in a form he believes to be the truth, even though he had not heard it from those who knew Edwin most.[14] He goes on to reassure his reader that even a tale that happened long before the days of any of those who are still alive, or in distant lands, can be passed on by faithful witnesses.[15] His phraseology further implies actual uncertainties when he identifies the man in Edwin's vision as Paulinus. Thus he states not that it was, but that 'it is said' to have been Bishop Paulinus: *Sub hac igitur specie dicunt illi Paulinum.*[16] Throughout this chapter the author's concern to stress reliability actually encourages some misgivings about the certainty of the details. Bede avoids this impression entirely. Firstly, he does not intimate any anxiety as to the source of his information, rather he just moves straight into the narrative of the event.[17] This is particularly relevant if one considers the anonymous *Vita* to be one of the earliest of the Northumbrian *vitae*. After all, if an author writing in the early eighth century implicitly expressed some doubt as to the veracity of the sources and noted that all the verifiable witnesses were dead, Bede writing several years later, was in an even weaker position. Secondly, Bede avoids phrases such as 'it is said', preferring to retell the story directly as if he is the source, consequently enhancing the credibility. Whereas the anonymous author emphasized the trustworthiness of his information and, thereby, to some extent introduced an element of doubt, Bede discussed this part of the narrative with assured confidence, offering his reader little room for misgivings.

Even acknowledging these difficulties, historians still leave Bede's list of native sources more or less intact, preferring to trust his reliability rather than question his methodology. If, however, one starts to argue that Bede's *historiae* are at their core rhetorical and, that, in fact the method of constructing religious discourse fundamentally depended on textual precedents and other literary conventions as much as oral tradition or eyewitness accounts, such acceptance of Bede's reliability must be scrutinized. Although it is, for example, extremely difficult to be sceptical of Bede's named sources in the *EH* (especially individuals such as Acca who was after all a contemporary of Bede's), one still needs to treat such sources with a degree of circumspection. Since Acca, like Bede, was a product of a tradition that placed a premium on the immersion of the self into the textual reality of the Bible and the patristic fathers, it is possible that Bede's oral informants themselves may have provided stories which accommodated signs and explanations of virtues (or their absence) already considered as having authority by the religious communities from which they came.[18]

The reader should be aware that not only may Bede have been deliberately misleading his audience about the accuracy of his informants' descriptions, but also of the extent to which any source or eyewitness account expressed information using previous textual images and known literary conventions. Even where the source could be an eyewitness, the account they transmitted could conceivably be full of such conventions and literary reminiscences. In this it is not so much that the *EH* is a mosaic of *personal* memories, but of *convention-based* memories. An example of this can be seen in *EH* V:1 where Bede records a miracle by Oethelwald related to him by one of the brothers for whom it was performed, Guthfrith.[19] The miracle involved Oethelwald, praying for the ending of the raging tempest that was preventing Guthfrith and a group of fellow monks from getting to Farne Island. The allusion to the New Testament here is obvious, and the calming of the sea by a saint was a common hagiographical *topos*.[20] However, in the text Colgrave has also noted both specific use of Ephesians (3:14) and an echo in one of the sentences to Virgil's *Aeneid*.[21] Such conventions imply that either Bede or his informant transcribed their experience using a formula dependent on textual sources. This is even more pertinent when one examines the records that have been supplied to Bede by monasteries that held the memories of long dead saints. A useful illustration of this can be found in *EH* III:28. Here Bede depicts Chad travelling on foot like the Apostles through the countryside.[22] Bede then gives a brief description of the scenery. As Neil Wright has commented, some have viewed this as an accurate representation of the contemporary English landscape.[23] In fact, Professor Whitelock suggested that Bede's use of the word *castella* in this case was a translation of the Old English *byrig* and could have referred to a nobleman's residence.[24] Nonetheless, Campbell noted that such a marked clustering of words for places usually occurred when Bede was following a written text – at least offering a hint that this was a textual construct.[25] In actuality Wright has shown that this geographical depiction was a direct allusion to Caelius Sedulius' *Carmen Paschale*, a poem that Bede quotes explicitly in his *De Arte Metrica*.[26] As Regis Boyer has commented, such landscape depictions were included in narratives for the purposes of credibility.[27] However, credibility and factual accuracy need not be the same thing.

This case provides another question. Was it Bede's informant or Bede himself that phrased the story? After all, while Bede is exceptionally candid about the individuals and monasteries from which he acquired information, he is notably reticent when it comes to the method of construction utilized for their or his narrative. Perhaps this actually brings the observer to the crux of the problem: Bede's Preface is very persuasive in the sense that it supplies a list of sources with which one can identify: learned men with written records and old traditions ('*uel monimentis litterarum uel seniorum traditione*').[28] The efficacy of this list, however, as of his other informants, is misleading. The naming of sources does not necessarily equate with the accuracy of the biographical or other information. It does, however, detract from the inter-textual and stylized elements of the text that, if left overt, would undermine the seeming 'credibility of the historical reality' of what was being recorded. Behind these sources is a tradition of text construction that relies on direct and indirect references to previous texts that were considered to have their own authority. The point is that until we have collated and read all of these texts we are left with sections of the *EH* that might *seem* to relate to actualities but are, in fact, merely allusions to other sources used in the narrative to enhance the associations between historical events of the Anglo-Saxons and the Christian literary past. I do not deny that work has been done already on elucidating the key religious and literary texts used by Bede for the creation of some of his images, but I would suggest that the implication of this in terms of historical accuracy is far more profound than the academic historical community is prepared to admit. The religious community in which Bede moved was highly text-orientated and the texts he produced reflected such a predilection. In this sense, his understanding of an historical truth as represented in the written word, despite what it might seem, is quite different from that of modern academic historians.

These points are as relevant to Bede's Northumbrian female saints as they are to his male saints. One cannot help but express a degree of caution concerning the local sources Bede utilized, for example, in his portrayals of Aethelthryth, Hilda, Aebbe, Eanflaed, and Aelfflaed. For the last two one can assume he derived some knowledge from those still living at Whitby, who had at least known Aelfflaed as their abbess. Although Bede does not cite a source, Wallace-Hadrill, rather than focus on the conventional characterization in the *EH*, assumed that Bede drew on a *vita* produced at Ely for his depiction of Aethelthryth.[29] The East Anglian informant named in the Preface, Abbot Esi, whilst unknown outside of Bede's text, could have forwarded the information, but it is equally possible that Bede constructed the image either by using the stories recounted by St Wilfrid, or, more likely, from using other texts found in his library at Wearmouth.[30]

NON-NATIVE SOURCES

The conventional nature of Bede's depiction of his Northumbrian female saints is a reasonably under-utilized, yet clearly useful resource for understanding his rhetorical strategies in terms of the application of direct reference and allusion to Late Antique Christian models. The work of Christine Fell, Susan Ridyard, Stephanie Hollis, Clare Lees, and Gillian Overing has added to our understanding and readings of Bede's Northumbrian women, but has perhaps not fully grasped the impact of Bede's compositional methods.[31] For potential textual models in the library at Wearmouth, one need look no further than patristic literature concerning virginity and the writings of Venantius Fortunatus; Wallace-Hadrill has already suggested a relationship, both linguistically and in approach, between Bede's elegiac poem to

Aethelthryth's virginity and Venantius' *De Virginitate*.[32] Venantius' *Life of St Radegund* may also have provided Bede with an image he used in the chapter preceding his poem.

It is noticeable that in his version of the *Life of St Radegund*, Venantius does not take an interest in those saintly functions particularly associated with her position as queen. In terms of this chapter this is most evident in the fact that he does not mention her relationship with the court, nor does he connect her with another common Merovingian hagiographical *topos,* the freeing of captives. For her period as queen Venantius concentrates on her helping of the poor, a *topos* associated with saints in general rather than those that are specifically queens.[33] From then on he focuses on Radegund's ascetic extremes: for example, avoidance of the sexual side of her marriage so that she might serve Christ better, her fasting, her aid to lepers, and her poor diet of lentils and vegetables.[34] Pauline Stafford has commented on the similarity of the terms that Bede uses to describe Radegund and Aethelthryth, preferring to view them as evidence of actual religious practice rather than as linked textually.[35] However, given Bede's predilection for the use of previously established convention, it is just, if not more, possible that he was in fact drawing on Venantius as a source. Overall Bede's depiction of Aethelthryth reads like a summary of Venantius' *Life of St Radegund*. Bede, like Venantius, concentrates on Aethelthryth's sexuality, although Bede's model is one of the virgin rather than a married woman enduring sex, such as Radegund.[36] (This could of course be explained by the fact that whereas Aethelthryth remained childless Radegund did not, and, consequently the *topos* of sexual renunciation was perhaps being manipulated to serve the individual.) Bede also mentioned Aethelthryth's eating habits and her steadfast approach to prayer.[37]

Bede, like Venantius, centres his account of Aethelthryth on her ascetic characteristics, and one cannot help thinking that what Wallace-Hadrill said of Venantius' *Vita* could be quite easily transferred to Bede's Aethelthryth:

'He confines himself to the ascetic and miracle worker and reveals nothing of the person.'[38]

In some respects, in his portrayal of Aethelthryth and Hilda Bede's emphasis is again on the ascetic and monastic duties relevant to any abbess, be she royal or not. In this, Bede, particularly where Aethelthryth is concerned, has perhaps exhibited some of the 'class-less nature' of female hagiography that Schulenberg has noticed.[39] However, whilst the actions of Aethelthryth may be viewed as typically monastic rather than typically royal, it should not be forgotten that her royal status was well established in both the narrative concerning her sanctity and, also in passing, twice elsewhere in the scheme of the *EH*. Thus, in depiction of Chad's death, it is related that Owine, who heard the joyful singing of the summoning angels, had been the chief officer of her household (*eratque primus ministrorum et princeps domus eius*).[40] Also, in IV:22 it is noted that Imma (a young man injured at the battle between Ecgfrith and Aethelred at the river Trent, who subsequently remained unfettered thanks to the masses being celebrated on his behalf), was one of Aethelthryth's ministers (*quia et ipse quondam eiusdam [Aedalthrydae] reginae minister fuerat*).[41] Whilst her virtues may have had a universal quality, in the context of the *EH* her social status was left in no doubt. Nonetheless, it is important to note that in the context of the details of Aethelthryth's holy life Bede says nothing of her pre-monastic, royal, secular duties (except by implication, that of sex and childbearing). Indeed, if one compares the sanctity of Aethelthryth with that of Hilda, particularly in terms of her giving counsel to kings and princes, it almost appears that Hilda is being given more political importance.

The point is that the inclusion of these *topoi* was directly related to the representation of the characters – they did not necessarily appertain to the actual individual but were attributes *one would expect* of a saintly person. These expectations were themselves informed by characteristics outlined in biblical imagery and in patristic writings. For example, one need look no further than Jerome to find a reason why a female saint would have been portrayed, as Aethelthryth is, wearing coarse garments. He made it quite clear that fine clothes denoted corruption and that virginal asceticism was marked out by the neglect of personal attire.[42] Essentially, the type of clothes depicted on a saint acted as a sign of their inherent sanctity. As Morse has pointed out, conventions were imbued with meaning.[43]

These examples demonstrate the extent to which an understanding of grammatical rhetoric has affected the text. Hagiographical *topoi* and conventions stem from the blurring of the boundaries of grammar outlined by Knappe.[44] Indeed, it would not be hard to argue here that these are the 'constructed elements' of a saint that Delooz has emphasized, and that they were designed in response to approaches of reading that developed out of grammatical studies.[45] Of course, if one takes these elements of the saint's character with their functions as described in the texts one should at least raise the question of whether there are remains which bear a relationship to the 'real' people.

This can be seen in another hagiographical convention employed by Bede in his depiction of Aethelthryth's rejection of her husband after marriage, a *topos* that is also found in both Venantius' and the contemporary *Life of St Radegund* by Baudonivia. Firstly, it should be noticed that there was one essential difference between Radegund and Aethelthryth, namely that Radegund, unlike Aethelthryth, was not a virgin. Nevertheless both had a struggle to get their respective husbands to accept their desire to serve Christ by leaving them and entering a monastery.[46] Thus in chapters 4, 5, 6, and 7 Baudonivia describes how Radegund rejected her husband and how, through prayer and the help of the bishop of Paris (Germanus), the king finally repented and allowed her to continue to serve Christ. The parallels with Aethelthryth, Ecgfrith and the support of Aethelthryth by Bishop Wilfrid are obvious. The embellishment of Radegund's story serves merely to emphasize the struggle that she was prepared to go through to follow Christ. It was, in essence, a testimony of her faith.

Does this, then, cast any light on Bede's Aethelthryth? Like Radegund's husband, Ecgfrith is portrayed as a threat to Aethelthryth following 'a path to Christ'. Indeed, Bede even depicted him as having attempted to bribe Wilfrid to get her to consummate their marriage and thereby forego the main testimony to her sanctity.[47] He also emphasizes that it is only 'with difficulty' that she finally gains permission to enter the monastic life.[48] If one compares Bede with Venantius and the other Merovingian texts it becomes clear that in many ways his depiction of the relationship between Ecgfrith and Aethelthryth is just a standard convention. Indeed, the image of a woman, especially a virginal woman being the object of male sexual desires had been well established by Ambrose in his treatise *De Virginitate*.[49] Here both Agnes and Pelagia are depicted in such a manner and by doing this Ambrose and his successors actually sexualized women's bodies in their texts to increase the significance of their choice to remain virgins.[50]

Nonetheless, Pauline Thompson has made a spirited attempt to suggest that the depiction of Aethelthryth's refusal to consummate her marriages is far more than merely a construct designed to obscure a reality of sterility in her sexual relationships.[51] To do this she has considered the possibility that Aethelthryth was highly influenced as a young woman in East Anglia by the Christian discourse concerning monastic life and the superiority of virginity, and as a consequence chose not to consummate her marriage on two different occasions.[52] However, whilst it is hard not to accept that some degree of transmission of the images of virginity was occurring outside the monastic enclaves, its extent is not clear; the issue of how an Anglo-Saxon *historia* text was constructed is not addressed. Hindsight played a critical role in how events came to be narrated.[53] Characterizations associated with events in *historia* were rhetorical devices to explain the outcome of these events rather than descriptions of a lived experience. Where Aethelthryth was concerned the hagiographers (possibly Bede or a writer in East Anglia) had to explain the incorruption of her body. As Burrus commented, a woman's body was an aspect of her religious integrity – incorruption was a sign of the extent of that integrity and required explanation.[54] The only conclusion to be drawn was that she had managed to get through two marriages without consummating either, which is exactly what Bede concludes.[55] The narrators had patristic precedents for arguing such a case and Aethelthryth provided a useful vehicle to carry the message of the superiority of virginity. Consider, for example, if her corpse had been corrupt. Would she then have been depicted more in the light of Radegund as having lived with the outward appearance of being a wife, *sub coniugis specie*?[56] If Thompson is correct and Aethelthryth had at least some knowledge of Radegund's life, surely the message that she would have gained from it would have been that one could fully participate in marriage and still become a holy woman. (The idea that virginity was alluded to in Radegund's case seems misplaced. Virginity was a specific state and the title 'virgin' was not usually applied to one who was not. The distinction would have been clear.)[57]

It is plain that Christian images of female holiness were extended to include women who had been married, by Anglo-Saxon authors such as Aldhelm when writing for female audiences. That the gender of the audience may have played a role in the extent of emphasis on virginity is obvious if one compares Bede's *EH* entries with texts written for a female readership. Thus, Aldhelm in his *De Virginitate* does refer to virginity as wielding the sceptre of the highest sovereignty among the virtues.[58] However, he also notes that alongside it must be the virtue of humility.[59] Indeed, for Aldhelm it was better that one reached the port 'battered' (having been sexually active) than be an arrogant virgin. For Aldhelm there was, in this sense, more humility in giving up carnal knowledge than never having had it in the first place. To his audience Aldhelm made it quite clear that virgins without virtue 'will be punished along with the foolish virgins carrying burned out lamps'.[60] This was an image that took into account that his audience of noble women turned nuns included at least some who had rejected their worldly marriages.[61] Aldhelm was producing virtuous stereotypes to which his female audience could relate. Bede, on the other hand, seems to have been writing for an audience of men who, presumably, did not need to relate to their female counterparts (at least not textually). Bede focused on the extent of Aethelthryth's virginity for the benefit of his predominantly male audience.

The nature of representation for Bede as a Christian historian meant he undertook rhetorical exposition, but this is not quite the same as him having access to and following Cicero's suggestions concerning that exposition. Where the use of *topoi* are concerned we hear the shouts of rhetoric in grammar rather than the conversation of the antique tradition. Underneath that shouting, however, whispers can be heard of the classical assumption that a story not known to have happened in fact may nevertheless be useful if it is congenial to the narrator's cause and meets one or more of the criteria of verisimilitude. These whispers are perhaps the bastardized form of antique rhetoric that has led Ray to hope Bede had direct access to Cicero.

The description of Aethelthryth, however, does throw up a link to antiquity that needs more comment. Ray noticed that the poem to Aethelthryth, coming as it does immediately after Bede's prose description, could be viewed in the light of Bede's biblically influenced understanding that *historia* could contain a medley of poetry, rhetoric, and metre.[62] Of interest here, though, is that Bede's poem to Aethelthryth's virginity could be seen not so much as an emulation of Venantius nor as a biblical convention, but as an example of *conversio* or paraphrase.[63] Peter Godman notes that this practice of turning poetry into prose and vice versa is first mentioned by Cicero in *De Oratore* and was considered further by Quintilian in his *Institutio Oratoria*.[64] If, in his studies, Bede was following these sources to aid him with his poetry then perhaps some of Ray's other assertions about the availability of such texts are accurate. It is clear that the practical use of verse as a suitable vehicle for formulating the moral significance of a prose statement in a lofty style was an acceptable practice to Bede, Aldhelm, and Alcuin.[65] Moreover, we know that the art of poetry, as well as being studied at Canterbury, Wearmouth, Malmesbury, and York, was also evidently studied at a convent on Thanet.[66] Were the tools for learning this practice original Latin authors such as Cicero and Quintilian? We should, at least, consider that the study of Virgil and Ovid could bring with it access to antique rhetorical traditions which may subsequently have been assimilated into early medieval concepts of grammar, but were nonetheless more than just acceptable Christianized textbook tools about poetry. There is, of course, as usual a caveat with Bede. In his poem to Aethelthryth he makes it quite clear that his subject matter is so much better than that of Virgil.[67] Moreover, his links in the poem to female martyrs such as Eulalia place him in the poetic culture of early Christian poets such as Prudentius.[68] When he came to write his *De Arte Metrica*, he mainly relied on such poets.[69] If Bede was drinking from the cup of Classical Antiquity he did so with a distinct grimace.

If the Northumbrian female saints were useful vehicles for conventional aspects of sanctity, the portrayals of Edwin, Oswald, and Oswine arguably were not, presenting Bede with a challenge. In his construction of images of episcopal and monastic sanctity he and his informants could and did draw upon a wealth of hagiographic sources for their models, such as those of Venantius and Sulpicius Severus.[70] Saintly lay rulers, on the other hand, exhibiting in actuality all the vagaries of royal power, were a relatively new topic for such an exercise. Nonetheless, in his depiction of these three individuals, Bede betrays signs of similar techniques of construction to those of their saintly male and female religious counterparts. As noted earlier, however, these techniques

depended more upon allusion and inference than on direct inter-
textuality and emphasize the suggestion of a discourse community
imbued with the patristic literature. His use of documentary evidence
reflected a manipulation of the Christian discourse available and showed
the extent to which the textual world of his predecessors influenced his
present understanding and representation of individuals from the recent
and not so recent past.

Wallace-Hadrill, Campbell, Mayr-Harting, McClure, and Stancliffe
have all identified the key texts to which Bede alludes or by which he is
influenced in his portrayal of the 'saint-kings' of Northumbria.[71] Clare
Stancliffe has provided a particularly thorough outline of these
Christianized kings and reads Bede as fitting their personalities and
actions into his portraits, though fashioning his descriptions from pre-
suppositions shaped by his reading. This book goes one step further
arguing that his reading shaped his pre-suppositions so much that it is
hard to get access to the personalities and the actions. Credibility, not
authenticity, was the primary rhetorical aim. That authenticity seems to
be present reflects Bede's artistry.

It is clear that biblical, particularly Old Testament, and patristic
sources supplied exemplars. Rufinus-Eusebius can be seen to have
particularly influenced Bede in his portrayal of Oswald as a pseudo-
Constantine.[72] Clemoes has commented that Oswald, like Constantine,
was identified with devotion to the Cross.[73] Clemoes' point can perhaps
be taken further by suggesting that Bede's discussion of Oswald's
triumphant victory over the tyrant Cadwalla is reminiscent of Eusebius'
discussion of Constantine's many victories, especially that over the tyrant
Licinius.[74] To enhance the similarities between the two events Bede
emphasizes Cadwalla's tyranny, saying that he was both a savage tyrant
(*tyrannus saeuiens*) and outrageous in his tyranny (*uaesanam Brettonici
regis tyrannidem*).[75] Oswald's victory, like that of Constantine before him,
was depicted as being over tyranny. Moreover, Bede's image of Oswald
holding under his sway all the peoples and kingdoms of Britain is perhaps
an allusion to Eusebius' picture of Constantine reuniting the Roman
Empire, 'bringing it all under their [Constantine and his son Crispus]
peaceful sway'.[76] In fact, Bede was not the first to allude to Oswald's
'imperial' image; in Adomnan's *Vita Columbae* Oswald is referred to as
'*totius Britanniae imperator*'.[77] The evidence here, then, suggests a

significant influence of Eusebius on Bede's portrayal of Oswald.

In terms of the imperial allusions it is pertinent that two of the characteristics that Bede associates with Oswald – his faith and his humility – are also traits attributed to the emperor Theodosius by his ecclesiastical panegyrists, Paulinus of Nola and Ambrose. Thus Paulinus praises Theodosius' faith and humility: *'ut in Theodosio non tam imperatorem quam Christi seruum, non dominandi superbia sed humilitate famulandi potentem, nec regno sed fide principem praedicarem'*.[78] Ambrose, too, in his obituary of Theodosius eulogizes his piety (*imperatoris pii*), his compassion (*imperatoris misericordis*), his faith (*imperatoris fidelis*), and his humility.[79] As Judith George has commented, these two ecclesiastical panegyrists were the initiators of a formulation of Christian kingly virtues which reflected the more general teaching of the Church concerning the virtues to which it was worth aspiring.[80] Arguably, they also provided Bede with a framework of kingly virtues on which to develop his image of his most saintly king, Oswald.

Gregory the Great's *Pastoral Care* also supplied Bede with imagery appropriate to the Christian conduct of kings.[81] Whilst Oswald's virtue of humility may well derive from Paulinus or Ambrose, it, like Oswine's, can also be linked to the *Pastoral Care*. Gregory made it clear that humility was a critically important virtue in ruling.[82] Oswine's bounteousness to nobles and commons alike also reminiscent of Gregory's admonitions that a ruler should be bounteous with his goods.[83]

The depiction of Edwin's thoughtfulness may also have been an image crafted from a knowledge of the *Pastoral Care*. In this, Gregory notes the importance of a ruler giving equal attendance to both his inner (spiritual) and outer (worldly) lives.[84] In Bede's portrayal of Edwin there is a consistent repetition of the theme of Edwin's solitary consideration of religion. In *EH* Book II:9 he is portrayed as sitting alone for long periods in silence deliberating on what he ought to do concerning conversion to Christianity.[85] Again in Book II:12 he is portrayed as having remained outside, 'in silent anguish of spirit and consumed with inward fire' (*cumque diu tacitis mentis angoribus et caeco carperetur igni*) following a faithful friend's warning of Raedwald's treachery.[86] This image is reiterated once more by Bede, who recorded that whilst Edwin hesitated to accept the Word of God from Paulinus, he used to sit alone (*solitarius sederet*) for hours at a time debating with himself.[87] In the midst of a representation of an Anglo-Saxon king this theme of solitary pensiveness is unusual. This feature is not attributed to Aethelberht, Oswald, or Oswine, and, in fact, this image, in the context of kingship, appears to be unique in Bede's *EH*. The *Pastoral Care*, however, provides an excellent model for such behaviour. As has been commented, in his *Pastoral Care*, Gregory placed great importance on the attendance by rulers to both inner and outer worlds. Bede's depiction of Edwin perhaps represented an interpretation of this part of the *Pastoral Care* giving a secular king the virtue of discernment. If read in this light, Edwin was a man engrossed in both the external world and, in his solitary ponderings, also in his internal one.

Clare Stancliffe has suggested that Edwin's hesitancy was an example of royal pride, acting as a foil for Oswald's whole-hearted commitment to Christianity.[88] However, viewed through the 'window' of Gregory's *Pastoral Care*, such hesitancy could actually be viewed as as much a virtue as a weakness. In fact, Bede at no time accuses Edwin of pride, a vice to which Gregory had paid special attention, and one which if Bede had meant to emphasize it, would surely have merited explicit mention. Nor in his depiction of the post-converted king is there any question of Edwin's commitment to his faith. He is shown as having established the wooden church of St Peter at York whilst still a catechumen and soon after his baptism he is said to have initiated the building of a magnificent stone church.[89] In Book II:15 Edwin's great devotion was illustrated by his persuasion of King Eorpwald to abandon idolatry. Bede also gives him the epithet 'soldier in the kingdom of Christ' (*Christi regno militauit*) for the six years of his reign following his conversion.[90]

By illustrating Edwin's thoughtfulness, Bede alluded not only to Gregory the Great, he also elaborately reiterated a theme which he first introduced in the narrative concerning Aethelberht of Kent. In Book I:26, Bede records that Aethelberht rejoiced in other people's conversions but compelled no-one to accept Christianity because he had learned from his teachers that converting to the Faith was a voluntary, not a compulsory act.[91] Elsewhere in the *EH*, Bede implicitly restates this, showing Edwin persuading Eorpwold of East Anglia, and Alhfrith apparently also verbally persuading Penda of the Middle Angles.[92] Arguably, the theme he is reiterating here is that kings should not enforce conversion. However, underneath this he is also intimating that the process of conversion must be an individual's choice whoever the 'missionary' is. Indeed, if one examines Bede's description of Oswiu's enticement of Sigeberht of East Anglia to accept Christianity, it is clear that Sigeberht's process of acceptance has similarities to that of Edwin.[93] Thus Bede portrays Sigeberht being persuaded by Oswiu's almost priest-like discussion of the falseness of idols and the power of God, but only after gaining consent from his friends and taking counsel with his followers does he accept baptism. In this sense Sigeberht, like Edwin, could be viewed as hesitating. Such hesitancy, however, was neither an absence of humility nor an act of royal pride, rather it was an indication that conversion was a serious act that required thought and a consequential voluntary acceptance.

It is in his depiction of another king, Ecgfrith, that Bede seems to allude to Gregory the Great's discussion of pride in his *Pastoral Care*. In the *EH* IV:26 Bede portrays Ecgfrith's death at the hands of the Picts as a punishment for his attack on the Irish and his subsequent sin of not listening to his friends, particularly Cuthbert, concerning this attack and to Egbert concerning the previous attack on the Irish.[94] The details of this particular account are not recorded elsewhere. In the anonymous *Life of St Cuthbert* and in Bede's *Life of St Cuthbert*, Ecgfrith's death is used only to illustrate the efficacy of Cuthbert's prophetic capabilities and to show his awareness of an event without being present.[95] Only the anonymous author implies that Ecgfrith's death was 'in accordance with the predestined judgement of God': *postremo tamen secundum praedestinatum iudicium Dei*.[96] In his *EH* Bede added the reason for God's judgement by implying a relationship between Ecgfrith's failure to listen to his friends and the outcome of the battle of Nechtansmere.

In the *Pastoral Care* Gregory made it quite clear that a ruler who becomes conceited about his own authority, and esteems himself wiser than any of those whom he sees he exceeds in power, will find 'within himself the pit of his own downfall'.[97] Ecgfrith's failure to listen to his friends, when viewed in the light of this, can be seen as the vice of pride, and Ecgfrith's pride came before his destruction. This particular part of Bede's narrative is highly instructive in illustrating the complexities of his methods of construction. It exhibits the Orosian tendency to associate adversity with the judgement of God. It also appears to develop one of Gregory the Great's themes concerning rulership. Finally, it warns the modern reader against taking accounts at face value without acknowledging the textual tradition in which they occurred. For a Christian historian the outcome of events required understanding in terms of God's intercession. Ecgfrith failed disastrously at Nechtansmere, leaving the kingdom to 'ebb and flow away'. (This later phrase is itself an echo of Virgil's *Aeneid*.[98]) Bede selected for this outcome a convention that associated Ecgfrith's personal conduct with his failure. As Morse has noted in his discussion of historical fictions, such characterization preceding events is a rhetorical device.[99] The truthfulness of Bede's statement is, in this case, less important than the message and, given the allusions to Orosius, Gregory the Great, and Virgil it is hard not to view his analysis as a textual construct.

Wallace-Hadrill noted that the Pseudo-Cyprian text *De duodecim abusiuis saeculi* played a role in Bede's construction of the image of Oswald.[100] Certainly, if one compares this document with the portrayals of Edwin and Oswine, it is arguable that this text provided Bede with an underlying framework for Edwin and Oswine as well. *De duodecim abusiuis saeculi* is a Hiberno-Latin document, dated by Kenny to 630–650, which discusses public morals under twelve headings: a wise man without works; an old man without religion; an adolescent without obedience; a rich man without alms-giving; a woman without modesty; a lord without virtue; the contentious Christian; a proud pauper; an unjust king; a neglectful bishop; a populace without discipline; a people without law.[101] Two of these chapters in particular, 'the lord without virtue' and the 'unjust king', appear to contain sentiments with which Bede could identify and virtues he could ascribe to his model kings.

Of Edwin Bede notes that no-one dared to lay hands on the drinking places Edwin established because they feared the king greatly, nor did they wish to, because they loved him dearly.[102] In 'a lord without virtue', Pseudo-Cyprian makes it clear that it is crucial for a lord to inspire both love and fear in his people, for unless he be both loved and feared his order will hardly stand.[103] The peace of Edwin's land which allowed for the freedom of movement of women and children, and the noting of Oswald's kindness and generosity to the poor and estranged (*pauperibus et peregrinis*) may also have been influenced by Pseudo-Cyprian's comments concerning kingly conduct. Thus he notes that the justice of the king includes being the defender of aliens, orphans, and widows and giving alms to the poor.[104]

Pseudo-Cyprian also makes it clear that a king needed to devote himself to prayers at certain hours: *certis horis oratianibus insistere*.[105] Oswald is the epitome of this. In Book III:12 he is noted as praying diligently, often from matins until daybreak.[106] As a result of Bede's subsequent comment on Oswald's posture in prayer, this point has been viewed as coming from a popular source that had maintained pagan overtones. Indeed, Chaney has suggested that this was not 'the customary posture for prayer but a ritual attitude perhaps used by his pagan predecessors'.[107] Nonetheless, if one looks at the context in which Bede places his description of Oswald's method of prayer, it is hard to believe that Bede would have included it if it had pagan overtones. Firstly, as Rollason observed, it appears that he suppressed other pagan elements associated with the cult of Oswald.[108] Secondly, in general, Book III:12 is the record of a miracle at Bardney, and the stress in the narrative is on how the diligence of Oswald's prayerfulness in life now led to his power of intercession after death.[109] This is hardly the most appropriate place in which to feature a traditional pagan element of worship.[110] More specifically, diligent prayer was a conduct necessary in a Christian king – as Pseudo-Cyprian had noted. To undermine this with a hint of continued pagan practice was not Bede's aim, and for him to record the posture, whatever its provenance, suggests that it was an acceptable way for a king to pray. The point, of course, is that the emphasis on Oswald's prayerfulness may represent a construct influenced by Bede's textual sources.

Royal largesse, particularly in giving alms to the poor, also appears to be a critical virtue identified by Bede in his portrayal of Oswald. However, this too has a profoundly conventional basis. Bede proves Oswald's generosity to the poor in his narrative concerning the Easter day meal. On this occasion, when faced with a gathering of the poor, Oswald (using the appropriate minister) sent out food and ordered that the plate on which it was served was to be broken and distributed among them.[111] The plausibility of this tale has been accepted most recently by Clare Stancliffe, who has suggested that because of the presence of an official, royal generosity was regarded as a regular activity but that Oswald's spontaneity was beyond the call of duty.[112] However, this particular story is also a perfect candidate for being in essence derived from a series of text-based sources. In general terms Gregory the Great outlined the importance of a ruler being bounteous in the giving of goods to others in his *Pastoral Care*.[113] More specifically, *De duodecim* listed alms-giving as a crucial act of a king.[114] These two texts alone, excluding the patristic homilies on alms-giving found in the writings of such individuals as St John Chrysostom, could have supplied Bede with this particular characteristic of Christian kingship.[115]

It is interesting to note at this juncture that royal largesse is also a feature of Isidore's portrayal of his most Christian king, Reccared. Reccared, Isidore narrates, 'deposited his wealth among the wretched and his treasures among the impoverished'.[116] Indeed, Isidore emphasizes that Reccared's generosity was a response to his knowledge that kingship had been conferred on him, so that he might enjoy it in a salutary manner, attaining a good end.[117] What is perhaps most pertinent, in this context, is that Reccared's generosity is not depicted as being limited to alms-giving to the poor. He is also noted as restoring wealth to private citizens, enriching many with gifts and conferring honours – representing a slightly more 'secular' bound generosity than Oswald's.[118]

In Bede's portrayal of Oswald it is possible that he deliberately focused on a virtue that was common to Church teaching and not just associated with being a king. The way Oswald was shown as expressing his alms-giving was obviously affected by his social standing but the virtue itself was crucial to Christian living in general (as were faith and humility). Alms-giving was a textually established virtue worth aspiring to and Oswald provided a perfect vehicle with which to emphasize it. Moreover, as Campbell observed, Bede's description of the minister ordered to dispense Oswald's alms is comparable to officials with a similar role called *consules*, found in Merovingian texts.[119] This might, of course, be coincidental, but the image Bede used could conceivably have been derived from some lost piece of continental hagiography. Additionally, this tale is completed with Aidan's blessing and prayer concerning the incorruptibility of Oswald's generous hand, surely a warning of the hagiographical nature of the story. This whole episode, with its respective conventions of alms-giving, the agents dispensing it and the fulfilment of Aidan's prayer (elaborated with direct speech, a notable tool of rhetoric), reads like a textual construct drawn together from a variety of sources.[120] Whilst it might reflect elements of historical truth, what is more significant is Bede's ability to manipulate the available textual culture and the consequential effect this would have on any representation of actuality.

Oswald's miracle stories provide further evidence for the influence of the textual culture in which Bede moved. The standard discussion of these miracles can still be found in Colgrave's article in *Bede's Life, Times and Works*, and, as he observed, there is not one detail in these miracles that cannot be found in *Acta Sanctorum* or elsewhere in the *EH* itself.[121] Oswald's miracles are at their core stylized and conventional, influenced by common trends in contemporary hagiography. The point is, of course, that originality was far less important than the effective transmission of a message. Bede's miracle stories concerning Oswald were designed to convey the message that the depth of Oswald's faith during his life was exhibited after his death by signs, and as a consequence that faith in one's lifetime rewarded the believer with power *post mortem*. This power after death is particularly well illustrated by the events of the translation of Oswald's relics to Bardney. Thus in III:11 the power of Oswald's sanctity brings about a heavenly light of revelation and ensures his acceptance by the monks there.[122] Wallace-Hadrill has accepted Bede's intimation that the monks of Bardney did not want to receive Oswald's relics because he had conquered them.[123] In this, he follows Patrick Wormald's suggestion that at the time of Oswald's translation Bardney was already a Mercian house and the prejudice being shown was provincial.[124] However, to illustrate provincial antagonism was not necessarily Bede's primary purpose in this narrative. Bede's focus was on the fact that whilst the monks were aware of Oswald's sanctity, they still refused him entry, and only a sign changed their mind. This is a hagiographical *topos* designed to emphasize that relics should be received with reverence by *all* the faithful.[125] It is perhaps pertinent to note in this context that earlier in his description of Oswald Bede comments specifically on the fitting respect with which Oswald's relics at St Peter's church, Bamburgh were venerated by all.[126] The issue of reverence was clearly of importance. Indeed, the works of Gregory of Tours could easily have supplied Bede with an emphasis on this subject. As Brown has noted, Gregory was acutely aware that the tombs and relics of the holy might lack the reverence they deserved and, in his portrayal of the Bardney monks, Bede was expressing similar sentiments.[127]

The fundamental question is whether these sentiments were purely textually based or if they reflected actual events. This part of Bede's narrative is more than possibly a construct. By stressing the monks' unwillingness to receive the relics, Bede or his informant set the scene in which a miracle would be required to persuade them of their error. The miracle itself followed a standard convention of a revelation by a divine column of light, a common *topos* found elsewhere in Bede and in Merovingian hagiography.[128]

The conventionality of Oswald's miracles may itself be significant, as they placed a relatively unusual saint, whose sanctity did not fit into the categories of confessor or martyr, within established hagiographical tradition. In Bede's portrayal of Oswald it is his faith rather than retirement to the celibate monastic life or death at the hands of a pagan that ensures his sanctity. This is excellently shown in Bede's account of events following Denisesburn. In this record Bede makes it clear that Oswald's faith caused the site where he erected the pre-battle cross to become a place of miracles. Therefore, Bede stated that innumerable miracles of healing were known to have been wrought in the place where Oswald erected the cross, 'doubtless as a token and memorial of the king's faith': *ad indicium uidelicet ac memoriam fidei regis.*[129] Bede reiterates this message in his description of the period following Oswald's death. Thus Oswald's great faith and devotion of heart were made clear by miracles.

Bede repeats the same message when discussing the miracles that occurred at the place where Oswald was slain. Here, rather than suggesting that Oswald's seeming martyrdom was the cause of miracles, he implies that they were a result of Oswald's great faith in God and his devotion of heart.[130] Bede further associates Oswald's care of the sick and the poor with the cures brought about by soil from the place where Oswald fell, suggesting that his alms-giving and help whilst he was alive were important factors in his sanctity.[131] Here Bede is implying that royal generosity rather than martyrdom brought about Oswald's saintly status. In a later miracle Bede returns to the theme of Oswald's faith as the cause of his sanctity. In Book III:12, following his narration of the cure of a boy's fever at Bardney, he notes that it should not be wondered at that Oswald's intercession should prevail, for while he ruled he was always accustomed to work and pray most diligently for the eternal kingdom.[132] According to Bede, Oswald's sanctity was established during his life and rested on his faith, his care of the poor and sick, his religious works, and his prayer. This unique image of royal sanctity fits neither into confessor, martyr nor virgin categories. The conventionality of the 'proofs' of this sanctity (the miracles) may have made the unique nature of Oswald's sanctity easier to assimilate. The point one is always drawn back to is, of course, that whilst the nature of Oswald's sanctity is atypical, both the virtues on which his sanctity rested and the miracles which proved the efficacy of these virtues can be found, like the rest of Bede's characterizations, in texts such as the *Pastoral Care* and *De duodecim*.

Up to this point the discussion has focused on the textual models that Bede chose to use in his portrayal of Northumbrian royal saints. However, as has been noted elsewhere, there is one image he avoided – that of martyrdom.[133] Despite the fact that Bede never used any explicit signs of martyrdom for either Edwin or Oswald, there has been a prevailing tendency among historians to consider both of these individuals as martyr-saints. In summary it is argued that ultimately, the historian is perhaps wrong to look at Oswald's sanctity solely in terms of martyrdom. Indeed, it is time to accept that Bede did not consider Oswald to be a martyr. Folz has queried whether the omission of the *topoi* and title of the martyr was merely a personal preference on Bede's part.[134] It may be possible to go further on this point and argue that at the time Bede wrote his *historia* even the sources of information from which he drew has reservations about designating Oswald a martyr. The miracle stories Bede presents appear to come from a variety of sources including popular tradition, Bardney, and Hexham – none of these sources seem to have given Bede the impression that Oswald was a martyr.[135] Essentially, Bede or his informants chose not to draw from textual images of martyrdom in their portrayal of Oswald, and similarly in their portrayal of Edwin. The absence of textual analogies is important, as one has seen, simply because textual referents were a crucial part of the method of construction.

In composing his images, then, Bede applied a methodology that involved two main approaches. Firstly, direct inter-textual referencing, using verbatim sentences and phrases, and secondly, indirect associations made by producing variations on themes concerning kingship and sanctity, found in sources housed in his library. Further to this it is more than likely that the clerical informants he so carefully names also used a similar method of image construction. The reality of the lives of the individuals Bede depicted was profoundly framed in textual allusions that give his narrative authority via association, thereby guaranteeing the validity of his message. In this sense the characters of Anglo-Saxon church history were instruments through which Bede could transmit not only the virtues and vices outlined in Christian literature but also the effects of living by them. Recognizing this should immediately make us cautious about focusing historical research purely on 'authentic' historical information and urge the reader to be constantly aware of the rhetorical nature of the *EH*.

Bede's portrayal of Oswine should also be viewed in this light. For information on this saint Bede had several potential 'authentic' sources. He could have received material from his own abbot Ceolfrith, who had begun his monastic life at Gilling and, therefore, would surely have been able to pass on material concerning any established cult. It is also conceivable that Lindisfarne was a source, given that Bede's depiction is inextricably linked to his narrative concerning Aidan. Bede's choice of one example to prove Oswine's great humility (*'et uno probare sat erit exemplo'*) is, after all, directly associated with this bishop.[136] Tynemouth, too, could have provided information.

Yet he says hardly anything about Oswine that is not conventional. His depiction of Oswine as a tall, handsome, bounteous, pleasantly spoken man, whose royal dignity was demonstrated in his character, appearance, and actions, reads like a stylized exemplary literary construction influenced by the Late Antique Christian writers.[137] In actuality Bede's depiction of Oswine is brief and offers the historian very little concerning the nature of his sanctity. Despite the paucity of material in III:14 Rollason, Folz, and most recently, Catherine Cubitt have accepted that Oswine was venerated as a saint soon after his death.[138] For Rollason, Bede's description of Oswine placed him at the beginning of 'a consistent tradition of the veneration of murdered royal saints'.[139] Folz preferred to place him in a category of royal martyrs: *'Le Roi Massacré'*.[140] Fundamentally, both historians have placed an emphasis on the continuity of the cult of St Oswine (although Folz does concede that it was the period following the revelation of Oswine's relics in 1065 that assured his cult rather than the earlier one).[141]

If one accepts the idea of an early cult for Oswine the question arises as to why Bede did not say more. To attempt to answer this question, one needs to determine whether a cult was indeed established – after all, if the evidence for this is scarce, this alone might answer why the Oswine narrative is so brief.

Dating the origin of the veneration of Oswine is impossible. Unlike Edwin and Oswald, there are no independent contemporary documents that mention him except for an obituary notice in the *Calendar of Willibrord*. Such a notice should not be confused as designating the status of sanctity; rather, it should be seen as an aspect of necrology.[142] Again unlike Edwin, there is no other surviving contemporary hagiographical information than Bede's account. The main *vita* concerning Oswine, *Vita Sanctissimi et Gloriossimi Oswini*, dates from the post-conquest period and seems to relate predominantly to the events surrounding his second translation on 23 August 1103.[143] He is nowhere to be found in Anglo-Saxon martyrologies or pre-conquest litanies.[144] Nor does Alcuin mention him in his York Poem. Following the death of Oswald, Alcuin notes the succession of Oswiu, and, apparently drawing from Bede, he comments on Oswiu's struggle to hold the throne. However, he talks only in general terms of Oswiu's 'feuds with his *own* relatives', not mentioning their names, and, most importantly, ignoring the episode with Oswine completely.[145] Godman has noted that this omission may relate to the fact that Oswiu was one of Alcuin's heroes.[146] Nevertheless, if Oswine were a 'martyr-saint' or one of a consistent tradition of venerated murdered saints, such an omission brings into question exactly what status such murder-related martyrdoms actually did have. More pertinently perhaps, it may also show that Alcuin's reading of the Bede text did not lead him to conclude that Oswine was a saint.

In actuality, the only nearly contemporary evidence that the observer has for Oswine is from Bede's *EH*. Rollason, whilst admitting some unease about this portrayal, has argued that Bede's almost hagiographical description of Oswine's character and humility in Book III:14 suggests that he was venerated as a saint.[147] Nevertheless, this relies on Bede's portrayal being hagiographical. If one actually looks at the characterization Bede uses it becomes clear that there are several rhetorical themes running through it and an image of sanctity was not necessarily what Bede intended.

The dilemma posed by the depiction of Oswine relates to the ambiguity of Bede's own comments. There is no definite statement that clearly suggests that Oswine was considered a saint; rather it is implied that Oswine was a good king, unjustly killed. Nonetheless, Folz has argued that the recorded personality of a saintly king was reconstructed around one fundamental characteristic (or sign).[148] Oswine's sign of sanctity, according to Folz, is essentially the humility attributed to him. However, Wallace-Hadrill's argument concerning royal humility and its relationship to Christian kingship, rather than sanctity, is still very persuasive.[149] This certainly corresponds with Bede's characterization of Oswine, which relates directly to his royal position rather than any saintly qualities: he was 'beloved by all', not because of any holiness, but rather because of the 'royal dignity which showed itself in his character, his appearance, and his actions'.[150] The story of the gift of the horse is not a simple hagiographic motif either. Rather, it works as a metaphor for the relationship between the church and a king. Thus one feels that Oswine's statement to Aidan '*quia numquam … tribuas*' relates more to the idea that kings should not interfere in how the church, and especially bishops, dispensed their gifts received from kings.[151]

Further to this, Kirby has commented that in this chapter Aidan's role is purely secondary. He argues that Bede's intention was less to illustrate the saintliness of Aidan than to extol that of Oswine.[152] Is this probable, however? For a start there are only two main episodes concerning Oswine. The first relates to the treachery that led to his death, and one cannot help feeling that this is one of the few times where Bede seems to pander to the whims of the aristocratic, heroic tastes of his audience.[153] Indeed, the type of narrative Bede uses in this case suggests that he is drawing upon a saga source. This becomes particularly evident if one compares this passage with Mayr-Harting's comments on Bede's use of saga.[154] Thus, it contains the treachery of a *comes*, whom Oswine believed to be a friend, the personal loyalty of his *miles*, Tondhere (*sibio fidissimo*), and it concerns, as Mayr-Harting so eloquently puts it, 'life and politics dramatically affected by individual actions, men innocently caught up in malevolent forces and overpowering tragedy'.[155] Also, as with the example of saga used by Bede in relation to Edwin outlined by

Mayr-Harting, there is a profusion of proper names: the *miles*, Tondhere;
the *comes*, Nunwold; and the murderous prefect, Aethelwine. What is
perhaps interesting in this case is that Bede does not dwell on the tale.
Indeed, he actively appears to have toned down its more heroic elements.
Unlike the saga account found in the Edwin narrative, there is no
elaborate embellishment concerning how Oswine was killed, just that he
was murdered. Bede has perhaps stripped the saga of its more dramatic
elements and presented the information as historical fact.[156]

The second incident to be described is associated directly with Aidan
and immediately precedes Bede's discussion of Aidan's miracles.[157] One
cannot help feeling that the source of this information was the same as
for the rest of the data on Aidan. If one looks at the text it does, indeed,
appear to be Aidan's rather than Oswine's character that is shown here,
for the story provides Bede with an opportunity to elucidate many of the
characteristics which he attributes to Aidan in Book III: 17. Thus in
chapter 17 Bede notes that Aidan 'relieved and protected the poor'. In
chapter 14 he shows him actively doing this by offering his horse to a
beggar.[158] Bede also shows Aidan using his priestly authority to reprove
Oswine. From this one could say that this whole chapter furnishes Bede
with a literary vehicle with which to swing the narrative from a
concentration on Oswine to one that looks more closely at the miracles
of his bishop.

Essentially *EH* Book III:14 does not contain within it evidence which
constitutes information relating to the possible veneration, in the late
seventh century, of Oswine as a saint.[159] It is perhaps pertinent in this case
that when Bede recorded the establishment of a monastery at Gilling, the
prayers that were to be said were for the redemption of the souls of both
Oswine and Oswiu; they were not asking for Oswine's intercession.[160]
Bede's Oswine, like his Edwin and Oswald, is a textual construct
composed from sources such as Gregory's *Pastoral Care* and sagas. In the
image he constructed he carefully avoided conventions that would prove
Oswine's sanctity, focusing on royal dignity rather than saintly virtues.

When reading the pages of the *EH* concerning the Northumbrian
kings and queens, particularly those now considered to be saints, the
observer needs to apply caution. Through sophisticated composition
techniques Bede used conventions from sources he knew to have
authority. He was able to do this in such a way that generally, textual

traits and rhetorical devices flow relatively smoothly in the narrative, leaving the reader with a secure sense of Bede's abilities as an historian rather than a skilful rhetorician.

COMPOSITE IMAGERY AS A NARRATIVE STRATEGY

The point considered above is significant because it raises the issue of to what extent Bede's portrayals of these three kings related in any way to their historical reality. Wallace-Hadrill himself noted that Bede never intended his depictions of Edwin, Oswald, and Oswine to 'constitute a careful synthesis of all that was knowable about them'.[161] In the light of the evidence cited above it is likely that in some cases Bede was not only drawing on and adapting what *was* known about them, but also actively creating what *is* now known about them. Clare Stancliffe too has remarked that Bede did not have one single stereotyped ideal of a Christian king, but used what he knew of the personalities and actions of the kings as a basis for drawing a series of portraits in which sometimes one quality is uppermost, sometimes another.[162] Yet what Bede knew of these personalities was clearly informed by the textual milieu in which he moved, not by any first-hand experience of them. The suggestion here is that to a great extent the characterizations of Edwin, Oswald, and Oswine are based on texts. Indeed, as Mayr-Harting also noted, Bede focused each of his kingly accounts on a particular virtue as if he [Bede] 'had in mind the way in which Anthony the Hermit, the most famous of all monks, had become acquainted with a number of ascetics and imitated each in the practice of the virtue for which that ascetic was outstanding'.[163] Given all that has been suggested about Bede's heavy reliance on varying textual themes, it is possible to see Mayr-Harting's comment in slightly firmer terms than he himself does. Bede probably did use the *Life of St Anthony* as a prototype for structuring his portrayal of individual virtues.

Essentially, what the observer is left with is a composite image of the virtues of kingship: Edwin's discernment and inner focus concerning religious matters; Oswald's faith and devotion; Oswine's humility. In addition to this Bede indicated an important vice of ruling – pride – using Ecgfrith as his vehicle. Such a composite image is a reminder that historians need to understand omissions and emphases in the light of the whole scheme of the *EH*. If an observer assumes access to biographical information concerning a king they are sure to be disappointed, for theirs is an expectation that does not accord with Bede's method of construction or aim. One also needs to take into account the fact that the virtues on which Bede focuses may have been more important to him than accurate association with the individual to whom he ascribes them. The success or failure of a king was viewed by Bede as relating directly to virtues or vices outlined in texts such as Gregory's *Pastoral Care*. If a king succeeded he would be described in terms of virtues, if he failed, in terms of vices (or perhaps he would be discreetly under-represented).

If one adds to the isolation of individual traits the focus on Edwin as the epitome of a royal convert and Oswald as the personification of the ideal secular saint, one can additionally suggest that the way Bede constructed his narrative was to avoid repetition. Essentially, Bede saw no point in repeating the same models. Certainly, if one examines the other convert kings in the *EH* it is clear that he does not give their conversion process quite as much space. Aethelberht's conversion narrative, whilst including listening to Augustine's words and allowing Augustine freedom of movement, is summed up with the line (I:25) 'At last the king believed'.[164] There is no image of solitary wanderings or visions. Similarly, brief notices can be found elsewhere in *EH*. With Oswald, Bede mentions that he was converted and received baptism in Iona (III:3) but there is no elaboration of the persuasion process.[165] Even Sigeberht of the East Saxons' conversion, at the exhortation of Oswiu, reads more like an abridged version of events than that of Edwin.[166]

This desire to avoid repetition could explain the absence in the *EH* of any hint of Edwin's sanctity. Arguably Bede only had space for one secular saint and that honour went to Oswald, whose cult (by the time Bede was completing the *EH*) had already achieved international fame. This sounds plausible. This is significant, for the omission of the cult material relating to Edwin has received attention both here and from other authors.[167] If compositional constraints were behind the silence the possibility of monastic or even provincial politics as causal factors would be lessened. However, there is one caveat. Although Bede avoided repeating an embellishment of the process of conversion, he did briefly record the event for several individuals. In just a few words Bede could have noted Edwin's subsequent elevation as a saint – he chose not to offer even an abridged statement. In this case it is hard not to assume that Bede was deliberately omitting information.

The lives of Edwin, Oswald, and Oswine, then, provided Bede with an opportunity to elaborate creatively on characteristics he knew from his monastic training to be of importance. By utilizing references to established authoritative texts he gave his Northumbrian kings a seeming continuity with the Late Antique period, linking their kingship and, in some cases, their sanctity with earlier Christian predecessors. Moreover, by drawing upon texts which had status within the monastic community, Bede both legitimized his own characterizations and disseminated early Christian ideals in a form that was perhaps more accessible to an Anglo-Saxon audience than the original sources. Additionally, through careful deployment of rhetorical devices and the avoidance of overt repetition in the portrayal of individual traits, Bede created a sense of credibility in his text that makes it seem as if he was writing historical fact. Nonetheless, the case study shows that the extent of textual construction places much of Bede's narrative concerning Edwin, Oswald, and Oswine in the realm of a form of historical apocrypha. While credible and well referenced on the surface level, but in an early medieval context, Bede's images do not in themselves mean that the narrative is either entirely or partially historically accurate. Only after the identification of the devices and textual allusions can one begin to get a hint of the historical (rather than inter-textual) record. Having done this, however, individual attributes portrayed in the *Ecclesiastical History* may be nothing more than a comprehensive set of literary references placed within annal-type information, disguised by Bede's undoubted rhetorical capabilities.

A similar approach to narrative can be illustrated in Bede's portrayal of the Northumbrian female saints. Christine Fell, when comparing Bede's Aethelthryth and Hilda, has suggested that they represent examples of Bede as hagiographer and Bede as historian respectively.[168] Essentially she is suggesting that the description of Aethelthryth is hagiography, whereas that of Hilda is more historical. To do this she has emphasized that Bede's picture of Aethelthryth focuses on her personal life-style and death, whilst the images of Whitby centre far more on events in the community than just the actions of one abbess. However, when approaching Bede's *EH* one should arguably be wary of making such stark distinctions between Bede the hagiographer and Bede the historian. In the first place, such a distinction implies that Bede perceived history in a similar way to more modern conceptions of history – as an analytical narration of events. As has been shown in chapter 4, Bede concentrates on the idea that *historia* should record the conventional deeds of good men (and by silent implication the odd good woman!). Thus his personal characterization of Aethelthryth's ascetic deeds is as much part of *historia* as the more apparently historical information (such as mentioning names, and outlining the general activities of a community) offered concerning Hilda.[169] Furthermore, Professor Fell's distinction may be somewhat anachronistic in this context when one considers that in his portrayal of Hilda, Bede also mentions the fulfilment of dreams and the occurrence of visions – hardly events one would today associate with 'history'.

The differences in portrayal may, however, relate more to the fact that in Book IV of the *EH* Bede was furnishing the reader with two different sets of attributes from which to draw a composite picture of the types of piety appropriate to female saints. Arguably, he did this in an effort to avoid repeating the same type of characteristics within the framework of the *EH*. Thus, Ridyard was right to note that Bede's account of Aethelthryth is an important interpretation of the sanctity of royal ladies, but it was by no means complete.[170] Only if one places chapters 19 and 23 together (Aethelthryth and Hilda respectively) is a more complete picture presented. From the two components of the lives of Aethelthryth and Hilda a larger image of female sanctity can be drawn. Thus with Aethelthryth Bede emphasizes the more 'personal' aspects of female piety, focusing the reader's attention on her virginity, her humility in terms of her woollen garments, her bathing habits, her fasting, her prayer, and her wish to be buried in a wooden coffin, in the ranks of the other nuns, as her turn came.[171] With reference to Hilda, however, Bede appears more anxious to depict the public, less 'personal' aspects of female piety. Consequently Bede concentrates more on her role as abbess, her establishment of a rule of life and her teaching at Hartlepool and then at Whitby.[172] Bede was perhaps intentionally developing some characteristics in one and some in the other in a manner that would encourage the reader to draw a composite picture of female sanctity.

This distinction is seen particularly clearly in terms of the role of these two women as teachers in their communities. Thus, in relation to

Aethelthryth, Bede notes that at Ely she became, by example of her heavenly life and teaching, the virgin mother of many virgins dedicated to God.[173] Yet in his following description Bede clearly concentrates on 'her heavenly life' rather than her teaching. With Hilda, however, the emphasis is exactly the opposite. Thus Bede describes in detail the instruction she gave:

> teaching them [members of her houses] to observe strictly the virtues of justice, devotion, chastity and other virtues too, but above all things to continue in peace and charity.[174]

Reges and *principes* sought and received her counsel when in difficulties and she compelled those under her direction to devote so much time to the study of holy Scriptures and so much time to the performance of good works.[175] Bede goes on to make a passing comment on Hilda's own 'devotion and grace', but does not elaborate it in the same way he does with Aethelthryth. In his depiction of Hilda his emphasis was on what she taught others to do; in his picture of Aethelthryth, it was on what she herself did.

Bede's elaboration of their respective deaths may also point to the idea that he was drawing a composite picture. Thus although Bede writes in depth about Hilda's death, he is, perhaps surprisingly, silent with regard to any elevation of her relics.[176] It seems unlikely that this silence is due to a paucity in Bede's sources, given his own evident contact with Hilda's monastery at Whitby.[177] As with Bede's description of the piety of Aethelthryth and Hilda, it is more plausible that his portrayal of these two saints needs to be considered in the context of the *EH* as a whole. Therefore, with Aethelthryth the stress is on the translation of her relics and the events surrounding that, whereas with Hilda it is on her actual death. For example, although Bede notes that some believed Aethelthryth to have prophesied her own death, his account of it is brief: When she died she was buried by her own command in a wooden coffin, in the ranks of the other nuns.[178] With Hilda, however, Bede writes in more depth, discussing her last day, her death and her 'ascension'.[179]

In drawing such a composite picture Bede has reproduced, without repetition, different aspects of piety associated with abbesses. Indeed, the lack of repetition is perhaps a crucial key to understanding Bede's portrayal. A comparison of Aethelthryth and Hilda possibly shows an example of how the overall structure of the *EH* influenced the way it was written. For Bede's *EH* to be a thorough 'History of the English Church' [*Historia...Anglorum Ecclesiastica*] he could not ignore either of these undoubtedly important female saints. Nevertheless, to accommodate both of them without repeating similar models, he was perhaps forced to divide the two components of a saintly life, namely personal and 'public' devotion, between Aethelthryth and Hilda. Bede's objective was not to present full lives for each of the saints he portrays, but to depict and accentuate particular ideals in the context of specific individuals. This has clear implications for his choice of material. To return briefly for example to Hilda, a recent reading of Bede's chapter on her life has suggested that he deliberately omitted covering Hilda's role at the Synod of Whitby at this point in the text, thereby reducing her agency.[180] The authors of this reflection, however, acknowledge this is not strictly speaking an omission because Bede covers her role elsewhere in the *EH*.[181] The point is that if Bede had a conceptual sense of a structural unity, repetition would need to be avoided. The saints in *EH* need to be studied in the work both as individuals in their own right, and also as people in the greater scheme of the work.

At this juncture it is worth considering Bede's portrayal of other saintly abbesses.[182] The paucity of information concerning the other major Northumbrian abbesses of the period, notably Eanflaed, Aelfflaed, and Aebbe, also suggests that Bede's stylistic objective was to avoid undesirable repetition. He does not study them in depth, partially because he has nothing to add to the models already focused on. Thus, of Eanflaed, Bede only offers information concerning her baptism, her flight to Kent following Edwin's death, her return to Northumbria to be Oswiu's queen, her burial at Whitby, the detail that she presided over Whitby with her daughter, Aelfflaed, and her role in Wilfrid's decision to go on pilgrimage.[183] He does not provide much detail of her life. In his discussion of Wilfrid's life he implies that she had some influence, but he really offers nothing on her role as queen or co-abbess.[184] Much the same can be said of Aelfflaed, whose appearances in the *EH* are even more scarce than those of her mother. Bede contents himself with merely mentioning her consecration to God when she was barely a year old, and the fact that as abbess of Whitby she received support from the retired bishop Trumwine in both the government of her monastery and in her life.[185] The audience learns nothing from Bede's *EH* about either the piety, sanctity, or even specific death days of these two individuals. Indeed, from a reading of Bede alone it would be difficult to conclude that either of these women played a critical role in Northumbrian church and secular politics.

Bede's silence concerning these two women has led Hollis to conclude that he deliberately chose to ignore elucidating images of them.[186] She has argued that essentially Bede felt 'considerable hostility' for the types of roles Aelfflaed, especially, played.[187] To show this she draws attention to the different picture Stephanus gives the observer of Aelfflaed's part in the proceedings at the council of Nidd.[188] She also states that Bede's overriding influence in his imagery of women was his love of patristic material, and that from his knowledge of such reading he would not offer pictures other than the orthodox ones the reader finds in Aethelthryth and Hilda.[189]

Whilst in general it seems that Hollis is quite right to point out that Bede wanted to produce 'rigidly orthodox' images of female sanctity for his readers, it is not so clear that many of the assumptions upon which Hollis has founded her conclusions can be accepted. For example, she talks of Bede's revisionist approach to Aelfflaed as a hostile rewriting of the relationship between her and Cuthbert.[190] Therefore, she notes both the silences in the *EH* concerning Aelfflaed and the changes Bede makes to the anonymous *Life of St Cuthbert*'s discussion of her meeting with Cuthbert. There can be no doubt that her absence in the *EH* is all too self-evident and it is hard, given Aelfflaed's apparent role as a 'counsellor', not to conclude that Bede was avoiding describing her.[191] Nevertheless, he had offered the image of the abbess as a counsellor in his portrayal of Hilda. Did he need to repeat the same role in the text of the *EH*?

Furthermore, one needs to question whether Bede's rewrite of the anonymous *Vita*'s discussion actually shows hostility to Aelfflaed. For instance, Hollis has argued that in the anonymous *Life of St Cuthbert* Aelfflaed appears as a confidential intimate of Cuthbert, citing as her evidence for this the fact that she alone is made privy to Cuthbert's future knowledge of his death.[192] She goes on to say that Bede radically redraws this relationship, and notes, to emphasize this point, that this is shown by the fact that no one else appears to have been told of this tale.[193] However she states that Bede changes the primary role Aelfflaed has by introducing the male witness Herefrith. Yet, from a reading of Bede's chapters on the events concerning Cuthbert's prophetic words to Aelfflaed, one cannot help but think that Bede only notes the fact that Aelfflaed discussed the matter with Herefrith because, in his usual obsessive way, he wished his audience to believe that he had received valid and accurate information from a reliable, named source. In this case, the mentioning of Herefrith is less something sinister, and more the workings of a pedantic author who wanted all of his writings to conform to certain rhetorical expectations.

I am not for one minute trying to deny that Bede does ignore Aelfflaed's obviously wider influence (as Hollis has shown); merely that this did not necessarily come out of a hostility to the actual person, but from a desire to produce models worthy of imitation. In fact, if one were to rely only on the anonymous *Life of St Cuthbert* for information concerning the 'expected' activities of Aelfflaed as abbess, one would be severely limited. The anonymous author tells the audience nothing of Aelfflaed other than her part in Cuthbert's prophecy. Indeed, it is Bede, who, in his Prose *Vita*, reiterates the conventional role of the abbess. There he implicitly portrays her as a wise and learned woman;[194] shows her to be the recipient of instruction from Cuthbert; and adds a new chapter to the anonymous author's information, where she receives a miraculous cure from Cuthbert's girdle.[195] Moreover, the titles Bede uses to describe Aelfflaed make it very difficult to conclude that he viewed her with considerable hostility. Thus he calls her the 'most venerable handmaiden of Christ' (*uenerabilis ancilla Christi*);[196] the 'most reverend virgin and mother of virgins' (*reuerentissima uirgo et mater uirginum*);[197] the 'most noble and holy virgin of Christ' (*nobilissima et sanctissima uirgine Christi*);[198] and eulogizes her, noting that she increased her own nobility by the much more potent nobility of the highest virtue (*ac regalis stemata nobilitatis potiori nobilitate summae uirtutis accumulabat*).[199] Compared with the rather understated titles of the anonymous *Life of St Cuthbert*, which refer to her only as 'virgin and royal abbess' (*uirgo et regalis Aelfleda*) and 'most faithful abbess' (*fidelissima abbatissa Aelfleda*), Bede's terminology is clearly not unfavourable.[200] To sum up, in his portrayal of Aethelthryth and Hilda in the *EH* Bede covered the role of a saintly abbess and did not find it necessary to repeat such information with other abbesses: one composite model drawn from two individuals was enough.

The development of a composite narrative is significant. It is time for those reading Bede's *EH* to consider its narrative integrity. The study of 'omission' and 'conspicuous absence' in a text allows the reader to examine possible rhetorical strategies, but has perhaps also led us to lose sight of the potential for a broader unity in that text which would have an impact on how an author would construct his writing. The underpinning assumption behind the analysis of what 'is missing' seems to be a sense that in each of the chapters Bede's intention was to represent a biographical characterization. We have, perhaps, been seduced by these apparently discrete segments of text, rather than questioning the possibility that Bede was, through composite imagery, accommodating a literary unity. Bede's notion of literary unity may differ from ours; it may even be seen as showing evidence of a biblical influence on his compositional process; but nonetheless a conception of a structural whole does seem to be present, representing a deliberate artistry not normally associated with the modern discipline of history.[201]

Conclusion
The Implications of Bede's Approach and Methods

THE IMPLICATIONS OF BEDE'S APPROACH AND METHODS IN TERMS of the study of Anglo-Saxon history seem stark. As onlookers of a period previous to our own we need to come to terms with the possibility that Bede's primary aim was not so much recording historical actuality as historical Christian convention, at least in the case of the personal and public actions of the individuals he identifies. Where the *Ecclesiastical History*, in particular, is concerned, at some level one is dealing with an embellished list of events expanded to meet the needs of a Church attempting to promote deeds worthy of aspiration. At times the embellishments may reflect an actuality, but without corroborative contemporary evidence we are not in a position to prove this.

Having acknowledged this, it is of note that the chronology of Bede's *Ecclesiastical History*, despite some minor inconsistencies, appears to be accurate – itself a factor in the rhetoric of persuasion. After all, if Bede was obsessive about chronology, surely he must have been equally obsessive about factual accuracy? Yet an interest in time does not necessarily exclude the provision of models within that framework constructed from a textual rather than an actual basis. In many regards Bede's *historiae* in general do not reflect 'reality' but only other texts – they are in this sense a post-modernist's delight.

The consequence that this has for the study of the *historiae* is that they demand of the historian a change in the questions applied to interpret the material, effectively shifting the boundaries of history into a wider discipline that involves the study of rhetoric and literary theory as well as the techniques for creating seemingly accurate reconstructions of the past. Indeed, where this later issue is concerned the *historiae* texts challenge the concept that one can reconstruct the Anglo-Saxon past from the evidence for one is always faced with the possibility that apart from the chronology Bede's images are fundamentally Late Antique in provenance. In some respects it is as if writers such as Jerome, Augustine, and Gregory the Great are still determining the questions one asks of the texts, for it is their interests that pervade Bede's apparent interpretation of events. This is not to negate the continued work undertaken by those historians examining the possibility that Bede was reflecting a historical actuality in terms of the actions of his saints, kings, queens, and noblemen, merely to recognize that in doing this the focus first should be the texts upon which Bede may have drawn.

Narrative manipulation, however, does not mean that political considerations are completely absent from the text, merely that these considerations may be clothed in conventions not originating in the contemporary period with which Bede was dealing. Bede's *historiae* themselves, for example, do appear to yield some information concerning the central issue of monastic superiority in the Northumbrian kingdom. Thus, as was shown in chapters 2 and 3, the composition of the text concerning the Irish, Easter, and the Northumbrian monasteries implies that Bede was consciously rewriting the historical record to maintain the superiority of his own community. Of pertinence here is the fact that although Bede was immersed in similar texts to his contemporaries, there is a fundamental act of colonization in Bede's works that sets them apart from their Ionan and even their Canterbury counterparts. In Northumbria at least, Bede developed a sense of Anglo-Saxon ecclesiastical history that isolated his own monastic affiliation as inherently orthodox and whispered that other monasteries all had a slight taint. This was not just insinuated in his writing, it was also achieved by the act of 'over-writing', which is a clear theme of Bede's book production at Wearmouth-Jarrow. At the beginning of chapter 1 a brief comment was made with regard to Bede's disparaging remarks concerning some of the learning of his contemporaries.[1] It is noticeable, that the first example selected is critical of a particular Irish exegete.[2] This is perhaps representative of Bede's views on the tortuous style and content of the Hiberno-Latin tradition; after all he also passes remark on Adomnan's style in his rewriting of '*The Holy Places*'.[3] Although I have argued for his use of *De duodecim*, his portrayal of the Northumbrian kings is suspected as being a deliberate attempt to write advice on Christian kingshsip in a more accessible format than housed in the Hiberno texts to which he had access. In current theoretical parlance it is hard not to see Bede as a 'text-based colonialist', competing with the local culture, overturning the Hiberno-influenced cultural norm and replacing it with a Rome-centred one. Whilst we view Bede for his orthodoxy now, the normative environment of the Northumbrian church was perhaps still less orthodox than Bede could stand. In this he was writing a different history from his immediate contemporaries.

We might, with further research, be able to take this one step further and identify a slight, but similar act of competition with the production of texts at Canterbury. The other examples referred to with regard to Bede's disdain in chapter 1 actually relate to Theodore of Canterbury and suggest that he had less respect for Theodore than we might have considered. Indeed, a closer reading of the *EH* hints at an incongruence in Bede's portrayal of this archbishop, with his subtle manipulations pointing towards Hadrian, not Theodore, as the man without religious practice peculiarities.[4] Bede's reticence about providing details of Theodore's scholarship, when examined in this light, suggests that he might well have known of Theodore's work, but perhaps did not wholeheartedly approve of it or perhaps viewed Canterbury's textual production as competition.[5] A comparison between the type, form, and content of books produced at Canterbury and those produced in Bede's *scriptorium* might make for an interesting read.[6] Was Bede filling in gaps, for example, or was he writing 'better' alternatives? The latter certainly seems the case with the *Life of St Anastasius*. By utilizing Late Antique Roman genre and rhetorical styles and by rewriting Roman, Irish, and British models Bede appropriated contemporary monastic literary culture and made it that of Wearmouth-Jarrow. The apparent rise in power of his monastery was both a cause and a consequence of this appropriation. Arguably, the subsequent popularity of Bede's writings has obscured the extent of his and his monastery's difference in the Northumbrian kingdom. Were one to read only Bede, his *historiae* would leave one with the abiding impression of Wearmouth-Jarrow's moral superiority over an Anglo-Saxon (not just Northumbrian) Church which had hitherto struggled with orthodoxy. If, as has been argued, this is what Bede set out to do, he accomplished it with aplomb.

When faced with the extent of Bede's reliance on generic association, a method of composition that included premeditated adaptation of the evidence to emphasize a particular agenda and dependence upon texts which related to a different time and place to create a history of his own people's church, it is difficult to prevent scepticism invading our responses to his *historiae*. The impression one could derive from both Bede's aim and his methods is that he deliberately set out to mislead his readers, implying a historical truth when in fact he was merely manipulating Late Antique Christian imagery to suit an ideological purpose with the intention of encouraging behavioural modification (imitation). This particular interpretation presents Bede as an ecclesiastical spin-doctor, spinning a narrative designed to promote a Christian uniformity in aspirations and practices.

Indeed, as Averil Cameron noted, the aim of Christian rhetoric was to persuade individuals towards certain acts.[7] Throughout the *EH* Bede can be seen to be employing rhetorical devices and themes to illustrate through narrative the personal actions worthy of Christian aspiration. Viewed in this light the virtues Bede illustrated were of more importance than historical accuracy. He merely uses seemingly historical episodes as vehicles to exhibit the principles at issue – a methodology not dissimilar to *Encomium*.[8]

However, Bede's machinations are only really sinister if one assumes that he knew his immediate audience would be ignorant both of his understanding of *historia* and of the methods he had applied – essentially, that he intended the text to be read by a large, unlearned group. One needs to question whether or not Bede's monastic audience would have perceived history as a discipline in its own right rather than as a form of rhetoric, and, therefore, governed by rhetorical rules of composition. As Roger Ray has observed, both Jerome and Augustine viewed history as a major form of rhetorical exposition.[9] Thus, one can perhaps assume that at least some of his monastic recipients would see nothing untoward in the structures of the *EH*. Indeed, his placing of the narrative into the genre of *historiae* may have been a conscious attempt to remind his readers of how to approach his texts.

Those in Bede's audience with a knowledge of Jerome and Augustine would not have expected the historical truth for which modern historians search. This is not to argue, as McCready has, that Bede believed from his reading of Cassian and Jerome that there were occasions that merited untruth or justified lying.[10] Rather, it is suggested that Bede's sense of historical truth, where personal and public individual actions were concerned, was bound up in a belief that these actions could only be explained through connection to authoritative literature; for this literature itself represented the truth – a point which he expected his audience to know and one which he emphasized by the generic placing of the text. In this sense Bede was not lying.

Moreover, whilst it is clear from Bede's own listing of his *historiae* texts that he viewed them as part of an individual genre, it is also evident that the methods he applied in constructing his narrative were not restricted merely to *historia* but were used elsewhere. His application of rhetorical methods, conventions and references was not an approach unique to him, it was a standard part of monastic life, devolved from Scriptural studies and exegesis. One need only examine the literature concerning Bede's biblical *Commentaries* or the research concerning hagiography to see that these methods were as much monastic as they were 'Bedan'. In this case a monastic audience would have been unlikely to have been fooled into a credulous acceptance.

Of course, the size of Bede's initial audience for the *EH* is unclear. It is fair to assume that the monks of his own monastery and those of Canterbury would have been expected to peruse the text and that subsequently, as other monasteries asked for copies, their inhabitants too would have read the work. However, there is no evidence to suggest, manuscript or otherwise, that (in Latin at least) it was produced for a mass audience. In this sense if the primary objective of the text was to attempt to dupe people deliberately into activities and behaviours they had not up until then been following, its immediate success would surely have been limited to those already attempting to live a Christian life.

Nonetheless, the apparent desire to provide readers with exemplars does imply that at some point Bede intended them to be widely received. Perhaps Canterbury asked Bede to provide them with a text that could be used to ensure conformity and pass on the Christian message in a manner that was seen to be more relevant to Anglo-Saxon life. If so, the text was aimed at a future audience of people in which some would receive the narrative literally and, therefore, might believe the authenticity of the history contained in it.

Yet if the text was limited mainly to a monastic readership initially, the probability of members of those communities not recognizing the textual allusions is surely slight. One caveat to this point of course is that, as was mentioned in chapter 1, literacy and erudition are not the same thing. The extent of Bede's textual knowledge as implied by the *EH* does seem fairly unusual, and whilst some of his allusions are obvious, many are not. Rather, they are blended so effectively into the text that modern researchers often cannot discern them. Viewed from a rhetorical perspective, Bede's brilliance lies in the fact that his narrative is often so plausible that historians have accepted much of it as authentic. Perhaps the same could be said of some of the monastic readers, especially where the extent of their libraries may have been limited.

Bede's understanding of the genre of *historia*, the methods he employed in his construction of *historiae* narratives and his desire to augment his own monastery in these texts all suggest that the historian should exhibit extreme caution when considering *historia* to be history. Historical episodes, however plausibly framed within these texts, need not reflect contemporary political considerations nor need they represent actuality. It is no longer appropriate for the historian to maintain the incongruent stand of acknowledging literary influences while still accepting the basis of the narrative as historically accurate. Rather, our search for the textual allusions should be placed foremost with the recognition that any historical gleanings we try to show may only be the result of our own assumptions concerning what we would expect to find in a text that calls itself a history. Indeed, it is time for those of us in Bedan studies to take up Allen Frantzen's challenge and deconstruct the typologies we have created to order our analysis of Bede, particularly the bibliographical categorization of his *historiae* texts as primary sources.[11] They clearly are not.

In terms of Bede's desire to augment his own monastery there is perhaps one final point that needs to be taken into consideration. His ability to rework authoritative texts into an Anglo-Saxon context is unquestionable, as is his apparent depth of knowledge implied by the textual allusions in the *EH*. This phenomenal exhibition of learning was in itself an act of augmentation for his monastery. Throughout both the *HA* and the *EH* Bede mentioned books. The possession and knowledge of such books brought with it status. In the *EH* in particular Bede 'showed off' both explicitly, by listing the books that individuals had written, and implicitly by textual allusion, his learning and by association the wealth of the community in which he learned. Bede was a product of a newly literate segment of aristocratic Anglo-Saxon society, one that placed great emphasis on the power of the word. In such an environment the sophistication of the narrative of his *historiae* was a form of status symbol. The power of it is shown by the fact that Bede's sanctity came more from his own writing than the manner of his life, death or miracles.

References

Introduction

1   For American scholarship cf. in
particular: R. Ray, 'Bede's *vera lex historiae*',
Speculum, 55 (1980), 1–21; 'What do we
know about Bede's Commentaries?',
Recherches de Théologie Ancienne et Médiévale,
49 (1982) 5–20; 'The Triumph of Greco-
Roman Assumptions in Pre-Carolingian
Historiography', in *The Inheritance of
Historiography 350-900*, C. Holdsworth & T.
P. Wiseman (eds), (Exeter, 1986) 67–84;
*Bede, Rhetoric, and the Creation of Christian
Latin Culture* (Jarrow, 1997). G. H. Brown,
Bede the Venerable (Boston, 1987); W. Goffart,
*The Narrators of Barbarian History AD
500–800* (Princeton, 1988).

2   Cf., for example, D. Kirby, *Bede's
Historia Ecclesiastica Gentis Anglorum: its
Contemporary Setting* (Jarrow, 1992), 3; I. N.
Wood, *The Most Holy Abbot Ceolfrith* (Jarrow,
1993).

3   P. Brown, *The Cult of Saints* (London,
1981).

4   This refers to a comment made by
Goffart, and specifically related to his
suggestion in *Narrators of Barbarian History*,
that previous historians such as Patrick
Wormald and James Campbell have
assumed that Bede lived a fundamentally
secluded monastic life, absorbed in a book-
learned past, and was the unconscious
plaything of his circumstances and
environment. Goffart's judgement seems
harsher than is necessary. W. Goffart, 'The
Historia Ecclesiastica: Bede's Agenda and

Ours', *Haskins Society Journal*, 2 (1990), 32;
Goffart, *Narrators*, 238, 325.

5   Cf., for example, A. Thacker, 'Lindisfarne
and the Origins of the Cult of St. Cuthbert',
in *Cuthbert, Cult & Comm.*, 103–22; 'Membra
Disjecta: The Body and the Diffusion of the
Cult of St. Oswald', in *Oswald: Northumbrian
King to European Saint*, C. Stancliffe & E.
Cambridge (eds). (Stamford, 1995), 97–127;
D. Rollason, *Saints and Relics in Anglo-Saxon
England* (Oxford, 1989); S. J. Ridyard, *The
Royal Saints of Anglo-Saxon England*
(Cambridge, 1988); D. P. Kirby, 'Bede, Eddius
Stephanus and the "Life of Wilfrid"', *English
Historical Review*, 98 (1983), 101–14; S. Hollis,
Anglo-Saxon Women and the Church
(Woodbridge, 1992); Clare Stancliffe,
'Oswald, "Most Holy and Most Victorious
King of the Northumbrians", in *Oswald:
Northumbrian King to European Saint*, C.
Stancliffe & E. Cambridge (eds) (Stamford,
1995), 33–83; C. Cubitt, 'Sites and Sanctity:
Revisiting the Cult of Murdered and
Martyred Anglo-Saxon Royal Saints', *Early
Medieval Europe*, 9 (2000), 53–83.

6   W. Goffart, *Narrators*; Kirby, *Bede's
Historia Ecclesiastica*; I. Wood, 'The Mission of
Augustine of Canterbury to the English',
Speculum, 69 (1994), 1–17.

7   W. Goffart, 'Bede's Agenda and Ours',
29.

8   C. Martindale, *Redeeming the Text: Latin
Poetry and the Hermeneutics of Reception*,
(Cambridge, 1993), 7; V. Gunn, 'Transforming
Subject Boundaries: The interface between

Higher Education teaching and learning theories and subject-specific knowledge', *Arts and Humanities in Higher Education,* 2/3 (2003), 265–80, p. 268; cf. also A. Frantzen, *Desire for Origins: New Language, Old English, and the Teaching Tradition* (London, 1990), 130.

9 Gregory the Great, *Moralia in Job,* i. 33, *Patristica Latina,* 542, c. Translated by Diana Greenway, 'Authority, Convention and Observation in Henry of Huntingdon's *Historia Anglorum', Anglo Norman Studies,* xviii (1995), 106.

10 On the issue of 'reading' experience cf. R. Markus, *Signs and Meanings: World and Text in Ancient Christianity* (Liverpool, 1996), 9, 47, 67.

11 R. Ray, 'What do we know about Bede's Commentaries', 16.

12 R. Ray, 'Triumph of Greco-Roman Assumptions', 76 ff.

13 *Bede, Commentary on the Acts of the Apostles,* L. T. Martin trans, 7:16, 71–7.

14 R. Ray, 'Triumph of Greco-Roman Assumptions', 76.

15 R. Ray, 'Triumph of Greco-Roman Assumptions', 77.

16 R. Ray, *Bede, Rhetoric,* 2.

17 R. Ray, *Bede, Rhetoric,* 7ff.

18 R. Ray, *Bede, Rhetoric,* 11 ff.

19 L. D. Reynolds *et al., Texts and Transmission: A Survey of Latin Classics,* (Oxford, 1983), 55ff.

20 G. Knappe, 'Classical rhetoric in Anglo-Saxon England', *ASE,* 27 (1998), 5–29.

21 M. B. Parkes, 'Rædan, areccan,

smeagan: how the Anglo-Saxons read', *ASE,* 26 (1997), 1–16.

22 G. H. Brown, *Bede the Educator* (Jarrow, 1996), 10.

23 R. Ray, *Bede, Rhetoric,* 6.

24 G. H. Brown, *Bede the Educator,* 13.

25 Cicero, *De Inventione,* I:xix, 55

26 Cicero, *De Inventione,* I:xix, 55.

27 *Isidori Hispalensis episcope – Etymologiarum siue originum,* W. M. Lindsey (O.C.T., 1911), Book I, ch. xli–xliv

28 R. Ray, *Bede, Rhetoric,* ??

29 Cicero, *De Inventione,* I:xix, 55

30 Chapter 4, 122 ff.

31 G. Knappe, 'Classical rhetoric', 7.

32 G. Knappe, 'Classical rhetoric', 13.

33 Cf. ch 7.

34 E. Auerbach, *Literary Language and its Public in Late Latin Antiquity and in the Middle Ages,* (London, 1965), 198.

35 T. Charles-Edwards, *Early Christian Ireland* (Cambridge, 2000), 76.

36 A. Cameron, *Christianity and the Rhetoric of Empire: The Development of Christian Discourse* (Oxford, 1991), 145.

37 C. B. Kendall, 'Bede's *Historia Ecclesiastica:* The Rhetoric of Faith', *Medieval Eloquence: Studies in the Theory and Practice of Medieval Rhetoric,* J.J. Murphy (ed.) (Berkeley, 1978), 145–72.

38 W. McCready, *Miracles and the Venerable Bede* (Toronto, 1994), 49.

39 B. Ward, *The Venerable Bede* (London, 1990), 114.

40 J. Campbell, 'Bede I', in *Essays*, 2.

41 J. O'Reilly, 'Introduction', *Bede: On the Temple*, S. Connolly trans. (Liverpool, 1995), xxxiii–xxxv.

42 J. McClure, 'Bede's Old Testament Kings', P. Wormald et al., *Ideal and Reality in Frankish and Anglo-Saxon Society* (Oxford, 1983), 76–98, .

43 *EH (P)*, I, lx.

44 *EH*, IV: 23, 406; Kendall, 'Bede's *Historia Ecclesiastica*', 169.

45 C. Fell, 'Hild, Abbess of Streonaeshalch', *Hagiography and Medieval Literature: A Symposium*, H. Bekker-Nielsen et al. (ed.) (Odense, 1981), 76ff ; S. Hollis, *Anglo-Saxon Women and the Church*, 248.

46 For a clarification of the difference between allegory and typology cf. R. A. Markus, *Signs and Meanings*, 11.

47 H. Mayr-Harting, 'Bede's Patristic Thinking as an Historian', in *Historiographie im frühen Mittelalter*, A. Scharer & G. Scheilbelter (eds) (München, 1994), 371.

48 J. Smith, 'The hagiography of Hucbald of St. Amand', *Studi Medievali*, 35 (3rd series, 1994), 517–542.

49 H. Mayr-Harting, *The Coming of Christianity to Anglo-Saxon England*, 3rd edn (London, 1991), 212. L. T. Martin 'Introduction', *The Venerable Bede: Commentary on the Acts of the Apostles*, Cistercian Studies Series: 117 (Kalamazoo, 1989) xvi; for the reference to St Augustine cf. Markus, *Signs and Meanings*, 23.

50 R. A. Markus, *Signs and Meanings,*. 23.

51 P. Meyvaert, 'Bede, Cassiodorus, and the Codex Amiatinus', *Speculum*, 71 (1996), 859.

52 H. Mayr-Harting, *Coming of Christianity*, 204. From the perspective of medieval rhetorical training, Suzanne Reynolds has also pointed out that medieval authors would resort to allegory to fulfil an ethical imperative: S. Reynolds, *Medieval Reading: grammar, rhetoric and the classical text* (Cambridge, 1996), 15.

53 Mayr-Harting makes it clear that although Theodore of Canterbury was a representative of the Antiochan literalist school of exegesis, in Anglo-Saxon England as far as the Bible was concerned, the tradition followed was that of the allegorists of the Alexandrian school. *Coming of Christianity*, 206.

54 For this understanding of *inventio*, cf. P. Ricoeur, 'History and Rhetoric', *The Social Responsibility of the Historian*, F. Bedarida (ed.) (Oxford, 1994), 10.

55 D. Greenway, 'Authority, Convention and Observation', 105 & 114.

56 These ideas were developed in response to Markus, *Signs and Meanings*, 49–69.

57 *EH*; *HA (History of the Abbots)*: *Historia Abbatum* in *EH (P)*, 364–87; *Life of St. Cuthbert*; *Vita S. Felicis* J. A. Giles (ed.), *Venerabilis Bedae Opera* (London, 1843–4), IV, 173–201; *Chronica Maiora* in *De Temporum Ratione*, C. W. Jones (ed.), *CCSL* CXXIIIB (Turnhout, 1978), 463–544; *Chronica Minora* in *De Temporibus*, C. W. Jones (ed.), *CCSL* CXXIIIA, 585–611; J. Dubois & G. Renaud, *Édition pratique de Bède, d l'Anonyme lyonnais et de Florus* (Paris, 1976).

58 J. McClure & R. Collins trans., *The Greater Chronicle*, *Bede: The Ecclesiastical History of the English People*, B. Colgrave (ed.),

(Oxford, 1994), 307–40. F. Wallis, trans.,
Bede: The Reckoning of Time (Liverpool, 1999),
157–238.

59   Cf. J. Dubois & G. Renaud, *Édition
pratique*.

60   Translations in D. Farmer (ed.), *The Age
of Bede* (Harmondsworth, 1985), 285–308; J.
N. Hillgarth (ed.), *Christianity and Paganism,
350–750* (Philadelphia, 1986), 153–60; C.
Albertson (ed.), *Anglo-Saxon Saints and
Heroes* (Fordham, 1967), 225–42.

61   M. Lapidge, 'Textual Criticism and the
Literature of Anglo-Saxon England', in
*Textual and Material Culture in Anglo-Saxon
England*, D. Scragg (ed.) (Cambridge, 2003),
113, n. 35.

62   Cf. Lapidge's comments with regard to
textual criticism, 'Textual Criticism and the
Literature', 107 & 119.

Chapter 1

1   Cf. in particular: F. H. Bäuml, '*Scribe et
Impera*' Literacy in Medieval Germany',
Frankia, 24/1 (1997), 123–32; R. McKitterick,
'The Audience for Latin Historiography in
the Early Middle Ages: Text Transmission and
Manuscript Dissemination', in *Historiographie
im frühen Mittelalter*, A. Scharer & G.
Scheibelreiter (eds) (München, 1994),
96–114; M. Innes, 'Memory, Orality and
Literacy in an Early Medieval Society', *Past
and Present*, 158:5 (1998), 1–36; J. C. Brown,
'Writing Power and Writing-Power: the rise
of literacy as a means of power in Anglo-
Saxon England', *Medieval Perspectives*, 15
(2000), 42–56.

2   Cf. for example: Letter to Plegwine,
where Bede mentions his irritation at the
less learned in his community; F. Wallis, *Bede:
Reckoning of Time*, 413; he also passes fairly
disparaging judgements on the works of
others: cf. his *Commentary on 2 Peter* – on

the ridiculous error of one exegete: D.
Hurst trans., *Bede the Venerable, Commentary
on the Seven Catholic Epistles*, (Kalamazoo,
1985), 133; referred to also by G. H. Brown,
Bede the Educator (Jarrow, 1996), 7; also
Bede's comment on the translation of the
Passion of St. Anastasius in the *EH*, which (if
Theodore was the original translator from
whom Bede worked) might suggest Bede
was less comfortable with, if not downright
critical of, some of Theodore's learning. Cf.
EH V:24, 568. On Theodore and the *Passion
of St. Anastasius* cf. A. C. Franklin, 'Theodore
and the *Passio S. Anastasii*', in *Archbishop
Theodore: Commemorative Studies on his Life
and Influence*, M. Lapidge (ed.) (Cambridge,
1995), 183ff. That Bede was not as
convinced by Theodore's learning as we
might suppose is perhaps further evidenced
by his reference to and apparent correction
of Theodore's explanation concerning 2
Corinthians 11:26 in Bede's *On Eight
Questions*, cf. W. T. Foley & A. Holder trans,
Bede: A Biblical Miscellany (Liverpool, 1999),
152.

3   Cf., for example, J. N. Stephens, 'Bede's
Ecclesiastical History', *History*, 62 (1977), 4;
Wallace-Hadrill, *Comm.*, 1.

4   P. Brown, *The Cult of Saints*, 13.

5   P. Brown, *The Cult of Saints*, 20.

6   P. Brown, *The Cult of Saints*, 4.

7   V. Gunn, 'Transforming Subject
Boundaries', 271 ff.

8   One of the most recent uses of two
groups with seemingly monolithic identities
and conceptions of understanding is found
in Catherine Cubitt's piece on the cult of
murdered royal Anglo-Saxon saints, where
she has used the concept of the 'ordinary
Anglo-Saxon', and discussed the interaction
between the 'learned' and the 'ordinary'.
Cubitt, 'Sites of Sanctity', 58.

9 Cf. R.A. Markus, *The End of Ancient Christianity* (Cambridge, 1990), 45f; *Signs and Meanings*, 214–22.

10 R. McKitterick, *The Carolingians and the Written Word* (Cambridge, 1989), 215–22.

11 K. Heene, 'Audire, Legere, Vulgo: An Attempt to Define Public Use and Comprehensibility of Carolingian hagiography', in *Latin and the Romance Languages in the Early Middle Ages*, R. Wright (ed.) (Philadelphia, 1991), 146–63.

12 V. Gunn, 'Transforming Subject Boundaries', 268.

13 K. Heene, 'Audire, Legere, Vulgo', 149.

14 A. Gurevich, *Medieval Popular Culture: Problems of Belief and Perception* (Cambridge, 1988), 51; K. Heene, 'Audire, Legere, Vulgo', 150.

15 G. H. Brown, *Bede the Educator*, 5.

16 J. Campbell, 'Bede 1', in *Essays*, 20.

17 M. Godden, 'King Alfred's Preface and the Teaching of Latin in Anglo-Saxon England', *EHR*, 472 (2002), 596–604.

18 Cf. H. Gneuss, 'The Study of Language in Anglo-Saxon England', in *Textual and Material Culture in Anglo-Saxon England*, D. Scragg (ed.) (Cambridge, 2003), 80; G. H. Brown, 'The Dynamics of Literacy in Anglo-Saxon England', in *Textual and Material Culture in Anglo-Saxon England*, D. Scragg (ed.), (Cambridge, 2003), 185.

19 A clear example of this Anglo-Saxon vernacular literacy is evident in Cuthbert's letter on the death of Bede, where he makes it clear that Bede was familiar with Anglo-Saxon poetry and was translating the Book of John into their own tongue (*nostram linguam*). *EH*, 580–82.

20 P. J. Geary, *Phantoms of Remembrance: Memory and Oblivion at the End of the First Millenium* (Princeton, 1994), 15. P. Geary has suggested that the paucity of evidence for the early medieval period at our disposal today is partly related to decisions made in the eleventh century about the utility of the masses of written material inherited from previous centuries. Whilst the validity of this claim is clear we are still unaware of the extent to which the documents that were destroyed were in the vernacular as much as in Latin. This is important because what the documentation might have shown is that even in the case of functional literacy Latin would not have been the predominant language used. If so, one would view a functional literacy based on Old English, which would suggest a differentiation between literacy used for practical purposes in the secular world and literacy used for exegetical and interpretative purposes in monasteries. Moreover, as will be argued, the probability that reading materials such as letters and history books were accompanied by other gifts given and received in some form of ceremony, suggests a culture focused more on the oral transmission of the information than on the written word. This is of relevance as it may well indicate the dichotomy between those who were expected to interpret texts through a process of reading, recognition, and reflection, and those who were to receive the narratives literally (or even *just* as physical gifts). Cf. B. Stock, *The Implications of Literacy: Written Language and Models of Interpretation in the Eleventh and Twelfth Centuries* (Princeton, 1983), 14.

21 S. Kelly, 'Anglo-Saxon Lay Society and the Written Word', in *The Uses of Literacy in Early Medieval Europe*, R. McKitterick (ed.) (Cambridge, 1990), 42–6.

22 Cf. G. Koziol, *Begging Pardon and Favour: Ritual and Political Order in Early Medieval France* (Ithaca, 1992), 297.

23 A. Gurevich, *Historical Anthropology of the Middle Ages*, J. Howlett (ed.), (Cambridge, 1992), 178.

24 *EH*, I: 32, 110.

25 *Bonifatii Epistolae*, no. 73,[initial?] Emerton trans, *Letters of St. Boniface*, 130–4.

26 *Bonifatii Epistolae*, nos. 74, 75, [initial?]Emerton trans., *Letters of St. Boniface*, 130–3.

27 R. McKitterick, *Carolingians and the Written Word*, 245.

28 This argument may be extended to include the symbolic value of the words in terms of how they were presented to potential observers. In a letter to the Abbess Eadburga (c.735), Boniface requests that the wording of a copy of the Epistles of St Paul be lettered in gold. Golden letters are themselves of intrinsic value in this case, regardless of whether the audience viewing them could read the words they represented. Cf. U. Schaefer, 'Ceteris Imparibus: Orality/Literacy and the Establishment of Anglo-Saxon Literate Culture', in *The Preservation and Transmission of Anglo-Saxon Culture*, P. E. Szarmach & J. T. Rosenthal (eds), 'Studies in Medieval Culture' XL (Kalamazoo, 1997), 301.

29 *EH*, V: 15, 508. Aldfrith is one of the few kings from this early period associated with learning (a sign perhaps of its uniqueness in the society), yet it is clear that Adomnan's gift was not just used personally by the recipient but rather was subject to copying.

30 M. Clanchy, *From Memory to Written Record: England 1066-1307* (Oxford, 1993, 2nd edn), 18.

31 *EH*, preface, 52–6; Cf Kendall, 'Bede's *HE*: the Rhetoric of Faith', 150.

32 D. Kirby, 'King Ceowulf of Northumbria and the *Historia Ecclesiastica*', *Studia Celtica*, xiv/xv (1979/80), 170f.

33 D. Kirby, *Bede's Historia*, 5.

34 B. Yorke, *Kings and Kingdoms of Early Anglo-Saxon England* (London, 1990), 23.

35 This is intimated by P. H. Blair, *The Moore Bede, Early English Manuscripts in Facsimile*, vol. IX (Copenhagen, 1959), 31.

36 R. McKitterick, *Carolingians and the Written Word*, 160.

37 S. Kelly, 'Anglo-Saxon Lay Society. and the Written Word', 61.

38 W. Levison, *England and the Continent*, 245: *Quod perspicue inuenire potes in libro secundo Ecclesiasticae Hystoriae, quem beatus presbiter Beda scripsit, capitulo xviii. et xvii. Ibique inuenires, quod ad ordinationem beati Honorii pontificis Doruuernensis ecclesiae sanctus Paulinus Lindocoloniam occurrit ibique eum ordinauit archiepiscopum, quod idem beatissimus Honorius papa in sua epistola confirmauit.*

39 *EH*, preface, 4.

40 F. H. Bäuml, 'Scribe et Impera', 126.

41 J. McClure, 'Bede's *Notes on Genesis* and the Training of the Anglo-Saxon Clergy', *The Bible in the Medieval World: Essays in Memory of Beryl Smalley*, Studies in Church History, Subsidia 4 (Oxford, 1985), 17. Cf. also M. B. Parkes, 'Rædan, areccan, smeagan: how the Anglo-Saxons read', *ASE*, 26 (1997), 1-16.

42 D. Rollason, 'Hagiography and Politics in Early Northumbria', in *Holy Men and Holy Women – Old English Prose Saints' Lives and their Contexts*, P. E. Szarmach (ed.) (New York, 1996), 96.

43 V. Gunn, 'Transforming Subject Boundaries', 271 ff.

44 For an outline of the different types of reading cf. Parkes, 'Rædan, areccan, smeagan', 1.

45 M. Herrin, 'The transmission and reception of Graeco-Roman mythology in Anglo-Saxon England, 670–800', *ASE*, 27 (1998), 87–103.

46 Augustine quoted in: *Saints and their Cults: Studies in Religious Sociology, Folklore and History*, S. Wilson (ed.) (Cambridge, 1983), 2.

47 Fichtenau discusses the existence of a similar intellectual elite and the practical value of their scholarship in *Living in the Tenth Century: Mentalities and Social Orders*, P. J. Geary trans. (London, 1991), 293.

Chapter 2

1 In terms of the notion of the vying for primatial status among monasteries and the sense of a hierarchy in the eleventh century at least, cf. P. Haywood, 'Gregory the Great as "Apostle of the English" in Post-Conquest Canterbury', *Journal of Ecclesiastical History*, 55:1 (2004), 19-57, especially 24-25.

2 For similar discussion of the situation amongst the Irish monasteries cf: L. M. Bitel, *Isles of the Saints: Monastic Settlement and Christian Community in Early Ireland* (New York, 1990), 157–59.

3 M. Herbert, *Iona, Kells and Derry: The History and Hagiography of the Monastic Familia of Columba* (Oxford, 1988), 134.

4 M. Herbert, *Iona, Kells, Derry*, 135; R. Sharpe trans., *Adomnan of Iona – Life of St. Columba* (Harmondsworth, 1995), 40.

5 M. Herbert, *Iona, Kells, Derry*, 136.

6 *EH*, III: 24, 292: *donatis insuper XII possessiunculis terrarum, in quibus ablato studio militae terrestris ad exercendam militiam caelestem supplicandumque pro pace gentis eius aeterna deuotioni sedulae monarchorum locus facultasque suppeteret. E quibus uidelicet possessiunculis sex in prouincia Derorum, sex in Berniciorum dedit.*

7 Colgrave and Rosemary Cramp have both assumed that the land grants for Hartlepool and Whitby came from Oswiu out of his package of endowments following the Battle of Winwaed. However, as noted, Bede does not explicitly state this. Bede also notes that the monasteries founded immediately after Winwaed were for monks to wage heavenly warfare – and one must question if he included nuns in this. Such vagueness on Bede's part is perhaps a sign to the reader to proceed with caution and avoid making connections he does not make. *EH*, 290, n. 1; R. Cramp, 'Monastic Sites', in *The Archaeology of Anglo-Saxon England*, D. M. Wilson (ed.) (Cambridge, 1976), 223.

8 *EH*, IV: 23, 406.

9 *EH*, IV:23, 406.

10 In III:24 Bede makes it clear that Hilda received a grant of ten hides at Whitby and built a monastery on that site: *conparata possessione X familiarum in loco, qui dicitur Streanaeshalch, ibi monasterium construxit.* However, in IV:23 Bede seems to imply some hesitancy in his knowledge, noting that Hilda either undertook to found or to set in order a monastery at Whitby: *contigit eam suscipere etiam construendum sive ordinandam monasterium in loco.* Such an alteration to his narrative raises one's suspicions as to motive, and given Bede's predisposition for playing down a monastery's initial status it is hard not to connect this change with something less innocent than lack of knowledge. It is perhaps additionally worth noting the indeterminacy of who gave this grant of land to Hilda.

11 *EH*, III:25, 296: *quia nimirum Osuiu a Scottis edoctus ac baptizatus, illorum etiam lingua optime inbutus, nil melius quam quod illi docuissent autumabat.*

12   *EH*, III:24, 292.

13   *EH*, III:26, 308.

14   *Life of St. Wilfrid*, 11, 22: *Reges deinde consilium cum sapientibus suae gentis post spatium inierunt, quem eligerent in sedem uacantem.*

15   *EH*, III:28, 314–16: *Interea rex Alchfrid misit Uilfridum presbyterum ad regem Galliarum, qui eum sibi suisque consecrari faceret episcopum ... imitatus industriam filii rex Osuiu misit Cantiam uirum sanctum ... Erat autem presbyter uocabulo Ceadda.*

16   J. M. Wallace-Hadrill, *Comm.*, 133.

17   Referred to by Wallace-Hadrill, *Comm.*, 237.

18   H. Mayr-Harting, *Coming of Christianity*, 130, noted the controversial nature of this issue in passing.

19   *EH*, III:28, 314: *que eum sibi suisque consecrari faceret episcopum.*

20   *EH*, V:9, 522: *cum consilio atque consensu patris sui Osuiu episcopum sibi rogauit ordinary.*

21   Cf. E. John, 'The Social and Political Problems of the Early English Church', *AGR*, 18 (1970), 46–50; Iso McClure and Collins (eds), *Bede – The Ecclesiastical History*, 398, n. 163.

22   *EH*, III: 23, 286.

23   *EH*, III: 29, 318.

24   *Life of St. Wilfrid*, 16, 34: *Nam culmina antiquata tecti distillantia fenestraeque apertae, auibus nidificantibus intro et foras uolitantibus, et parietes incultae omni spurcitia imbrium et auium horribiles manebant.*

25   *Life of St. Wilfrid*, 19, 40.

26   2 Kings, 11. This allusion is perhaps not the most positive Stephanus could have chosen for 2 Kings; 2 Kings 12 makes it obvious that Joash became displeased with his priests, including Jehoiada, for collecting treasure but not using it to repair the 'house of the Lord' and had to demand that they do so. Was Stephanus actually alluding to the cause of the rift between Ecgfrith and Wilfrid?

27   *Life of St. Wilfrid*, 19, 40: *Ecfritho rege in concordia pontificis nostri uiuente, secundum multorum testimonium regnum undique per uictorias triumphales augebatur.*

28   *Life of St. Wilfrid*, 17, 36. H. Mayr-Harting, *Coming of Christianity*, 157.

29   *HA*, 4, 367.

30   *EH (P)*, ii, 358: *reges saeculi, cognito uirtutum eius studio, locum ei monasterii construendi non ab aliqua minorum personarum ablatum, sed de suis propiis donatum dare curabant...*; L. T. Martin & D. Hurst trans., *Bede the Venerable: Homilies on the Gospels*, I (Kalamazoo, 1991), 129.

31   *Life of St. Wilfrid*, 22, 44: *Nam Inaegustaldesae, adepta regione a regina sancta Aethelthrithae*; H. Mayr-Harting, *Coming of Christianity*, 157.

32   *EH*, IV:19, 392: *quia sciebat illam nullum uirorum plus illo diligere.*

33   *Life of Saint Wilfrid*, 2, 6.

34   *Life of Saint Wilfrid*, 2, 3, 6 & 8.

35   *HA*, 1, 364: *Denique cum esset minister Oswiu regis, et possessionem terrae suo gradui competentem illo donante perciperet.*

36   *HA*, 4, 367.

37   D. P. Kirby, *The Earliest English Kings*, (London, 1991), 106.

38 *HA*, I, 364.

39 *HA*, 6, 369.

40 *HA*, 7, 370; *Life of St. Ceolfrith*, 12, 392.

41 In fact, the wealth of Biscop's monastery leads to another query. As Campbell has noted, the key to much of the success and nature of Wearmouth-Jarrow was that its founder was rich enough to make extensive purchases overseas. Indeed, Bede takes great delight in describing Biscop as a *religius emptor*, a religious tradesman (*HA*, 5). However, Bede notes in the first chapter that Biscop was one of King Oswiu's ministers: *esset minister Oswiu regis* (*HA*, I). This is important for both Chadwick and Thacker have noted that Bede's use of the word *minister* usually implied a young landless bachelor of noble birth in the immediate entourage of the king. The question is, where did a man of no more standing than *minister*, who had rejected what land had been given to him, find either the money or the gifts to exchange for the objects he purchased? To answer the question a useful comparison can be made with another *vita*, albeit slightly later, the *Life of St. Willibrord*, by Alcuin. In chapter 6 of this text the mayor of the Palace, Pippin, is indicated as having sent Willibrord to be consecrated bishop by Pope Sergius. Willibrord is dispatched to Rome, 'with distinguished company, bearing gifts appropriate to the Pope' (*Et sic cum honorifica legatione et numeribus apostolicae auctoritatis condignis Romam directus est*); having received the pallium, Willibrord was then given by the Pope, without hesitation, 'whatever he desired or asked for in the way of relics of saints or liturgical vessels'. The implication of gift exchange is clear. The point is, however, that one can infer from the text that Pippin supplied Willibrord's gifts. Is it not possible that the kings with whom Biscop had direct contact supplied him with similar gifts for exchange? It is interesting to note that on Biscop's first three trips to Rome, firstly and secondly from Britain, and thirdly from Lerins, the aspects upon which Bede places an emphasis relate not to the collection of any tangible objects but rather to the amassing of knowledge, evidence perhaps that knowledge was in itself a precious commodity that brought prestige to its 'owner'. It is, in fact, not until the fourth trip that the great number of actual objects start to be described. In this context one should be aware that Bede notes Biscop was going to Cenwalh on returning from his fourth trip: '*At ingressus Brittanniam, ad regem se Occidentalium Saxonum nomine Counualh conferendum patauit, cuius et ante non semel amicitiis usus, et beneficiis erat adiutus*' (*HA*, 4). Did Cenwalh supply funds for this trip? Bede comments, after all, on the fact that Cenwalh had helped Biscop. What did he mean by this ambiguous statement? Also Biscop's fifth trip, undoubtedly his most profitable in terms of gains for the monastery, occurred after Ecgfrith had given land to establish Wearmouth. It is conceivable that Ecgfrith was more than just a patron of land. Unfortunately, our sources remain silent on this and only inferences can be made from the scarce comments. Nevertheless, there would appear to be a thriving economy in terms of a sacred object gift exchange network. Indeed, religious objects are clearly a trading commodity. J. Campbell, 'Elements in the Background to the *Life of St. Cuthbert* and his Early Cult', *Cuthbert, Cult & Comm.*, 17; M. Chadwick, *Studies in Anglo-Saxon Institutions* (Cambridge, 1905), 339; A. Thacker, 'Some Terms for Noblemen in Anglo-Saxon England, c. 650–900', *Anglo-Saxon Studies in Archaeology and History*, 2, D. Brown (ed.), *BAR*, 92 (1981), 202; Alcuin, *The Life of St. Willibrord, The Anglo-Saxon Missionaries in Germany*, C. H. Talbot (ed.) (London, 1954), 8; W. Levison, *MGH:SRM*, vii, 7–8, 121–22.

42 *HA*, 4, 367.

43 *HA*, 7, 370.

44 I. Wood, *The Most Holy Abbot Ceolfrid* (Jarrow, 1995), 3 & 5.

45 *EH*, III: 23, 286.

46 I. Wood, *The Merovingian Kingdoms 450–751* (Harlow, 1994), 192 ff.

47 *EH*, III:24, 292.

48 But cf. Wood's caution on this point, *Abbot Ceolfrid*, 3.

49 *HA*, 3, 366.

50 *HA*, 6, 369: *Ecgfridum regem uoluisse ac licentiam dedisse nouerat, quo concedente et possessionem terrae largiente ipsum monasterium fecerat.*

51 Anon. *Life of St. Cuthbert*, I: 3, 64; IV: 1, 11; Prose *Life of St. Cuthbert*, 24, 238.

52 *EH*, IV:5, 352: *Vt plures episcopi crescente numero fidelium augerentur..*

53 *EH*, IV:12, 370.

54 Cf. Rollason, 'Hagiography and Politics in Early Northumbria', 103.

55 *Life of St. Wilfrid*, 32, 64 & 172: *Statuimus atque decernimus, ut Deo amabilis Wilfrithus episcopus episcopatum, quem nuper habuerat, recipiat, salua definitione superius ordinata; et quos cum consensu concilii ibidem congregandi elegerit sibi adiutores episcopos…secundum regulam superius constitutam a sanctissimo archiepiscopo promoti ordinentur episcopi.*

56 *Life of St. Ceolfrith*, 11: 391. In this context it is perhaps pertinent that Theodore's later letter to Aldfrith asking for a reconciliation between Wilfrid and Aldfith, requested he do it for the sake of the redemption he do it for the sake of the redemption of the soul of King Ecgfrith: *et pro redemptione animae Ecgfrithi regis. Life of St. Wilfrid*, 43, 88.

57 *EH*, III:14, 256.

58 *EH*, III:24, 293.

59 I. N. Wood, *Abbot Ceolfrid*, 3.

60 I. N. Wood, *Abbot Ceolfrid*, 3.

61 *EH*, IV:28, 438. In the reign of Ecgfrith one sees the change in relations between sacred and civil power on which C. Cubitt has commented. Thus, the function of selecting and deposing bishops appears increasingly to be in the hands of Theodore. However, this hypothesis should not be accepted without caution as in the case of the Northumbrian, Tunberht, Bede does not specifically state that he was deposed by Theodore, merely that he was deposed. C. Cubitt, *Anglo-Saxon Church Councils, 650–850* (London, 1995), 11–12.

62 *Life of St. Wilfrid*, 54, 116.

63 *EH*, IV:23, 408: *De medio nunc dicamus quia, cum in utroque Hildae abbatissae monasterio lectioni et obseruationi scripturarum operam dedisset, tandem perfectiora desiderans uenit Cantiam ad archiepiscopum beatae recordationis Theodorum. Vbi postquam aliquandiu lectionibus sacris uacauit, etiam Romam adire curauit.*

64 *EH*, IV:23, 406: *hoc est filia nepotis Eduini regis, uocabulo Heririci, cum quo etiam rege ad praedicationem beatae memoriae Paulini primi Nordanhymbrorum episcopi fidem et sacramenta Christi suscepit, atque haec, usquedum ad eius uisionem peruenire meruit, intemerata seruauit.*

65 A. Thacker, '*Membra Disjecta*', 106.

66 Gregory of Tours, *Liber Historiarum X*, B. Kauch & W. Levison (eds), *MGH SRM*, I/1 (1951), IX, 40.

67 *Vita Glodesinda: Vita Antiquior*, in *Acta Sanctorum*, July 25, 198–224, ch. 15, 205: *Quod nequaquam habitatores ipsius monasterii ansi sunt facere, nisi per licentiam atque jussionem Regis*. McNamara, *Sainted Women*, 146.

68   Thus the anonymous author of the *Historia de sancto Cuthberto* states: 'And King Ecgfrith and Archbishop Theodore gave to St. Cuthbert in the city of York all the land that lies from the wall of the church of St. Peter as far as the great gate towards the west, and from the wall of the church of St. Peter as far as the city wall to the south. They also gave him the vill that is called Crayke…': '*Et rex Ecgfridus et Theodorus archiepiscopus dederunt sancto Cuthberto in Eboraca ciuitate totam terram quae iacet a muro aecclesiae Sancti Petri usque ad magnam portam uersus occidentem, et a muro aecclesiae sancti Petri usque ad murum ciuitatis uersus austrum. Dederunt etiam ei villam quae uocatur Creca…*', D.Rollason (ed.), *Symeon of Durham, Libellus de Exordio atque Procursu istius hoc est Dunhelmensis Ecclesie* (Oxford, 2000), 46-48.; also *Symeonis Monachi Opera Omnia*, T. Arnold (ed.), I (1885), 199; T.J. South (ed.) *Historia de sancto Cuthberto* (Cambridge, 2002), 46-47.

69   G. Bonner, 'St. Cuthbert at Chester-le-Street', *Cuthbert, Cult & Comm.*, 388; L. Simpson, 'The King Alfred/Saint Cuthbert Episode in the *Historia sancto Cuthberto*: Its Significance for mid-tenth century English History', *Cuthbert, Cult & Comm.*, 397; Rollason (ed.), *Symeon of Durham*, xlii-xliii

70   M. Roper, 'Wilfrid's Landholdings in Northumbria', *Saint Wilfrid at Hexham*, D. Kirby (ed.) (Newcastle, 1974), 76.

71   M. Roper, 'Wilfrid's Landholdings', 76; A.T. Thacker, 'Lindisfarne and the Origins', 115.

72   *Tunc sanctus abbas Boisil statim notum fecit regi Osuingio sanctam uisionem beati Cuthberti, et quod plenus esset spiritu sancto. Tunc rex et omnes meliores Angli dederunt sancto Cuthberto omnem hanc terram quae iacet iuxta fluvium Bolbenda…*', D. Rollason (ed.), *Symeon of Durham*, 44. T. J. South (ed) *Historia de sancto Cuthberti*, 43; T.Arnold, *Symeonis Monachi* 197.

73   T.J. South (ed.) *Historia de sancto Cuthberti*, 43; T.Arnold, *Symeonis Monachi* 197, n. A.

74   R. Folz, *Les saints rois du Moyen Âge en Occident (VIe-XIIIe siecles)* (Brussels, 1984), 29.

75   T.J. South (ed.) *Historia de sancto Cuthberto*, 48; T.Arnold, *Symeonis Monachi* 199.

76   M. Roper, 'Wilfrid's Landholdings', 76, n. 21.

77   *EH*, IV:28, 436; Anon. *Life of St. Cuthbert*, IV: 1, 110; Prose *Life of St. Cuthbert*, 24, 238.

78   *EH*, IV:28,438: *unanimo omnium consensu ad episcopatum ecclesiae Lindisfarnensis eligeretur.*

79   *EH*, IV:28, 438: *Electus est autem primo in episcopatum Hagustaldensis ecclesiae pro Tunbercto, qui ab episcopatu fuerat depositus; sed quoniam ipse plus Lindisfarnensi ecclesiae, in qua conuersatus fuerat, dilexit praefici, placuit ut Eata reuerso ad sedem ecclesiae Hagustaldensis, cui regendae primo fuerat ordinatus, Cudberct ecclesiae Lindisfarnensis gubernacula susciperet.*

80   Anon., *Life of St. Cuthbert*, III: 6, 104: *Ipse etiam paululum tacens dixit, Illum autem non minus tibi esse fratrem usurpaueris, quam alterum. Hoc quippe et incredibile uidebatur, diligentius tamen interrogauit, in quo loco esset. Ipse uero patienter sustinens eam ait, O serua Dei, quid miraris licet sit in aliqua insula super hoc mare? Illa iam cito rememorauit de Aldfrido qui nunc regnat pacifice fuisse dictum, qui tunc erat in insula quam Ii nominant.*

81   C. Stancliffe, 'Cuthbert and the Polarity between Pastor and Solitary', *Cuthbert, Cult & Comm.*, 22.

82   *HA*, 9, 373: *Adtulit inter alia, et pallia duo oloserica incomparandi operis, quibus postea ab Aldfrido rege elusque consiliariis, numque*

Ecgfridum postquam rediit iam interfectum
repperit, terram trium familiarum ad austrum
Uuiri, iuxta ostium conparauit.

83   *HA*, 15, 381.

84   Herbert, *Iona, Derry, Kells*, 143–45.

85   *Life of St. Wilfrid*, 44, 90.

86   *Life of St. Wilfrid*, 44, 90.

87   *EH*, III:25, 294: *Sed et episcopus loci ipsius*
Eadberct ablata harundine plumbi lamminis eam
totam, hoc est et tectum et ipsos quoque
parietes eius, cooperire curauit.

88   A. T. Thacker, 'Lindisfarne and the
Origins of the Cult of Saint Cuthbert',
Cuthbert, Cult & Comm., 112.

89   C. Stancliffe, 'The Polarity between
Pastor and Solitary', 27.

90   M. Herbert, *Iona, Derry, Kells*, 138,
restated 145.

91   W. Goffart, *Narrators*, 270.

92   W. Goffart, *Narrators*, 296, cf. I. N.
Wood, *Abbot Ceolfrid*, 10; concerning
Wearmouth-Jarrow and the Rule of St.
Benedict see H. Mayr-Harting, *The Venerable*
Bede, the Rule of St. Benedict and Social Class
(Jarrow, 1976), 8; P. Hunter-Blair, *The World of*
Bede (Cambridge, 1970), 199.

93   D. A. Bullough, 'The Missions to the
English and the Picts and their Heritage (to
c. 800)', *Die Iren und Europa im früheren*
Mittelalter, H. Lowe (ed.) (Stuttgart, 1982), i.,
87–8.

94   D. A. Bullough, 'Missions to the English',
94.

95   *Life of St. Wilfrid*, 55, 92.

96   *Life of St. Wilfrid* 59, 128.

97   *Life of St. Wilfrid*, 59, 128: *Ad quem*
sanctus pontifex noster de exilio cum filio suo
proprio ueniens, de Hrypis quasi ad amicum
nuntios emisit, quibus austere et dure, persuasus
a consiliariis suis, pro antiqua nequitia
respondebat, dicens: "Per salutem meam iuro, nisi
de regno meo in spatio sex dierem discesserit, de
sodalibus eius quoscumque inuenero, morte
peribunt." Ec post haec aspera uerba,
coniuratione facta adversum eum, de regno quod
duos menses habuit, expulsus est.

98   *Life of St. Wilfrid*, 60, 128: *Nam in unum*
locum iuxta fluvium Nid ab oriente congregati
rex cum principibus et tres episcopi eius cum
abbatibus necnon et beata Aelfleda abbatissa.

99   *Life of St. Wilfrid*, 60, 130.

100   Bede, *Metrical Life of St. Cuthbert: Vita*
Sancti Cuthberti metrica, W. Jaager (ed.)
Metrische Vita Sancti Cuthberti (Palaestra, 198;
1935), ch. 21, li. 582–85.

101   *HA*, 15, 380.

102   W. Goffart, *Narrators*, 264.

103   W. Goffart, *Narrators*, 259.

104   A. T. Thacker, 'Membra Disjecta', 107–9.

105   W. Goffart, *Narrators*, 284; Rollason,
Saints and Relics, 113.

106   W. Goffart, *Narrators*, 284

107   A. T. Thacker, 'Membra Disjecta', 110.

108   *Life of St. Wilfrid*, 47, 99.

109   *Life of St. Wilfrid*, 47, 99.

110   *Life of St. Wilfrid*, 47, 99.

111   I. N. Wood, *Abbot Ceolfrid*, 10.

112   *Life of St. Ceolfrith*, 3, 389: *Qui mox*

ordinatus ob studium discendi maxime uitae monasterialis et gradus, quem subierat, instituta, Cantiam petiit.

113 *Life of St. Ceolfrith*, 4, 389: *adeo ut nemo per id temporis uel in aecclesiastica uel in monasteriali regula, doctior illo posset inueniri.*

114 *Life of St. Ceolfrith*, 4, 389: *nec tamen uel gradus, uel eruditionis, uel etiam nobilitatis suae intuitu, ut quidam, ab humilitatis statu valuit reuocari."*

115 *Life of St. Ceolfrith*, 4, 389: *quin in omnibus regulari se satagebat mancipare custodiae.*

116 *Life of St. Ceolfrith*, 5, 389 & 6, 390.

117 *Life of St. Ceolfrith*, 6, 390: *sic nimirum, sic memorabilis abbas Benedictus, cum esset in omnibus monasterii disciplinis instructissimus, in construendo suo monasterio Ceolfridi quaesiuit auxilium, qui et regularis obseruantiam uitae pari doctrinae studio firmaret.*

118 *Life of St. Ceolfrith*, 8, 390.

119 *Life of St. Ceolfrith* 11, 391–2.

120 *Life of St. Ceolfrith* 16, 393.

121 W. Goffart, *Narrators*, 285.

122 C. Stancliffe, 'The Polarity between Pastor and Solitary', 28.

123 D. A. Bullough, 'The Missions to the English', 96.

124 D. P. Kirby, *Bede's Historia Ecclesiastica*, 4.

125 D. P. Kirby, *Bede's Historia Ecclesiastica*, 12.

126 D. P. Kirby, *Bede's Historia Ecclesiastica*, 4.

127 In the context of this premise the comments of Michelle P. Brown with regard to the influences upon and possible provenance of the Lindisfarne Gospels are particularly pertinent. She has noted that a textual exemplar for the Lindisfarne Gospels came from Wearmouth-Jarrow, and that the stylistic aspects of these Gospels suggest that they were produced in the first quarter of the eighth century, contemporary that is with Bede's rewriting of the *Life of St. Cuthbert*. Unlike Brown, however, I would suggest that this is not about the fusion of two traditions with an eye to establishing a new identity for Northumbria, but further evidence of the influence and power of Wearmouth-Jarrow and Lindisfarne's need to be linked to it. From this it is very tempting to reconsider David Dumville's suggestion that the Lindisfarne Gospels originated from Bede's monastery. Cf. M. P. Brown, *In the beginning was the Word: Books and Faith in the Age of Bede*, Jarrow Lecture (Jarrow, 2002), 18 ff; 20; 25; 35, n. 108.

128 *HA*, 2, 365.

129 *HA*, 3, 367.

130 *HA*, 5, 368.

131 *HA*, 6, 369.

132 P. Wormald, 'Bede and Benedict Biscop', in *Famulus Christi*, G. Bonner (ed.) (London, 1976), 149.

133 I. N. Wood, *Abbot Ceolfrid*, 7.

Chapter 3

1 A. Thacker, 'Bede and the Irish', in *Beda Venerabilis: Historian, Monk and Northumbrian*, L. A. J. R. Honwen and A. A. MacDonald (eds), (Groningen, 1996), 31–59, cf. 37–8.

2 W. Goffart, *Narrators*, 310.

3 *EH*, II: 4, 146: *Siquidem ubi Scottorum in praefata ipsorum patria, quomodo et Brettonum* *in ipsa Brittania, uitam ac professionem minus ecclesiasticam in multis esse cognouit, maxime quod paschae sollemnitatem non suo tempore celebrarent sed...*

4   A. Thacker, 'Bede and the Irish', 39 cf. W. Goffart, 'Bede's Agenda', 36.

5   W. Goffart, *Narrators*, 310.

6   H. E. J. Cowdrey, 'Bede and the "English People"', *Journal of Religious History*, 11 (1981), 501–23.

7   *EH*, III:4, 222: *Namque ipsi australes Picti, qui intra eosdem montes habent sedes, multo ante tempore, ut perhibent, relicto errore idolatriae fidem ueritatis acceperant, praedicante eis Uerbum Nynia episcopo reuerentissimo et sanctissimo uiro de natione Brettonum, qui erat Romae regulariter fidem et mysteris ueritatis edoctus.*

8   *EH*, III: 4, 224.

9   *EH*, III:4, 224.

10   *EH*, III:18, 268.

11   *EH*, III:4, 224: *de cuius uita et uerbis nonnulla a discipulis eius feruntur scripta haberi. Uerum qualiscumque fuerit ipse...*

12   J. M. Wallace-Hadrill, *Comm.*, 94.

13   *EH*, 225, n. 2.

14   A. Thacker, 'Lindisfarne and the Origins', 112.

15   *EH*, III:4, 222: *habere autem solet ipsa insula rectorem semper abbatem presbyterum, cuius iuri et omnis prouincia et ipsi etiam episcopi ordine inusitato debeant esse subiecti, iuxta exemplum primi doctoris illius...*

16   A. Thacker, 'Bede and the Irish', 54.

17   One cannot help wondering if Bede's

note on the size of the monastery's initial land holding (five hides) was in fact a snub rather than a compliment to a monastery apparently lacking in material wealth in terms of its original grant. After all, whilst Bede favoured individual poverty for monks, if one contemplates the celebratory depiction of wealth at Wearmouth-Jarrow in his *History of the Abbots*, it is clear that he did not necessarily favour corporate poverty.

18   J. Campbell, 'Bede I', in *Essays*, 19.

19   W. Goffart, *Narrators*, 313.

20   *EH*, III: 25, 306: *Etsi enim patres tui sancti fuerunt, numquid uniuersali, quae per orbem est, ecclesiae Christi eorum est paucitas uno de angulo extremae insulae praeferenda? Etsi sanctus erat ac potens uirtutibus ille Columba uester, immo et noster si Christi erat.*

21   *EH*, III:5, 226: *Ab hac ergo insula, ab horum collegio monachorum, ad prouinciam Anglorum instituendam in Christo missus est Aidan...*

22   *EH*, III:3, 218.

23   *EH*, III:3, 218.

24   *EH*, III:17, 264.

25   *EH*, III:25, 296.

26   For example, *EH*, III:17, 266: *studium uidelicet pacis et caritatis, continentiae et humilitatis; animum irae et auaritae uictorem, superbiae simul et uanae gloriae contemtorem; industriam faciendi simul et docendi mandata caelestia; sollertiam lectionis et uigiliarum; auctoritatem sacerdote dignam redarguendi superbos ac potentes; pariter et infirmos consolandi ac paupares recreandi uel defendendi clementiam.*

27   *EH*, III:25, 296.

28   *EH*, III:26, 308.

29 *EH*, III:23, 288: *quod nunc Laestingaeu vocatur, et religiosius moribus iuxta ritus Lindisfarnensium, ubti educatus erat, instituit...*

30 *EH*, III:23, 286–8.

31 *EH*, III:19, 268: *multos et exemplo uirtutis et incitamento sermonis uel incredulos ad Christum conuertit uel iam credentes amplius in fide atque amore Christi confirmauit.*

32 *EH*, III:19, 272.

33 *EH*, III:19, 268.

34 A. Thacker, 'Bede's Ideal of Reform', in *Ideal and Reality in Frankish and Anglo-Saxon Society: Studies presented to J. M. Wallace-Hadrill*, P. Wormald et al. (eds) (Oxford, 1983), 146.

35 *Vita Sancti Fursei*, B. Krusch (ed.), *MGH: SRM*, iv (1902), 434–40.

36 W. Goffart, *Narrators*, 325–8.

37 D. Kirby, *Bede's Historia Ecclesiastica*, 7.

38 *EH*, III:25, 298.

39 *EH*, IV:23, 406.

40 *EH*, IV:23, 406.

41 J. M. Wallace-Hadrill, *Comm.*, 163.

42 *EH*, IV:23, 408.

43 *Life of St. Wilfrid*, 54, 116.

44 As noted in chapter 2, the reason for the ambiguity surrounding the founding of Whitby is also questionable.

45 W. Goffart, *Narrators*, 266 & 304ff.

46 *EH*, 122, n. 1; P. Meyvaert, *Bede and Gregory the Great* (Jarrow, 1964), 5. This point is further emphasized when one takes into account Alan Thacker's suggestions concerning the cult of Gregory the Great. He notes that a textual version of Gregory's cult was brought to England but that the Whitby author garbled its contents as a result either of incompetence or because he was dependent on a third-party report. Given Bede's fastidiousness about accuracy and perhaps given the less authoritative nature of this text because of its garbled state, it should not be surprising that Bede avoided it. A. Thacker, 'Memorializing Gregory the Great: the Origin and Transmission of a Papal Cult in the Seventh and Early Eighth Centuries', *Early Medieval History*, 7 (1998), 82.

47 W. Goffart, *Narrators*, 262.

48 W. Goffart, *Narrators*, 309.

49 J. M. Wallace-Hadrill, *Comm.*, 86.

50 *EH*, II, 16, 192; *EH*, II: 20, 206; *EH*, III: 25, 296 respectively.

51 *EH*, IV: 2, 334.

52 S. Hollis, *Anglo-Saxon Women*, 179 & 185ff.

53 *Life of St. Wilfrid*, 43, 88.

54 *Life of St. Wilfrid*, 59, 128.

55 *Life of St. Wilfrid*, 60, 128, 130.

56 *Life of St. Wilfrid*, 60, 132.

57 A. Thacker, 'Monks, Preaching and Pastoral Care in Early Anglo-Saxon England', in *Pastoral Care Before the Parish*, J. Blair & R. Sharpe (eds) (Leicester, 1992), 149.

58 A. Thacker, 'Monks, Preaching and Pastoral Care', 150.

59 A. Thacker, 'Monks, Preaching and Pastoral Care', 149.

60 *EH*, III:24, 292.

61   *EH*, IV:26, 428.

62   *EH*, III:25, 298.

63   *EH*, V:19, 520.

64   *EH*, V:1, 454.

65   *EH*, V:1, 454: *qui multis annis in monasterio, quod dicitur Inhrypum, acceptum presbyteratus officium condignis gradu ipse consecrabat actibus…*

66   *EH*, V: 19, 516.

67   *Life of St. Wilfrid*, 66, 142–43 & 68, 146–8.

68   *EH*, III:2, 216.

69   *Life of St. Wilfrid*, 22, 45; M. Roper, 'The Donation of Hexham', in *Saint Wilfrid at Hexham*, D. Kirby (ed.) (Newcastle, 1974), 169–71.

70   reference to Chapter 3, footnote reference 46 (after typesetting?)

71   J. M. Wallace-Hadrill, *Comm.*, 191.

72   *EH*, IV:19, 392.

73   *EH*, IV:12, 370; V:3, 458; V:11, 484; IV:29, 442; IV:19, 390.

74   *EH*, preface, 6; IV:27, 430; IV:27, 484; IV:28, 434, IV:29, 440; IV:29, 440; IV:29, 444.

75   *EH*, V:20, 530.

76   *EH*, IV:28 & 29.

77   Cf *EH*, II:14; *Life of St. Wilfrid*, 16, 32–4.

78   J. M. Wallace-Hadrill, *Comm.*, 170.

79   J. M. Wallace-Hadrill, *Comm.*, 170; A. Thacker, 'Bede's Ideal of Reform', 144.

80   *EH*, V:2, 456.

81   *EH*, III:13, 252; IV:14, 376; V:19, 526.

82   *EH*, V:20, 530; *HA*, 5, 368.

83   *EH*, V:20, 530; *HA*, 6, 369 & 4, 367.

84   *EH*, V:20, 530; *HA*, 5, 368.

85   *EH*, V:20, 530; *HA*, 6, 369.

86   *EH*, V:20, 530.

87   *EH*, V:20, 532.

88   J. M. Wallace-Hadrill, *Comm.*, 195.

89   *EH*, IV:18, 388.

90   *EH*, IV:18, 388.

91   *EH*, V:21, 534ff.

92   *EH*, V:21, 532.

93   *EH*, V:21, 550.

94   Cicero, *De Inventione*, I:20, 43ff; Anon., *Ad Herennium*, 13 ff.

95   Cicero, *De Inventione*, I:20, 43.

96   *EH*, III:1, 214: *Unde cunctis placuit regum tempora computantibus ut, ablata de medio regum perfidorum memoria.*

97   D. P. Kirby, *Bede's Historia Ecclesiastica*, 5–6.

98   D. P. Kirby, *Bede's Historia Ecclesiastica*, 3.

99   M. Lapidge, *The Anglo-Saxon Library* (Oxford, 2006), 37. One should not rule out either the status afforded by the sheer size of this monastery. To get a sense of the scale and importance of the physical aspect of Wearmouth-Jarrow one should explore the thorough archaeological report made by Rosemary Cramp of the excavations undertaken between 1959 and 1988. For a possible framework within which to interpret some of this material in the light of space, ideology and power, see also the work of Deirdre O'Sullivan. R. Cramp, *Wearmouth and Jarrow Monastic Sites* (Swindon, 2005), especially 31–115 and 348–365; D. O'Sullivan, 'Space, silence and shortages on Lindisfarne. The archaeology of asceticism,' *Image and Power in the Archaeology of Early Medieval Britain: Essays in Honour of Rosemary Cramp*, H. Hamerow & A. MacGregor (eds) (Oxford, 2001), 33-52.

100 Chapter 2, 68ff. (cross reference to this book, needs added after typesetting

101 *Epistolam ad Ecgberctum, EH (P)*, i, 412: *Quapropter uelim sollerter illum admoneas, ut in diebus uestris statum nostrae gentis ecclesiasticum in melius, quam hactenus fuerat, instaurare curetis. Quod non alio magis, ut mihi uidetur, potest ordine perfici, quam si plures nostrae genti consecrentur antistites.*

102 *Epistolam ad Ecgberctum, EH (P)*, i, 413: *Quapropter commodum duxerim, habito maiori concilio et consensu, pontificali simul et regali edicto prospiciatur locus aliquis monasteriorum, ubi sedes fiat episcopalis. Et ne forte abbas uel monachi huic decreto contraire ac resistere temptauerint, detur illis licentia, ut de suis ipsi eligant eum, qui episcopus ordinetur, et adiacentium locorum, quotquot ad eandem diocesim pertineant, una cum ipso monasterio curam gerat episcopalem.*

Chapter 4

1   Cf. for example, R.C. Van Caenegem, *Guide to the Sources of Medieval History* (Amsterdam 1978); *Typologie des Sources du Moyen Age Occidental*, L. Genicot (ed.), (Turnhout).

2   *Isidori Hispalensis episcopi – Etymologiarum siue originum*, W.M. Lindsey (ed.) (O.C.T., 1911), Book I, chs. XLI–XLIV.

3   A. G. Holder, 'Allegory and History in Bede's Interpretation of Sacred Architecture', *American Benedictine Review*, 40 (1989), 116.

4   R. Ray, 'What do we Know About Bede's Commentaries?', 15.

5   Heather Dubrow, *Genre* (London, 1982), 8–9.

6   J. W. Halporn, 'Literacy history and generic expectations, *Passio* and *Acta Perpetua*', *Vigilae Christianae*, 45 (1991), 223; Coats has also commented on the problems created by a unique text: G.W. Coats (ed.), *Saga, Legend, Tale, Novella, Fable, Narrative forms in Old Testament Literature*, (Journal For Study of the Old Testament) Supplement series, 35 (1985), 20.

7   W. Goffart, *Narrators*. not necessary – it is the underpinning theme of the whole book

8   H. Dubrow, *Genre*, 8.

9   H. Dubrow, *Genre*, 31.

10   J. Wallace-Hadrill, *Comm.*, 2; Campbell, 'Bede I', in *Essays*, 5. R. A. Markus, *Bede and the Tradition of Ecclesiastical Historiography* (Jarrow, 1975), 3.

11   R. A. Markus, *Bede and the Tradition of Ecclesiastical Historiography*, 8.

12   J. Wallace-Hadrill, 'Gregory of Tours and Bede: Their views on the Personal Qualities of Kings', *Frühmittelalterliche Studien*, 2 (1968), 31.

13   Cf. W. Goffart, *Narrators*, 4.

14   W. Goffart, *Narrators*, 4.

15   B. Croke and A. M. Emmett (eds), 'Historiography in Late Antiquity – An Overview', in *History and Historians in Late Antiquity* (Oxford, 1983), 9.

16 Isidore, *Historia Gothorum Vandalorum Sueborum*, T. Mommsen (ed.), *MGH:AA XI*, 267–303, in *Isidore of Seville, History of the Kings of the Goths, Conquerors and Chronicles of Early Medieval Spain*, K. B. Wolf, trans. (Liverpool, 1990), 81—110.

17 Gregory the Great. *Dialogues* Bk III:31, A. De Vogue & P. Autin (eds), vol. 2 (Paris, 1978–80), 388.

18 Isidore, *Historia Gothorum*, 287–88.

19 Isidore, *Historia Gothorum*, 273: *In reliquis autem etsi praeda hostium patuit, feriendi tamen inmanitas refrenata est.*

20 Isidore, *Historia Gothorum*, 273.

21 Isidore, *Historia Gothorum*, 289.

22 K. B. Wolf, Isidore *History*, 104–5; Isidore, *Historia Gothorum*, 290: *Prouincias autem, quas pater proelio conquisiuit, iste pace conseruauit, aequitate disposuit, moderamine rexit.*

23 K. B. Wolf, Isidore *History*, 105; Isidore, *Historia Gothorum*, 290: *Fuit autem placidus, mitis, egregiae bonitatis tantamque in uultu gratiam habuit et tantam in animo benignitatem gessit, ut in omnium mentibus influens etiam malos ad affectum amoris sui adtraheret.*

24 K. B. Wolf, Isidore *History*, 105; Isidore, *Historia Gothorum*, 290: *adeo liberalis ut opes priuatorum et ecclesiarum praedia, 'quae paterna labes fisco adsociauerat', iuri proprio restauraret* and *Multos etiam ditauit rebus, plurimos sublimauit honoribus.*

25 Isidore, *Historia Gothorum*, 289.

26 The question one of course asks is whether or not in the context of this *historia*, Isidore, even if he had knowledge of Reccared performing miracles, would have included them. After all they would have been a deviation from his task.

27 K. B. Wolf, Isidore *History*, 106; Isidore, *Historia Gothorum*, 291: *fuit autem eloquio nitidus, 'sententia doctus', scientia litterarum 'ex parte' inbutus.*

28 Isidore, *Historia Gothorum*, 289.

29 *Pauli Orosii Historiarum Aduersum Paganos libri VII*, C. Zangemeister (ed.), *CSEL*, v (Vienna, 1882), 1-600, 539; R. J. Deferrari, trans., *Paul Orosius – The Seven Books of History Against the Pagans*, Fathers of the Church, 50 (Washington, 1964).

30 Isidore, *Historia Gothorum*, 273.

31 Isidore, *Etymologiae*, I, 41ff.

32 W. Goffart, *Narrators*, 243 ff.

33 W. Goffart, *Narrators*, 245.

34 W. Levison, 'Bede as Historian', *BLTW*, 133.

35 On the process of legitimating a text through its identification with a particular genre, cf. R. Morse, *Truth and Convention in the Middle Ages: Rhetoric, Representation and Reality*, (Cambridge, 1991), 6 and restated 238.

36 Bede: *EH*, Bk. V: 24, 568–70; for further discussion of this cf. P. Mayvaert, 'Bede the Scholar', *Famulus Christi*, G. Bonner (ed.) (London, 1976), 35.

37 Gregory of Tours, *Historiae*, X: 31.

38 For example, J. M. Wallace-Hadrill, *Comm.*, 2; A. Thacker, 'The Social and Continental Background', 186.

39 J. M. Wallace-Hadrill, *Comm.*, 2.

40 J. M. Wallace-Hadrill, *Comm.*, 3, 'Equally important within the divine plan were the lives of holy men.'

41 *EH*, III:17, 264–6: *sed quasi uerax historicus simpliciter ea, quae de illo siue per illum sunt gesta, describens et quae laude sunt* *digna in eius actibus laudans, atque ad utilitatem legentium memoriae commendans.*

42 R. Ray, 'The triumph of Greco-Roman Rhetorical Assumptions', 78; J. J. Campbell, 'Bede I', in *Essays*, 10.

43 Cf. A. Cameron, *Christianity and the Rhetoric of Empire*, 144–6 and 185; in relation to this it is interesting to note that Bede's practice of focusing on virtue (*virtutes*) rather than vice (*vitia*) is reproduced in his *Liber de schematibus et tropis*. Franklin notes that in his construction of this text, Bede departed from his sources and the long established genre they represented by omitting *vitia*. She goes on to note that Bede's purpose here was not to teach pupils how to avoid vice but how to recognize virtues in their spiritual reading. C. V. Franklin, 'Grammar and Exegesis: Bede's *Liber de schematibus et tropis*, in C. D. Lanham (ed.), *Latin Grammar and Rhetoric: From Classical Theory to Medieval Practice* (London, 2002), 63–91, especially 70–71.

44 D. Greenway 'Authority, Convention and Observation', 114.

45 N. Wright, 'Gildas' – *De Excidio Britonum*, M. Winterbottom (ed.) and trans., *Gildas: The Ruin of Britain and Other Works*, (London, 1978), 87–142.

46 N. Wright, 'Gildas' Geographical Perspective: Some Problems', in *History and Literature in Late Antiquity and the Early Medieval West* (Aldershot, 1995), no. 1, 85.

47 Gildas, *Ruins of Britain*, 120.

48 M. Winterbottom, 'Gildas', *Ruins*, 17 (trans); 90: *haec erecta ceruice et mente, ex quo inhabitata est, nunc deo, interdum ciuibus, nonnumquam etiam transmarinis regibus et sublectis Ingrata consurgit.*

49 Gildas, *Ruins of Britain*, 91.

50 Gildas, *Ruins of Britain*, 92.

51 Orosius, *Historiarum Aduersum Paganos*, 1-600. W. Goffart, *Narrators*, 299.

52 *EH*, I:7, 28–35 and 28, n.2.

53 *EH*, I:4, 24: *et mox effectum piae postulationis consecutus est, susceptamque fidem Brittani usque in tempora Diocletiani principis inuiolatam integramque quieta in pace seruabant.*

54 M. Winterbottom, 'Gildas', *Ruins of Britain*, 19 (trans); 91: *Quae, licet ab incolis tepide suscepta sunt, apud quosdam tamen integre et alios minus usque ad persecutionem Diocletiani tyranni nouennem.*

55 Gildas, *Ruins of Britain*, 98: *cuius nunc temporibus nostris suboles magnopere avita bonitate degeneravit; EH*, I: 16, 52–4.

56 *EH*, I:17, 18, 19, 20, 21, 54–66.

57 *EH*, I:17, 54.

58 W. Goffart, *Narrators*, 299–301.

59 *EH*, I:22, 68.

60 *EH*, I:22, 68.

61 J. M. Wallace-Hadrill, *Comm.*, 30.

62 W. Goffart, *Narrators*, 299–301.

63 R. W. Hanning, *The Vision of History in Early Britain: From Gildas to Geoffrey of Monmouth* (London, 1966), 78.

64 *EH*, I:22, 68: *quin multo digniores genti memoratae praecones ueritas, per quos crederet, destinauit.*

65 *EH*, I:22, 142: *ut etiam temporalis interitus ultione sentirent perfidi, quod oblata sibi perpetuae salutis consilia spreuerunt.*

66 Cf. R. Ray, 'The Triumph of Greco-Roman Rhetorical Assumptions', 78.

67 McCready has suggested that Bede's writing was similar to that of these two writers. However, the evidence shows rather that Bede was changing the emphasis of their narratives. Cf., McCready, *Miracles and the Venerable Bede*, 48.

68 Orosius, *Historiarum Aduersum Paganos*, Prologue, 7: *sicut pie gubernari egenum opis oportet ita iuste corripi inmoderatum libertatis necesse est.*

69 Orosius, *Historiarum Aduersum Paganos*, Bk VII: 43, 563: *ab initio mundi usque in praesentem diem, hoc est per annos quinque milia sescentos decem et octo, cupiditates et punitiones hominum peccatorum, conflictationes saeculi et iudicia Dei quam.*

70 Orosius, *Historiarum Aduersum Paganos*, Bk VII: 28, 502.

71 Orosius, *Historiarum Aduersum Paganos*, Bk VII: 33, 519.

72 Orosius, *Historiarum Aduersum Paganos*, Bk VII: 36, 536.

73 *EH*, Preface, 2: *seu mala commemorat de prauis, nihilominus religiosus ac pius auditor siue lector deuitando quod noxium est ac peruersum, ipse sollertius ad exsequenda ea quae bona ac Deo digna esse cognouerit, accenditur.*

74 *EH*, III:I, 214; *EH*, III:24, 290.

75 *EH*, III:7, 232–6.

76 *Vita S. Felicis*, J. A. Giles (ed.), *Venerabilis Bedae Opera* (London, 1843-4), IV, 173–201.

77 Isidore, *Etymologiae*, I: ch. XLI, li. 18; cf. R. Ray, 'Bede's *vera lex historiae*', 15.

78 G. Constable, 'Past and Present in the Eleventh and Twelfth Centuries – Perceptions of Time and Change', in *Culture and Spirituality in Medieval Europe* (Aldershot, 1996), no. IV, 137.

79 For example, cf. B. Colgrave, 'Bede's Miracle Stones' in *BLTW*, 202.

80 P. Meyvaert, 'Bede the Scholar', 53.

81 *Chronica Maiora* in *De Temporum Ratione*, C. W. Jones (ed.), *CCSL* CXXIIIB (Turnhout, 1978), 463–544. Also *Bedae: Chronica Maiora*, T. Mommsen (ed.), *MGM:AA*, XIII (Berlin, 1898).

82 F. Wallis, *Bede: The Reckoning of Time*, 157–238; J. McClure & R. Collins, Bede, *Ecclesiastical History*, 305–40. Moreover, in analytical terms, until recently only Jones, Hanning and Blair have attempted to examine the *Chronicle* in terms of Bede's other historiographical works. C. W. Jones, *Saints Lives' and Chronicles in Early England* (New York, 1947); R. W. Hanning, *The Vision of History*; P. H. Blair, 'The Historical Writings of Bede', in *La Storiografia Altomedievale*, Settimone di Studio, XVII (Spoleto, 1970), 197–221.

83 A list of the sources can be found in: T. Mommsen, *Chronica Maiora*, pp. 227–9.

84 C. W. Jones, *DTR*, 242.

85 C. W. Jones, *DTR*, 241.

86 R. W. Hanning, *Vision of History*, 71–78.

87 J. McClure & R. Collins, Bede, *Ecclesiastical History*, 331; T. Mommsen, *Chronica Maiora*, 309, no. 531: *Idem missis Brittaniam Augustino, Mellito et Iohanne et aliis pluribus cum eis monachis timentibus Deum ad Christum Anglos conuertit. Et quidem Aedilberectus mox ad Christi gratiam conuersus cum gente Cantuariorum, cui praeerat, proximisque prouinciis etiam episcopum doctoremque suum Augustinum, sed et ceteros sacros antistites episcopali sede donabat. Porro gentes Anglorum abquilone Humbri fluminis sub regibus Aelle et Aedilfrido sitae necdum uerbum uitae audierant.*

88 *EH*, I:23, 68–70.

89 *EH*, I:23, pp.68–70.

90 P. H. Blair, 'Historical Writings', 210.

91 R. Davis, trans., *The Book of Pontiffs (Liber Pontificalis)* (Liverpool, 2000, rev. edn), 63; *Liber Pontificalis*, L. Duchesne & C. Vogel (eds) (3 vols; Paris, 1886–1956), I:66, 312.

92 P. H. Blair, 'Historical Writings', 209–10.

93 *EH*, 79, n.3.

94 *EH*, Preface, 4.

95 *EH*, I:30, 106.

96 For details of this accusation cf. P. H. Blair, *The World of Bede* (Cambridge, 1970), 266–8.

97 T. Mommsen, *Chronica Maiora*, 311, n. 541: *Anno Heracli regni XVI indictione XV Eduinus excellentissimus rex Anglorum in Brittania transumbranae gentis ad aquilonem predicante Paulino episcopo, quem miserat de Cantia uenerabilis archiepiscopus Iustus. Uerbum salutis cum sua gente suscepit anno regni sui XI, aduentus autem Anglorum in Brittaniam plus minus anno CLXXX eique Paulino sedem episcopatus Eburaci donauit*

98 *EH*, II:9, 162–6.

99 T. Mommsen, *Chronica Maiora*, 309, n. 531; 311, n. 541; 313, n. 534: *Theodorus archiepiscopus et Hadrianus abbas, uir aeque doctissimus, a Vitaliano missi Brittaniam plurima ecclesias Anglorum doctrinae ecclesiasticae fruge fecundarunt.*

100 T. Mommsen, *Chronica Maiora*, 319, n. 586.

101 T. Mommsen, *Chronica Maiora*, 529.

102 Gregory the Great, *Dialogues*, A. De Vogue & P. Antin (eds) (3 vols. *SC* 254, 260, 265; Paris, 1978–80), vol. 2, 388.

103 W. Levison, 'Bede as Historian', in *BLTW*, 122.
104 *DTR*, Jones, 538, li. 14–17: *inprimis martyrii uirtue coronet, dein ceteros fideles corripiens uel martyres Christi gloriosissimos uel damnatos apostatas faciat.*

105 T. Mommsen, *Chronica Maiora*, 315, n. 562.

106 T. Mommsen, *Chronica Maiora*, 316, n. 570.

107 *DTR*, C. W. Jones, 542, li. 2–5: *Et haec est octaua illa aetas semper amanda, speranda, suspiranda fidelibus, quando eorum animas Christus incorruptibilium corporum munere donatus ad perceptionem regni caelestis contemplationemque diuinae suae maiestatis inducat...*

108 C. W. Jones, *Saints' Lives and Chronicles*, 22, notes that less than a fiftieth goes to miracles. This is interesting for Goffart has suggested that miracles were historical events and that is why they were contained in history. However, if they were considered to be events they would be more likely to be found in Chronicles. They are placed in *historia* because they are the deeds of a person rather than a historical event. W. Goffart, *Narrators*, 245.

Chapter 5

1 *Historia Abbatum*, in *EH(P)*, 364-87.

2 P. Wormald, 'Bede and Benedict Biscop', 151; A. Thacker, 'Social and Continental Background'.

3 D. W. Rollason, *Saints and Relics*, 76.

4 J. W. Halporn, 'Literacy History and Generic Expectations', 231.

5   P. Meyvaert, 'Bede the Scholar', *Famulus Christi*, 19–39, 53ff; P. Wormald, 'Bede and Benedict Biscop', 151; W. Levison, 'Bede as Historian', 129.

6   P. Wormald, 'Bede and Benedict Biscop', 151.

7   P. Wormald, 'Bede and Benedict Biscop', 151; A. Thacker, 'Social and Continental Background', 148.

8   D. A. Bullough, 'Hagiography as Patriotism: Alcuin's "York Poem" and the Early Northumbrian "Vitae Sanctorum"', *Hagiographie, cultures et sociétés ive–xiie siecles* (Études Augustiniennes, Paris, 1981), 345.

9   R. Morse, *Truth and Convention in the Middle Ages*, 138; on general discussion of hagiography cf. P. H. Delehaye, *The Legends of the Saints and Introduction to Hagiography* (London, 1907), especially 2; 98; A. J. Gurevich, *Categories of Medieval Culture*, G. Campbell trans. (London, 1985), 43.

10   A. Thacker, 'Social and Continental Background', 184.

11   A. Thacker, 'Social and Continental Background', 186.

12   *HA*, 1, 364: *Religiosus Christi famulus Biscopus cognomento Benedictus, aspirante superna gratia, monasterium construxit...*

13   *HA*, cf. respectively, ch., 1, 2, 4, 6, 7.

14   *HA*, 6, 368.

15   P. Meyvaert, 'Bede, Cassiodorus, and the *Codex Amiatinus*', 837; *HA*, 15, 379: *Siquidem inter cetera monasterii necessaria quae longo regendi tempore disponenda conperiit, etiam plura fecit oratoria; altaris et aecclesiae uasa, uel uestimenta omnis generis ampliauit; bibliothecam utriusque monasterii, quam Benedictus abbas magna caepit instantia, ipse non minori geminauit industria; ita ut tres pandectes nouae translationis*

16   *HA*, 15, 379.

17   *HA*, 20, 385.

18   Anonymous *Life of St. Ceolfrith: Vita Sanctissima Ceolfridi*, C. Plummer (ex) *Venerabilis Baedae Opera Historica*, 2 vols. (Oxford, 1896); Translated in C. Albertson, *Anglo-Saxon Saints and Heroes* (Fordham, 1967). Badly translated by D. S. Boutflower, *The Life of Ceolfrid* (Lampeter, 1991).

19   *HA*, 15, 379ff.

20   *HA*, 18, 382ff & 20, 385.

21   C. W. Jones, *Saints' Lives and Chronicles*, 28.

22   *Life of St. Honoratus*, by St Hilary; *Life of St. Augustine*, by Possidus, *Early Christian Biographies*, R. J. Deferrari (ed.) (Washington, 1957).

23   *Life of Augustine*, 31; *HA*, 11, 375: *Bibliothecam quam de Roma nobilissimam copiossimamque aduexerat... sollicite seruari integram, nec per incuriam foedari, aut passim dissipari praecepit.*

24   *Life of Honoratus*, ch. 3:17, 374.

25   *Life of Honoratus*, ch. 3:17, 374.

26   *HA*, 5, 368.

27   *HA*, 5, 368.

28   *Life of St. Wilfrid*, 8, 166ff.

29   Cf., *HA*, ch. 1, 4, 7.

30   *Life of St. Wilfrid*, 17, 34.

31   *Life of St. Wilfrid*, 17, 36: *quae omnia et alia nonnulla in testimonium beatae memoriae eius in ecclesia nostra usque hodie reconduntur.*

32 *Vitae Sanctae Geretrudis,* version 'A', B. Krusch (ed.), *MGH: SRM,* ii (Hanover, 1888), ch.2.

33 P. Wormald, 'Bede and Benedict Biscop', 152.

34 *Baedae Opera Homilectica,* D. Hurst (ed.), *CCSL* CXXII (Turnhout, 1955), 88–94, 93, 1.172ff.

35 B. Ward, *The Venerable Bede* (Guildford, 1990), 71ff.

36 *De Templo,* D. Hurst (ed.), *CCSL* CXIX, 143–234, 147, 1. 736ff: *Domus Dei quam aedificauit rex Salomon in Hierusalem in figuram facta est sanctae uniuersalis ecclesiae quae a primo electo usque ad ultimum ...per gratiam regis pacifici, sui uidelicet Redemptoris, aedificatur.*

37 Cf. C. Jenkins, 'Bede as Exegete and Theologian', *BLTW,* 181.

38 *Vita S. Felicis,* 198: *Ablata autem omni foeditate ruderum ac sordium earundem, perstabat beatus antistes Paulinus ecclesiam quam coeperat, ad perfectum deducere: cujus aedificium omne tribus annis perfecit, et in picturis atque omni ornatu.*

39 *EH,* cf. I:33; II:3, 6.

40 *Le Liber Pontificalis, Texte, introduction et commentire,* L. Duchesne (ed.), 2 vols. 1886–92; Translation, *The Book of Pontiffs,* R. Davis trans. (Liverpool, 1989).

41 R. Davis, *Book of Pontiffs,* iii.

42 J. Herrin, *The Formation of Christendom,* (London, 1987), 162, cf. for example, Ceolfrith's letter to the Picts: *EH,* V:21.

43 *Liber Pontificalis,* ch. 34 and 66.

44 *Liber Pontificalis,* ch. 34, 170.

45 *Liber Pontificalis,* ch. 34, 172–87.

46 *Liber Pontificalis,* ch. 66, 312.

47 *Liber Pontificalis,* ch. 66, 312.

48 Gregory of Tours, *Histories,* X: 3:1.

49 A. Thacker, 'Social and Continental Background 144.

50 A. Thacker, 'Social and Continental Background 140.

51 A. Thacker, 'Social and Continental Background 140ff, J. McClure, 'Bede and the Life of Ceolfrid', *Peritia,* 3 (1984), 71–84, esp. 82.

52 P. Brown, 'Relics and Social Status in the Age of Gregory of Tours', *Society and the Holy in Late Antiquity* (London, 1982), 236.

53 Michel Sot, *Gesta Episcoporum, Gesta Abbatum:* Typologie des Sources (Turnhout, 1981), 32–3; 'Annals and Chronicles', *New Catholic Encyclopedia* (New York, 1966), 552.

54 M. Sot, *Gesta,* 13.

55 *New Cath. Encyc.,* 552.

56 *Gesta Sanctorum Patrum Fontanellensis Coenobii (GAF),* F. Lohier & R. P. J. Laporte (eds) (Paris, 1935). Also *Gesta Abbatum Fontanellensium,* S. Loewenfeld (ed.), (Hanover, 1886).

57 Concerning its composite nature cf. P. Grierson, 'Abbot Fulco and the Date of the *Gesta Abbatum Fontanellensium',* *EHR,* lv (1940), 275; and I. Wood, 'Saint Wandrille and its Hagiography', *Church and Chronicle in the Middle Ages – Essays Presented to John Taylor,* I. Wood & G.A. Loud (eds) (London, 1991), 4. It is also of note that when the 1935 editors of *GAF* outlined its sources they failed to make any connection between it and the *HA,* indicating perhaps the extent to which the *HA* has been undervalued as a historiographical text. Cf. *GAF,* xxxiii–xxxviij.

58   *HA* 4, 367; 6, 369; 9, 373; 15, 379–80.

59   *GAF,* IX: 2, 66ff (Loewenfeld, 13, 38–9).

60   *GAF,* XII: 2, 88 (Loewenfeld, 16, 47):
*Pentateucum Moysi codicem unum, minorum
prophetarum codicem unum, expositio sancti
Augustini in euangelio Iohannis codices duos,
librum Enkiridian sancti Augustini codicem unum,
omeliare diuersorum autorum uolumen unum.*

61   *GAF,* XII:3, 89ff (Loewenfeld, 16, 48).

62   *GAF,* XIII:4, 103 (Loewenfeld, 17, 54)

63   *HA,* 2, 365: *et non pauca scientiae
salutaris quemadmodum et prius hausta
dulcedine.*

64   *HA,* 10, 374: *uirum scientia quidem
scripturarum sufficienter instructum.*

65   *HA,* 18, 383: *Romam quoque temporibus
beatae memoriae Sergii papae accurrens, et non
paruo ibidem temporis spatio demoratus,
quaeque sibi necessaria iudicabat, didicit,
descripsit, retulit.*

66   *HA,* 11, 375.

67   I. N. Wood, 'Saint Wandrille', 7.

68   I. N. Wood, 'Saint Wandrille', 7.

69   *GAF,* XII:2, 88 (Loewenfeld, 16, 47):
*Scolam in eodem coenobio esse instituit,
quoniam pene omnes ignaros inuenit litterarum.*

70   *HA,* 1, 4, 7, 15.

71   I. N. Wood, 'Saint Wandrille', 9.

72   *GAF,* I:4, 5 (Loewenfeld, 1, 13): *Deinde
hortatu praefati praesulis ac possessionem
terrae largiente Echinoaldo … hoc Fontanellense
coenobium una cum uenerando nepote sue
Godone nouo opere construxit.*

73   Cf. I. N. Wood, 'Saint Wandrille', 8.

74   *GAF,* XII:1, 84 (Loewenfeld, 16,46); I.
N. Wood, 'Saint Wandrille', 9.

75   *HA,* 5, 368.

76   *HA,* 6, 369–70.

77   *GAF,* IV:3, 42 (Loewenfeld, 8, 28): *Hic
dimisit in hoc coenobio Fontenellensi calicem
aureum et patenam auream pensantes libras
quatuor et uncias duas, turiculum auream unam
pensantem libras quinque, capsam auro et
gemmis decoratam continentem pignera
diuersorum sanctorum.*

78   *GAF,* XI:2, 80 & XII:2, 88 (Loewenfeld,
15, 44 & 16, 47 respectively).

79   Cf. I. N. Wood, 'Saint Wandrille', 7.

80   *HA,* 20, 385; *GAF,* II:4, 20 (Loewenfeld,
2, 17–19).

81   *HA,* 6, 369; cf. I. N. Wood, 'Saint
Wandrille', 8.

82   For example *GAF* names Benignus'
father as Maurino and his mother as Inga
(III:1, 22; Loewenfeld, 3:20); Hugo's parents
are named as Drogonis and Adeltrude (IV:1,
37; Loewenfeld, 8:26); Wando's father,
Baldric is also noted (IX:1, 63; Loewenfeld,
13:47); as are Austrulfi's parents, Sindulfo
and Wilberta, (X:1, 71; Loewenfeld, 14: 40);
Witlaic's parents, Irmino and Witbolda (XI:
1, 78: Loewenfeld, 15:440); Gervold's
parents, Walchario and Walda (XII:1, 84;
Loewenfeld, 16:45); Ansigisus' parents,
Anastasio and Himilrada (XIII: 1, 92;
Loewenfeld, 17: 49). Bede on the other
hand made no attempt to name Biscop's
parents, contenting himself instead merely
with noting that Biscop was of noble
lineage: *Nobile quidem stirpe gentis Anglorum
progenitus, HA,* 1, 364.

83   Cf. I. N. Wood, 'Saint Wandrille', 6.

84   It is perhaps possible to state that
though the Carolingians introduced the title
Gesta it would seem that this particular

sub-genre of *historia* (which subsequently became a genre in its own right) was isolated by Bede first! Cf. M. Sot, *Gesta*, 'les *gesta* sont un genre historiographique carolingien', 35.

Chapter 6

1   H. Delehaye, *Cinq Leçons sur la Méthode hagiographique*, Société des Bollandistes, *Subsidia hagiographica*, 21 (Brussels, 1934), 59; W. Levison, *England and the Continent in the Eighth Century* (Oxford, 1946), 169; J. Dubois, *Les martyrologes du Moyen Âge latin*, Typologie des sources du moyen age latin, fascimile 26 (Turnhout, 1978), 39.

2   One need only glance at its bibliographical entry in *Clavis Patrum Latinorum* to see how relatively untouched it has been: *Clavis Patrum Latinorum*, E. Dekkers (ed.) (Turnhout, 1995), no. 2032, 664. F. Lifshitz, 'Bede, *Martyrology*', in *Medieval Hagiography: An Anthology*, T. Head (ed.) (London, 2001), 169–98.

3   H. Quentin, *Les martyrologes historiques du moyen age. Etude sur la formation du martyrologe romain*, (Paris, 1980); Dubois & Renaud, *Édition pratique*. Passing comments on Bede's *Martyrology* are made by W. Goffart, *Narrators*, 247–8; P. Blair, *The World of Bede*, 277.

4   *EH*, xxvi.

5   H. Quentin, *Les martyrologes historiques*, 18.

6   H. Quentin, *Les martyrologes historiques*, 20.

7   For the list of materials Bede drew on cf. Quentin, *Les martyrologes historiques*, 111.

8   J. Dubois, *Les martyrologes*, 31; Michael Lapidge, 'The Saintly Life in Anglo-Saxon England', *The Cambridge Companion to Old English Literature*, Malcolm Godden & Michael Lapidge (eds) (Cambridge, 1991), 250; W. Goffart, *Narrators*, 247.

9   H. Delehaye, *Cinq Leçons*, 60.

10   *EH*, 570: *Martyrologium de nataliciis sanctorum martyrum diebus, in quo annes, ques inuenire potui, non solum qua die uerum etia quo genere certaminis uel sub quo indice mundum uicerint diligenter adnotare studui.*

11   J. M. McCulloh, 'Historical martyrologies in the Benedictine Cultural Tradition', *Benedictine Culture, 750–1050*, W. Lourdaux & D. Verhelst (eds), *Medievalia Lovansensia*, series I/studia XI (Leuven, 1983), 127.

12   M. Lapidge, 'The Saintly Life', 250.

13   H. Quentin, *Les martyrologes historiques*, 110; cf. also *Martyrologium Hieronymiamum*, H. Quentin & H. Delehaye (eds), *Acta Sanctorum*, November, vol. II, part 2 (Brussels, 1931), 4; J. Dubois & G. Renaud, *Édition Pratique*, 5: Bede: *Natale Alamachi qui, iubente Alypio urbis praefecto, cum diceret: Hodie octauae dominicae diei sunt: cessate a superstitionibus idolorum et a sacrificiis pollutis, a gladiatoribus hac de causa occisus est.* MH (Epternache Mss): *natale coronae qui iubente asclepio urbis praefecto, cum diceret hodie octauiae dei caeli sunt cessate a superstitionibus idolorum et sacrificias pullutis a gladiatoribus hac de causa occisus est.*

14   H. Quentin, *Les martyrologes historiques*, 110; J. Dubois & G. Renaud, *Édition Pratique*, 49 & 55.

15   F. Lifshitz, Bede, *Martyrology*, 184. H. Quentin, *Les martyrologes historiques*, 58; J. Dubois & G. Renaud, *Édition Pratique*, 49 & 55: *V Non. Mai. Romae, sanctorum Alexandri papae et Eventii et Theoduli presbyterorum: quorum primus post uincula et carceres, equuleum, ungulas et ignes, punctes creberrimus per tota membra peremptus est: sequentes et*

ipsi post longam carceris sustinentiam, ignibus examinati et ad ultimum decollati sunt sub Aureliano iudice tempore Traiani principis.

16 F. Lifshitz, Bede, *Martyrology*, 179. H. Quentin, *Les martyrologes historiques*, 104; for other details of Felix's life, cf. *Vita S. Felicis*, 173–201; J. Dubois & G. Renaud, *Édition Pratique*, 13: *XIX KL. FEB. In Campania, natale sancti Felicis presbyteri et confessoris: de quo inter alia scribit Paulinus episcopus quia cum a persecutoribus in carcerem mitteretur, et cochleis ac testulis uinctus superpositus iaceret, per noctem ab Angelo solutus atque eductus sit.*

17 *EH(P)*, I, clii.

18 H. Delehaye, *Cinq Leçons*, 49.

19 Rufinus-Eusebius, *Die Kirchengeshichte*, E. Schwartz & T. Mommsen (eds), *Eusebius Werke*, 2: 2, *Die griechischen chrislichen Schriftsteller*, (Leipzig, 1903–1909), VIII:3,743, li. 23ff.

20 Rufinus-Eusebius, *Die Kirchengeshichte*, VIII:7,755, li. 30ff–757, li.4: *quidam ex ipsis post uerbera, post ungulas, post flagella aliosque diuersi generis horribiles cruciatus flammis traditi sunt, alii in mare praecipitati, nonnulli etiam capite caesi, ita ut sponte ceruices suas securibus darent, nonnulli inedia consumpti, alii patibulis adfixi, in quibus quidam more peruerso capite deorsum presso et pedibus in sublime sublatis.* Translated by H. J. Lawlor & J. E. L. Oulton, *Eusebius – The Ecclesiastical History and the Martyrs of Palestine*, vol. I (London, 1927), 5, 263.

21 Cf. A. Palmer, *Prudentius on the Martyrs*, (Oxford, 1989), 227; M. Roberts, *Poetry and the Cult of the Martyrs: The Liber Peristephanon of Prudentius* (Ann Arbor, 1993) 42.

22 M. Roberts, *Poetry and the Cult of Martyrs*, 55

23 Jerome, *Ad Innocentium Presbyterum de Septies Percussa*, in *Jerome: Select Letters*, F. A. Wright trans., (London, 1954), 7 ff.

24 D. Scourfield, 'Chastity on Trial: History and Fiction in Jerome, Letter 1', Classics Research seminar, University of Glasgow, 2001; on declamations and torture cf. M. L. Clarke, *Rhetoric at Rome: A Historical Survey* (London, 1996 rev. edn), 91 ff; S. F. Bonner, *Roman Declamation in the Late Republic and Early Empire* (Liverpool, 1969), 59.

25 D. W. Robertson trans., *Saint Augustine: On Christian Doctrine*, Library of Liberal Arts, 80, 119: *Quoniam si acutum et fervens adsit ingenium, facilius adhaeret eloquentia legentibus et audientibus eloquentes quam eloquentiae praecepta sectatibus. De doctrina christiana*, IV. lii. 4

26 Prudentius, *Peristaphanon Liber*, in *Prudentius*, H. J. Thomson trans., vol. II, 98–345; Aldhelm, *Carmen de virginitate*, in *Aldhelm: The Poetic Works*, M. Lapidge & J. L. Rosier, trans. (Cambridge, 1985), 102–70.

27 Prudentius, *Peristaphanon*, Cassian, 221 ff; Agnes, 339 ff. F. Lifshitz, Bede, *Martyrology*, Cassian, 189, Agnes, p. 180; reference to stylistic approach 176.

28 H. Quentin, *Les martyrologes historiques*, 47; M. Lapidge, 'The Saintly Life', 251.

29 W. Goffart, *Narrators*, 247; this inaccuracy may have been caused by his use of the text by Dubois and Renaud which begins its entries on 24th December, *Édition Pratique*, I.

30 *Kalendarium siue martyrologium*, C. W. Jones (ed.), *CCSL*, CXXIIIC (Turnhout, 1980), 565: 'A further reason to those suggested is that it was not at all clear in the eighth century when the liturgical year began: some proposed March 25, some the first Sunday in Advent, some Christmas. At least every one agreed that January 1 in the Julian calendar was New Year, and at least a reasonable date for the beginning of the martyrological calendar.' G. H. Brown, personal communication, May 2004.

31 *Bedae Opera Didascalica,* C.W. Jones (ed.), *CCSL,* CXXIIIA (Turnhout, 1975), xiv, n.3.

32 C.W. Jones, *Kalendarium,* 565.

33 C.W. Jones, *Kalendarium,* 565.

34 *Bedae: Chronica Maiora,* T. Mommsen (ed.), *MGH:AA* XIII (Berlin, 1898), 289, n. 346: *CM: Perpetua et Felicitas apud Kartaginem Africae in castris bestiis deputatae pro Christo nonis Martiis.* H. Quentin, *Les martyrologes historiques,* 88: *Mart.: Apud Cartaginem, Perpetuae et Felicitatis, quae bestii sunt deputatae, sub Severo principe, et cum Felicitas parturiret in carcere, omnium militum qui simul patiebantur precibus impetratum est octavo mense pareret.*

35 J. McClure & R. Collins, Bede, *Greater Chronicle,* 311; *Chronica maiora,* 286, n.310: *Traianus ann MVIIII mens VI d. XV... Alexander quoque Romanae urbis episcopus martyrio coronatur et VII ab urbe miliario uia Numentana, ubi decollatus est, seppelitur.*

36 Cf. H. Quentin, *Les martyrologes historiques,* 58; J. Dubois & G. Renaud, *Édition Pratique,* 80.

37 J. McClure & R. Collins, Bede, *Greater Chronicle,* 319; *Chronica maiora,* 295, n.406: *IIIICCLVIII Nam et oceani limbum transgressa Albanum, Aaron et Iulium Britaniae cum aliis pluribus uiris ac feminis felici cruore damnauit.*

38 F. Lifshitz, Bede, *Martyrology,* 186; H. Quentin, *Les martyrologes historiques,* 105. J. Dubois & G. Renaud, *Édition Pratique,* 112: *X Ki. JUL. In Brittania, sancti Albani martyris: qui tempore Diocletiani in Verolamio ciuitate, post uerbera et tormenta acerba, capite plexus est: sed illo terram cadente, oculi eius qui eum percussit pariter cedierunt. Passus est cum illo etiam unus de militibus, eo quod eum ferire iusses noluerit, diuino utique perterritus miraculo, quia uiderat beatum martyrem sibi, dum ad coronam martyrii properaret, alueum amnis interpositi auando transmeabilem reddidisse.*

39 *Chronica maiora,* 289.

40 H. Quentin, *Les martyrologes historiques,* 88.

41 *Chronica maiora,* 286.

42 H. Quentin, *Les martyrologes historiques,* 58.

43 *Chronica maiora,* 287; H. Quentin, *Les martyrologes historiques,* 100.

44 *Chronica maiora,* 295; H. Quentin, *Les mart. historiques,* 105.

45 F. Lifshitz, Bede, *Martyrology,* 184; H. Quentin, *Les martyrologes historiques,* 103; J. Dubois & G. Renaud, *Édition Pratique,* 72: *VI KAL. MAI Depositio sancti Marcellini papae; qui cum Ecclesiam IX ann. M. IIII rexisset, temporibus Diocletiani et Maximiani, ab eodem Diocletiano pro fide Christi cum Claudio et Cyrino et Antonino capite truncatus est, et post dies XXXV sepultus est uia Salaria, in cubiculo, a Marcello presbytero et diaconibus, cum hymnis VI Kal. Mai.*

46 J. McClure & R. Collins, Bede, *Greater Chronicle,* 318–19; *Chronica maiora,* 295, n. 405: *IIIIXCCLVIII Secundo autem persecutionis anno Dioclitianus... Haec persecutio tam crudelis et crebra flagrabat, ut intra unum mensem XVII milia martyrum pro Christi passi inueniantur.*

47 F. Lifshitz, Bede, *Martyrology,* 186, but note correction: it is not that she was sixteen years old when buried but that she had been buried for sixteen years (cf. Bede *EH,* IV:19, 394); H. Quentin, *Les martyrologes historiques,* 106: *IX KL. IUL. Sanctae Aethelthrydae uirginis et reginae, in Brittania: cuius corpus cum sedecim annis esset sepultum, incorruptum inuentum est.*

48 J. McClure & R. Collins, Bede, *Greater Chronicle,* 335–6; *Chronica maiora,* 315, n. 562: *Sancta et perpetua uirgo Christi Edilthryda filia Annae regis Anglorum et primo alteri uiro permagnifico et post Ecfrido regi coniux data*

postquam XII annos thorum incorrupta seruauit
maritalem, post reginam sumto uelamine sacro
uirgo sanctimonialis efficitur, nec mora etiam
uirginum mater et nutrix pia sanctarum, accepto
in construendum monasterium loco, quem Eilge
uocant, cuius merita testatur etiam mortua caro,
quae post XVI annos sepulturae cum ueste, qua
inuoluta est, incorrupta repperitur.

49 *Chronica maiora*, 310, n. 539: *IIIDXCI*
Heraclius an. XXVI. Anastasius Persa Monachus
nobile pro Christo martyrium patitur.

50 *Chronica maiora*, 310, n. 539.

51 H. Quentin, *Les martyrologes*
historiques, 106.

52 H. Quentin, *Les martyrologes*
historiques,, 57.

53 H. Quentin, *Les martyrologes*
*historiques,,*58.

54 H. Quentin, *Les martyrologes historiques,*
respectively, 59, 60, 61, 62, 64, 65, 72, 74, 76,
77, 81, 83, 86, 103, 105.

55 For discussion of Christian concepts of
time and their effect on the medieval
mentality, cf. A. J. Gurevich, *Categories of*
Medieval Culture, G. L. Campbell trans.
(London, 1985), 110ff.

56 W. Goffart, *Narrators*, 247.

Chapter 7

1 T. Reuter, 'Pre-Gregorian Mentalities',
JEH, 45 (1994), 472.

2 D. Kirby, 'Bede's Native Sources for the
Historia Ecclesiastica', *BJRL*, 48 (1965–66),
341–71.

3 D. P. Kirby, 'Bede's Native Sources', 344.

4 P. J. Geary, *Phantoms of Remembrance*,
3–22.

5 P. J. Geary, *Phantoms of Remembrance*,
11.

6 P. J. Geary, *Phantoms of Remembrance*, 9.

7 P. J. Geary, *Phantoms of Remembrance*,
15; Matthew Innes makes the point that
Notkar's concept of literary truth was
centred on conformity of reported actions
to remembered textual models. Applying
such a hypothesis to Bede could mean that
he only reiterated images of the individuals
that seemed to match the textual model.
Whilst this cannot be ruled out, it is striking
that the models Bede presents, once a
corresponding text has been identified, are
so obviously textual reminiscences.
Essentially, we just cannot be sure. Innes,
'Memory, Orality and Literacy', 15.

8 D. Kirby, 'Bede's Native Sources', 345.

9 D. Kirby, 'Bede's Native Sources', 346.

10 *EH*, III:17, 266

11 D. Kirby, 'Bede's Native Sources', 346.

12 *EH*, IV:19, 390.

13 D. Kirby, 'Bede's Native Sources', 347.

14 *Anon. Life of St. Gregory*, 16, 98: *Quod non*
tam condenso quomodo audiuimus uerbo, sed
pro ueritate certantes, eo quod credimus factum
breui replicamus et sensu, licet ab illis minime
audiuimus famatum qui eius plura pre ceteris
sciebant.

15 *Anon.Life of St. Gregory*, 16, 98: *Nec*
tamen quod tam spiritaliter a fidelibus traditur,
tegi silentio per totum rectum rimamur, cum
etiam sepe fama cuiusque rei, per longa
tempora terrarumque spatia, post congesta,
diuerso modo in aures diuersorum perueniet.
Hoc igitur multo ante horum omnes qui nunc
supersunt, gestum est dies.

16 Anon. Life of St. Gregory, 16, 100.

17 EH, II:12,174–83.

18 R. Markus, Signs, 9. For a useful parallel cf. Matthew Innes, who has noted that in Notkar's Gesta Karoli, oral traditions were being coloured by written models and were subject to literary interference. M. Innes, 'Memory, Orality and Literacy', 17.

19 EH,V:1,454–6.

20 J. M. Wallace-Hadrill, Comm., 174.

21 EH, 455 n.4; J. M. Wallace-Hadrill, Comm., 175.

22 EH, III:28, 316.

23 N. Wright, History and Literature in Late Antiquity and the Early Medieval West, Variorum Reprints (Aldershot, 1995), ix.

24 EH, 317, n.3.

25 J. Campbell, 'Bede's Words for Places', Names, Words and Graves, P. H. Sawyer (ed.) (Leeds, 1979), 39.

26 N. Wright, History and Literature, ix; M. Irvine, 'Bede the Grammarian and the Scope of Grammatical Studies in Eighth Century Northumbria', ASE, 15 (1986), 33.

27 R. Boyer, 'An Attempt to Define the Typology of Medieval hagiography', Hagiography and Medieval Literature – A Symposium, H. Bekker-Nielsen et al. (eds) (Odense, 1981), 29.

28 EH, Preface, 4.

29 J. M. Wallace-Hadrill, Comm., 159.

30 EH, Preface, 7.

31 For example, C.E. Fell, 'Hilda, Abbess of Streonaeshalch,' Hagiography and Medieval Literature: A Symposium, H. Bekker-Nielson et

al. (eds) (Odense, 1981), 76–99; C. Fell, et al., Women in Anglo-Saxon England and the Impact of 1066 (Oxford, 1986); S. Ridyard, The Royal Saints of Anglo-Saxon England: A Study of West Saxon and East Anglian Cults (Cambridge, 1988); S. Hollis, Anglo-Saxon Women and the Church: Sharing a Common Fate (Woodbridge, 1992). C. Lees & G. Overing, Double Agents: Women and Clerical Culture in Anglo-Saxon England (Philadelphia, 2001); Carol Neuman de Vegvar has commented that the royal women monastics have not been neglected in the scholarship on early Anglo-Saxon England, noting that since the nineteenth century writers have focused on the individual accomplishments of these women. However, it is perhaps worth noting that apart from Lena Eckenstein's work, Women Under Monasticism, published in 1896, relatively little (at least when compared to the academic outpourings on men) was actually produced concerning women in history generally, let alone Anglo-Saxons, until the late 1970s. Neuman de Vegvar's optimism perhaps covers the discontinuity of publications in the field of Anglo-Saxon women's history until the last quarter of the twentieth century. Cf. Neuman de Vegvar, 'Saints and Companions to Saints: Anglo-Saxon Royal Women Monastics in Context', Holy Men and Holy Women: Old English Prose Saints' Lives and Their Contexts, P. E. Szarmach (ed.) (New York, 1996), 51.

32 J. M. Wallace-Hadrill, Comm., xxix

33 Venantius, Life of St. Radegund, Vita Sanctae Radegundis Liber 1: Venantius Fortunatus, in MGH: SRM, 2, B. Krusch (ed.) (Hanover, 1888), 3, 366.

34 Venantius, Vita Radegundis, 5, 367; 6, 367; 19, 370; 21,371.

35 P. Stafford, Queens, Concubines and Dowagers: The King's Wife in the Early Middle Ages (London, 1983), 182.

36 EH, IV.19, 390–2.

37   *EH*, IV:19, 392.

38   J. M. Wallace-Hadrill, *Frank. Church*, 86; reiterated in slightly amended form by J. Kitchen, *Saints' Lives and the Rhetoric of Gender: Male and Female in Merovingian Hagiography* (Oxford, 1998), 26.

39   J. T. Schulenberg, 'Saints' Lives as a Source for the History of Women', *Medieval Women and the Sources of Medieval History* (London, 1990), 287.
40   *EH*, IV:3, 338.

41   *EH*, IV:22, 405.

42   A. Cameron, *Christianity and the Rhetoric of Empire*, 177.

43   R. Morse, *Truth and Convention*, 73.

44   G. Knappe, 'Classical rhetoric', 7.

45   P. Delooz, 'Towards a Sociological Study of Canonized Sainthood in the Catholic Church', *Saints and their Cults*, S. Wilson (ed.) (Cambridge, 1983), 195.

46   Baudonivia, *Life of St. Radegund, Vita Sanctae Radegundis* Liber 2: Baudonivia, in *MGH: SRM*, 2, B. Krusch (ed.) (Hanover, 1888), 4, 381; partial translation of Baudonivia in M. Theibaux, *The Writings of Medieval Women*, 13, series B, Garland Library of Medieval Literature (New York, 1987); also translated in McNamara *et al.*, *Sainted Women*. On this point see also, M. Warner, *Alone of all her Sex: The Myth and the Cult of the Virgin Mary* (London, 1976), 68.

47   *EH*, IV:19, 392.

48   P. Thompson wonders why Ecgfrith was resistant to Aethelthryth's desire to enter monastic life, implying that in political terms it did not make sense. As a convention designed to note exactly what Aethelthryth needed to overcome to fulfil her religious desires, Ecgfrith's response is less puzzling, cf. P. Thompson, 'St.

Aethelthryth: The Making of History from Hagiography', *Studies in English Language and Literature: 'Doubt wisely' – Papers in Honour of E. G. Stanley*, M. J. Toswell & E. M. Tyler (eds) (London, 1996), 485.

49   V. Burrus, 'Word and Flesh – The Bodies and Sexuality of Ascetic Women in Christian Antiquity', *Journal of Feminist Studies in Religion*, 10 (1994), 29.

50   V. Burrus, 'Word and Flesh', 29; the preservation of virginity in marriage is found elsewhere in Late Antique Latin and Greek *vitae*. For example, in the anonymous fifth century text, *The Life of Olympias*, it is noted that she was a bride for a few days to Nebridius 'but in truth she did not grace the bed of anyone and her body too remained uncorrupt', cf. E. A. Clark, *Women in the Early Church*, (Minnesota, 1983), 224.

51   P. Thompson, 'Saint Aethelthryth', 476.

52   P. Thompson, 'Saint Aethelthryth', 480–4.

53   Cf. comments in this chapter on Bede's portrayal of Ecgfrith, 162 .

54   V. Burrus, 'Word and Flesh', 30.

55   *EH*, IV:19, 392: *Nam etiam signum diuini miraculi, quo eiusdem feminae sepulta caro corrumpi non potuit, indicio est quia a uirili contactu incorrupta durauerit.*

56   Baudonivia, *Vita Radegundis*, 1, 380; 5, 381.

57   P. Thompson, 'Saint Aethelthryth', 483.

58   Aldhelm, *De Virginitate* – 'The Prose De Virginitate', in *Aldhelm: The Prose Works*, M. Lapidge & M. Herren trans. (Ipswich, 1979), 61.

59   Aldhelm, *De Virginitate*, 67.

60   Aldhelm, *De Virginitate*, 71.

61 Aldhelm, *De Virginitate*, 52.

62 R. Ray, 'What do we know about Bede's Commentaries', 15.

63 J. M.Wallace-Hadrill, *Comm*, 160.

64 P. Godman (ed.), *Alcuin:The Bishops, Kings, and Saints of York: Alcuin, Versus de Patribus Regibus et Sanctis Euboricensis Ecclesiae* (OMT, 1982), lxxix.

65 P. Godman, *Alcuin: Bishops, Kings and Saints*, lxxxiii.

66 Cf. Letter of Leofgyth to Boniface, *English Historical Documents*, I, 735.

67 *EH*, IV:20, 396–400.

68 Prudentius, *Peristephonan*, III, 142–56; shortened version of Prudentius: Aldhelm, *Carmen de virginitate*, 147.

69 M. Herrin, 'Transmission and reception of Graeco-Roman mythology', 87.

70 Cf. A. Thacker, 'Social and Continental Background', 879. Cf. also: H. Mayr-Harting, 'Bede's Patristic Thinking', 367–4.

71 J. Wallace-Hadrill, 'Gregory of Tours and Bede: Their Views on the Personal Qualities of Kings', *Frühmittelatterliche Studien*, 2 (1968), 31–44, 37–8; J. Campbell, 'Bede's Reges and Princips', in *Essays*, 85–98, 97; J. Campbell, 'Bede I', in *Essays*, 4; H. Mayr-Harting, 'Bede's Patristic Thinking', 370–4; J. McClure, 'Bede's Old Testament Kings', *Ideal & Reality in Frankish and Anglo-Saxon Society*, P. Wormald (ed.) (Oxford, 1983), 76–98; C. Stancliffe, 'Oswald, Most Holy and Most Victorious King of the Northumbrians', *Oswald, Northumbrian King to European Saint*, C. Stancliffe & E. Cambridge (eds) (Stamford, 1995).

72 C. Stancliffe, 'Oswald', 63. As Mayr-Harting notes, Bede says a distinctively Constantinian thing about Oswald, Edwin,

and Oswine; Mayr-Harting, 'Bede's Patristic Thinking', 370.

73 P. Clemoes, *The Cult of St. Oswald on the Continent* (Jarrow, 1983).

74 *EH*, III:1,212–14; Rufinus-Eusebius, *Die Kirchengeshichte*, X: 8, 895, li. 10 ff.

75 *EH*, III:1, 212–14.

76 Rufinus-Eusebius, *Die Kirchengeshichte*, X: 9, 901, li. 4 ff.

77 Adomnan, *Life of Columba*, Bk.i:1, 16.

78 Paulinus of Nola, *Epistle*, 28, 6. *CSEL*, 29, J. Hartel (ed.), (Vienna, 1894), 247.

79 Ambrose, *De Obitu Theodosii*, in *Sancti Ambrosii Opera, CSEL*, 73, ed. O. Faller (Vienna, 1955), ch. 12, 377; humility is covered by Ambrose, ch. 27, 384ff.

80 J. W. George, *Venantius Fortunatus – A Latin Poet in Merovingian Gaul* (Oxford, 1992), 39.

81 R. A. Markus, 'Gregory the Great on Kings, Rulers and Preachers in the Commentary on *I Kings*', *The Church and Sovereignty c590–1918*, D. Wood (ed.) (Oxford, 1991), 7.

82 Gregory the Great, *Pastoral Care: Sancti Gregorii Magni, Regulae Pastoralis Liber*, in *PL* 77 (Paris, 1896), II:6, 34: *Seruanda itaque est et in corde humilitatis.*

83 Gregory the Great, *Pastoral Care*, I:10, 23: *Qui ad aliena cupienda non ducitur, sed propria largitur.*

84 Gregory the Great, *Pastoral Care*, II:7, 38 ff: *Ut sit rector internorum curam in exteriorum occupatione non minuens, exteriorum prouidentium in internorum sollicitudine non relinquens.*

85 *EH*, II:9, 166: *Sed et ipse, cum esset uir natura sagacissimus, saepe diu solus residens ore*

*quidem tacito sed in intimis cordis multa secum
conloquens, quid sibi esset faciendum, quae
religio seruanda, tractabat.*

86   *EH*, II:12, 178.

87   *EH*, II:12, 180.

88   C. Stancliffe, 'Oswald', 62.

89   *EH*, II:14, 186.

90   *EH*, II:20, 202.

91   *EH*, I:26, 78: *Didicerat enim a doctoribus
auctoribuis quesuae salutis seruitium Christi
uoluntarium, non coacticium esse debere.*

92   *EH*, II:15, 188; *EH*, III:21, 278.

93   *EH*, III:22, 380–2.

94   *EH*, IV:26, 428: *multum prohibentibus
amicis et maxime beatae memoriae
Cudbercto.... Sed quoniam anno praecedente
noluerat audire reuerentissimum patrem
Ecgberctum,... datum est illi ex poena peccati
illius, ne nunc eos, qui ipsum ab interitu reuocare
cupiebant, audiret.*

95   Anon. *Life of Cuthbert*, III:6, 104 &
Bede's *Life of Cuthbert*, ch. 24, 238; and Anon.
Life of Cuthbert, IV:8, 122; Bede's *Life of
Cuthbert*, ch. 27, 242–4 respectively.

96   Anon. *Life of Cuthbert*, IV:8, 122.

97   Gregory the Great, *Pastoral Care*, II:6,
35: *Miro ergo judicio intus foueam dejectionis
inuenit, dum foris in culmine potestatis extollit.*

98   B. Colgrave, *EH*, 428, n.3.

99   R. Morse, *Truth and Convention*, 104.

100   J. Wallace-Hadrill, *Comm.*, 88.

101   Pseudo-Cyprianus, *De duodecim abusivis
saeculi*, *CSEL* (ed.), iii, 3., 152ff; J. Kenney, *The*

*Sources for the Early History of Ireland:
Ecclesiastical* (Dublin, 1966), 281–2.

102   *EH*, II:16, 192: *contingere prae
magnitudine uel timoris eius auderet uel amoris
uellet.*

103   *De duodecim*, 160: *nisi enim ametur
dominus et metuatur, ordinatio illius constare
minime potent.*

104   *De duodecim*, 166: *aduenis et pupillis et
uidius defensorem; pauperes eleemosynis.*

105   *De duodecim*, 166.

106   *EH*, III:12, 250: *quia a tempore matutinae
laudis saepius ad diem usque in orationibus
persteterit.*

107   W. Chaney, *The Cult of Kingship in Anglo-
Saxon England* (Manchester, 1970), 116; cf.
also R. Folz, 'Saint Oswald Roi de
Northumbrie – Etude d'hagiographie
Royale', *AB*, 98 (1980), 51.

108   D. Rollason, *Saints and Relics*, 127.

109   *EH*, III:12, 250: *Nec mirandum preces
regis illius iam cum Domino regnantis multum
ualere apud eum, qui temporalis regni quondam
gubernacula tenens magis pro aeterno regno
semper laborare ac deprecari solebat.*

110   It is perhaps of relevance here to take
into consideration the study of S. Lerer,
who, using the case of Imma (*EH*, IV:22,
400–1), extrapolates that Bede deliberately
suppressed pagan modes of understanding
rather than encouraging them to be
remembered through textualization. It is
surely unlikely that Bede would have
wanted a specific model remembered in the
context of Oswald. Cf. S. Lerer, 'The
Releasing Letters: Literate Authority in
Bede's Story of Imma', *Literacy and Power in
Anglo-Saxon Literature* (London, 1991), 33, 38,
39.

111 *EH*, III:6, 280.

112 C. Stancliffe, 'Oswald', 65.

113 Gregory the Great, *Pastoral Care*, I:10, 23.

114 *De duodecim*, 166.

115 Cf. For example, St. John Chrysostom, Homily 78 (John 16. 5–15). *Saint John Chrysostom – Commentary on St. John the Apostle and Evangelist*, Homilies, 48–88, T. A. Goggin, trans. (Washington, 1959), 349.

116 Isidore, *Historia Gothorum*, 56, 290: *thesauros suos in egenis recondens.*

117 Isidore, *Historia Gothorum*, 56, 290: *sciens ad hoc illi fuisse conlatum regnum, ut eo salubriter frueretur, bonis initiis bonum finem adeptus.*

118 Isidore, *Historia Gothorum*, 55, 290: *aedo liberalis, ut opes priuatorum et ecclesiarum praedia; 56, 290: Multos etiam ditauit rebus, plurmos sublimauit honoribus.*

119 J. Campbell, 'The First Century of Christianity', in *Essays*, 54.

120 Cf. R. Morse, *Truth and Convention*, 47.

121 B. Colgrave, 'Bede's Miracle Stories,' *BLTW*, 219.

122 *EH*, III:11, 246.

123 J. Wallace-Hadrill, *Comm*, 104.

124 J. Wallace-Hadrill, *Comm*, 104.

125 *EH*, III:11, 246: *Sed miraculi caelestis ostensio, quam reuerenter eae suscipiendae a cunctis fidelibus essent, patefecit.*

126 *EH*, III:6, 230.

120 P. Brown, 'Relics and Social Status in the Age of Gregory of Tours', *Society and the Holy in Late Antiquity* (London 1982), 235.

128 See, for example, Gregory of Tours' description of the light over the relic of the True Cross at Poitiers: Gregory of Tours, *Liber in Gloria Martyrum*, B. Krusch (ed.), *MGH: SRM*, I (Hanover, 1885), 484–561, 490.

129 *EH*, III:2, 214.

130 *EH*, III:9, 242: *Cuius quanta fides in Deum, quae deuotio mentis fuerit, etiam post mortem uirtutum miraculis claruit.*

131 *EH*, III:9, 242.

132 *EH*, III:12, 250: *qui temporalis regni quondam gubernacula tenens magis pro aeterno regno semper laborare ac deprecari solebat.*

133 V. Gunn, 'Bede and the Martyrdom of St. Oswald', *Martyrs and Martyrologies*, D. Wood (ed.) Studies in Church History, 30 (1993), 57–66.

134 R. Folz, 'Saint Oswald roi de Northumbrie: étude d'hagiographie royale', *AB*, 98 (1980), 59.

135 Cf. *EH* III:2, 9, 10 (Popular tradition); *EH* III:11, 12 (Bardney); *EH* III:13 (Hexham). The suggestion is that one should no longer accept that Bede's material on Oswald came predominantly from Hexham (D. Kirby, 'Bede's Native Sources', 350).

136 *EH*, II:14, 256: *Erat autem rex Osuini et aspectu uenustus et statura sublimis et affatu iucundus et moribus ciuilis et manu omnibus, id est nobilibus simul atque ignobilibus, largus; unde contigit ut ob regiam eius et animi et uultus et meritorum dignitatem ab omnibus diligeretur.*

137 *EH*, II:14, 256.

138 C. Cubitt, 'Sites of sanctity', 66.

139 D. Rollason, 'Cults of murdered royal saints', 12.

140 R. Folz, *Les saints rois*, 28.

141 R. Folz, *Les saints rois*, 29.

142 *The Calender of Saint Willibrord*, H.A.
Wilson (ed.), HBS, lx (London, 1918), xxii;
C. Cubitt, 'Sites of sanctity', 80.

143 R. Folz, *Les saints rois*, 29.

144 See, for example, *English Kalenders
Before AD 1100*, F. Wormald (ed.), HBS, lxxii,
(London, 1934), 1 – texts; *Anglo-Saxon Litanies
of the Saints*, M. Lapidge (ed.), HBS, 106,
(London, 1991).

145 P. Godman, *Alcuin: Bishops, Kings and
Saints*, 44, l. 505 ff.

146 P. Godman, *Alcuin: Bishops, Kings and
Saints*, 1.

147 D. Rollason, 'Cults of Murdered Royal
Saints', 3.

148 R. Folz, *Les saint rois*, 223.

149 J. Wallace-Hadrill, *Early Germanic
Kingship in England and on the Continent*
(Oxford, 1971), 85.

150 *EH*, III:14, 256; cf. also A. J. Gurevich,
Categories of Medieval Culture, 161.

151 *EH*, III,14, 258; J. Wallace-Hadrill, *Early
Germanic Kingship*, 85–6.

152 D. P. Kirby, 'Bede's Native Sources', 351;
restated in *Saint Wilfrid at Hexham*, D.P.
Kirby (ed.) (Newcastle, 1974), 14.

153 Cf. P. Wormald, 'Bede, Beowulf, and the
Conversion of the Anglo-Saxon Aristocracy,'
in *Bede and Anglo-Saxon England*, R.T. Farrell
(ed.), BAR, Brit. Ser. 46 (Oxford, 1978).

154 H. Mayr-Harting, *The Coming of
Christianity*, 223–4.

155 *EH*, III:14, 256; H. Mayr-Harting, *The
Coming of Christianity*, 224.

156 On this occasion giving the narrative
the feel of historical authenticity may not
have been Bede's only aim. Mayr-Harting
has also commented on the relationship
between this part of Oswine's story and the
allegorical allusion to Luke, 14:31. Here is a
perfect example of where Bede seems to
be relying on an Anglo-Saxon source and
yet manipulates the story to fit into
Christian allegory. It is clear that there is
some interface between the Anglo-Saxon
past and Bede's *EH* but even these
examples have been subjected to literary
interference; H. Mayr-Harting, 'Bede's
Patristic Thinking', 368.

157 *EH*, III:15, 16, 17.

158 *EH*, III:14, 258, compare with 17, 266.

159 Both Wallace-Hadrill and Rollason
have implied some unease concerning *EH*
III:14 being a hagiographical depiction: J.
Wallace-Hadrill, *Comm.*, "Bede's treatment
[of Oswine] does not follow a normal
hagiographical pattern', 108; D. Rollason,
'Cult of Murdered Royal Saints', 'Bede's
almost hagiographical description of
Oswine', 3. Such expressed unease possibly
has its origins in the fact that this chapter
was never intended to be viewed as
hagiography. From this the validity of
Rollason's hypothesis relating to the early
veneration of murdered royal saints needs
to be reassessed.

160 *EH*, III:14, 256: *in quo pro utriusque regis,
et occisi uidelicet et eius qui occidare iussit,
animae redemtione cotidie Domino precis offeri
deberent*

161 J. Wallace-Hadrill, 'Gregory of Tours
and Bede', 43.

162 C. Stancliffe, 'Oswald', 62.

163 H. Mayr-Harting, *The Coming of Christianity*, 255. Mayr-Harting was not the only person to note this use of an individual to highlight a particular characteristic. D. Wilcox commented too that Bede subordinated individuals to abstract character traits and that this was at the expense of their own basic reality. Cf. D. Wilcox, 'The Sense of Time in Western Historical Narratives from Eusebius to Machiavelli', in *Classical Rhetoric and Medieval Historiography*, E. Breisach (ed.) (Kalamazoo, 1985), 204–6.

164 *EH*, I:26, 76.

165 *EH*, III:3, 218. However, given the unorthodox nature of Iona it is unlikely that Bede would have used Oswald as the vehicle for the process of conversion.

166 *EH*, III:22, 280–2.
167 J. Wallace-Hadrill conjectured that Bede perhaps disbelieved some part of the Whitby claim; J. Wallace-Hadrill, *Early Germanic Kingship*, 82.

168 C. Fell, 'Saint Ædelfryð: a Historical Hagiographical Dichotomy Revisited', *Nottingham Medieval Studies*, 38 (1994), 25–6.

169 Pauline Thompson has made a similar observation in relation to Aethelthryth, noting a need to modify Fell's dichotomy. Cf. P. Thompson, 'St. Aethelthryth', 477.

170 S. Ridyard, *Royal Saints*, 82.

171 *EH*, IV:19, 392.

172 *EH*, IV:23, 406–10.

173 *EH*, IV:19, 392.

174 *EH*, IV:23, 408.

175 *EH*, IV:23, 408.

176 *EH*, IV:23, 408.

177 S. Hollis, *Anglo-Saxon Women and the Church*, 248.

178 *EH*, IV:19, 392.

179 *EH*, IV:23, 410 ff.

180 C. Lees & G. Overing, *Double Agents*, 27.

181 C. Lees & G. Overing, *Double Agents*, 27.

182 The following points are a response to Hollis' comment that politically influential abbesses with powerful family connections are 'conspicuously absent' from Bede's *EH* (*Anglo-Saxon Women and the Church*, 179). In this context, it is perhaps interesting to note that Rosenthal has argued the opposite case to Hollis concerning Bede. Instead she concentrates on the *Anglo-Saxon Chronicle* as being noteworthy for the 'total absence' of holy virgins and saints. Rather than seeing Bede's works in misogynistic terms she views him as offering a more 'hospitable' image of women. The apparent contradiction between these two academics' perception is perhaps evidence that making comments which isolate one text from the universal silence of women at this time is problematic. Quantitatively women tend to be notable for their absence in general.

183 *EH*, II:9, 165; II:20, 204; III:15, 260; III:24, 292; III:25, 296; IV:26, 430; V:19, 518.

184 *EH*, V:19, 518.

185 *EH*, III:24, 290; IV:26, 428.

186 S. Hollis, *Anglo-Saxon Women and the Church*, 179ff.

187 S. Hollis, *Anglo-Saxon Women and the Church*, 179.

188 S. Hollis, *Anglo-Saxon Women and the Church*, 180–1; She makes a particularly

compelling argument for the importance of
Aelfflead in Northumbria.

189 S. Hollis, *Anglo-Saxon Women and the
Church*, 189.

190 S. Hollis, *Anglo-Saxon Women and the
Church*, 187.

191 S. Hollis, *Anglo-Saxon Women and the
Church*, 184.

192 S. Hollis, *Anglo-Saxon Women and the
Church*, 185.

193 S. Hollis, *Anglo-Saxon Women and the
Church*, 187.

194 Prose *Life of Cuthbert*, XXIV, 234.

195 Prose *Life of Cuthbert*, XXXIV, 262 &
XXIII, 230.
196 Prose *Life of Cuthbert*, XXIII, 230.

197 Prose *Life of Cuthbert*, XXIV, 234.

198 Prose *Life of Cuthbert*, XXXIV, 262.

199 Prose *Life of Cuthbert*, XXIII, 230.

200 Anon. *Life of Cuthbert*, III:4, 102 & IV:10,
126. If one compares Bede's epithets with
those of the *Life of St. Wilfrid* they are clearly
equally favourable. Thus the *Life of St. Wilfrid*
calls her '*sancta uirgo et abbatissa*' (*Life of St.
Wilfrid*, 43, 88); '*sapientissima uirgo*' (*Life of St.
Wilfrid*, 59, 128 & 60, 132); '*beatissima Aelfleda
abbatissa*' (*Life of St. Wilfrid*, 60, 130).

201 R. Alter, *The Art of Biblical Narrative*
(London, 1981), 133ff.

Conclusion

1   Chapter 1, 19[NB page nos will
change], n. 2.

2   George Hardin Brown has noted the
exegete Bede had in mind was the Irishman,

Hilary, cf. G. H. Brown, *Bede the Educator*, 7;
Bede's insinuations about Irish learning
might also lie under his comment
concerning rhythmic verse (*de rithmo*) in the
penultimate chapter of his *De Arte Metrica*.
Here Bede discusses how rhythmic verse
(which he says is a harmonious arrangement
of words that is scanned by the number of
syllables judged in accordance with the way
they sound to the ear) is the verse of the
common poets. However, he later notes
that the rhythmical attempts of common
poets are inevitably done awkwardly,
whereas the learned poets do it skilfully.
When translating this text Kendall
commented that this reference is most
likely to refer to the non-quantitative Latin
poems like many of those found in the Irish
Liber Hymnorum. It is, in the light of this
argument, tempting to infer that Bede was
in some way deprecating certain types of
Irish poetry. Cf. *Bede: Libri II De Arte Metrica
et De Schematibus et Tropis – The Art of Poetry
and Rhetoric*, C.B. Kendall trans.
(Saarbrücken, 1991), 161.

3   Bede, *On Holy Places*, W. T. Foley & A.
Holder trans., *Bede: A Biblical Miscellany*
(Liverpool, 1999), 4 & 25.

4   From such a reading of the *EH*, Bede's
comments or choice of material with
regard to the Council of Hatfield might not
be so much proof of Theodore's orthodoxy,
as an implication that there were some valid
concerns which were only sorted out at
this time. This would challenge Henry
Chadwick's argument: cf. H. Chadwick,
'Theodore, the English Church and the
monothelete controversy', *Archbishop
Theodore: Commemorative Studies on his Life
and Influence* (Cambridge, 1995), especially
89ff.

5   Franklin questions whether Bede was
unaware of the level and nature of
Theodore's scholarship. Lapidge too seems
inclined to consider Bede was lacking in
knowledge, implying that Bede would have
possibly tempered his remarks had he been

aware that the *Life of St. Anastasius* was by
Theodore. Given the importance of
monastic networks, the evidence that
suggests that individual learning had
particular value within Anglo-Saxon society,
and Bede's apparent correction of Theodore
in *On Eight Questions*, a lack of knowledge of
Theodore's work on Bede's part seems
increasingly unlikely. Cf. Franklin, 'Theodore
and the *Passio S. Anastasii*', 202; M. Lapidge,
'The Career of Archbishop Theodore', in
Anglo-Latin Literature 600–899 (London,
1996), 112.

6   The identification of more of
Theodore's scholarly legacy by Michael
Lapidge and his colleagues perhaps makes
the potential for at least some comparison
possible. The corpus of Aldhelm's works
could be included also. Cf. the relevant
chapters in M. Lapidge, *Anglo-Latin Literature
600–899*.

7   A. Cameron, *Christianity and the Rhetoric
of Empire*, 120.

8   R. Morse, *Truth and Convention*, 90.

9   R. Ray, 'The Triumph of Greco-
Rhetorical Assumptions', 67.

10   W. McCready, *Miracles and the Venerable
Bede*, 225.

11   A. J. Frantzen, 'Literature, Archaeology,
and Anglo-Saxon Studies: Reconstruction
and Deconstruction', *Sutton Hoo: Fifty Years
After*, R. Farrell & C. Neuman de Vegvar
(eds), *American Early Medieval Studies*, 2
(1992), 25.

Bibliography

Primary Sources

Adomnan, *Vita Sancti Columbae*, A. O. Anderson & M. O. Anderson (eds), *Adomnan's Life of Saint Columba* (London, 1961); R. Sharpe trans., *Adomnan of Iona – Life of Saint Columba* (Harmondsworth, 1995).

Alcuin, *Vita Sancti Willibrordi*, W. Levison (ed.), *MGH: SRM*, 7, 81–141; *The Life of St Willibrord*, C. H. Talbot (ed.), *The Anglo-Saxon Missionaries in Germany* (London, 1954), 3–22.

Alcuin, *Versus de Patribus Regibus et Sanctis Euboricensis Ecclesiae*, P. Godman (ed.), *The Bishops, Kings and Saints of York* (Oxford, 1982).

Aldhelm, *The Prose Works*, M. Lapidge & M. Herren (eds) (Ipswich, 1979).

Aldhelm, *The Poetic Works*, M. Lapidge & J. L. Rosier (eds) (Cambridge, 1985).

Ambrose, *De Obitu Theodosii*, O. Faller (ed.), *Sancti Ambrosii Opera*, CSEL, 73 (Vienna, 1955).

Anonymous (Pseudo Cicero) *Rhetorica ad Herennium*, H. Caplan trans.,(London, 1954).

Anonymous, *Vita Sanctissima Ceolfridi Abbatis*, C. Plummer (ed.), *HE (P)*, I, 388–404.

Anonymous, *Vita Sancti Cuthberti*, B. Colgrave (ed.), *Two Lives of Saint Cuthbert* (Cambridge, 1940), 60–139.

Anonymous, *Vita Sancti Gregorii Magni*, B. Colgrave (ed.), *The Earliest Life of Gregory the Great* (Cambridge, 1985).

Augustine, *De Sancta Virginitate*, in *Seventeen Short Treatises of St. Augustine* (Oxford, 1847), 308–52.

Baudonivia, *Vita Sanctae Radegundis*, liber 2, B. Krusch (ed.), *MGH: SRM*, 2 (Hanover, 1888).

Bede, *Chronica Minora, Chronica Maiora*, T. Mommsen (ed.), *MGH: AA*, xiii (Berlin, 1898), 231–327; J. McClure & R. Collins trans., 'The Greater Chronicle', *Bede: The Ecclesiastical History of the English People* (Oxford, 1994), 307–40.

Bede, *De Locis Sanctis Libellus*, J. A. Giles (ed.), *Venerabilis Bedae Opera*, 4 (London, 1843–44), 402–43; *On Holy Places*, in *Bede: A Biblical Miscellany*, W. T. Foley & A. Holder trans., (Liverpool, 1999).

Bede, *De Templo*, D. Hurst (ed.), *CCSL* CXIX (Turnhout, 1969), 143–234; S. Connolly trans., *Bede: On the Temple* (Liverpool, 1995).

Bede, *De Temporum Ratione*, C. W. Jones (ed.), *CCSL* CXXIIIB (Turnhout, 1978), 263–460; F. Wallis trans., *Bede: The Reckoning of Time* (Liverpool, 1999).

Bede, *Epistolam ad Ecgberctum*, C. Plummer (ed.), *HE (P)*, I, 405–23.

Bede, *Historia Abbatum*, C. Plummer (ed.), *HE (P)*, I, 364–387.

Bede, *Historia Ecclesiastica*, C. Plummer (ed.), *HE (P)*, I, 5–360; B. Colgrave & R. A. B. Mynors (eds), *Bede's Ecclesiastical History of the English People* (Oxford, 1969).

Bede, *Kalendarium siue Martyrologia Quasi Bedae Cura et Opere*, C. W. Jones (ed.), *CCSL* CXXIIIC (Turnhout, 1980), 567–78.

Bede, *Martyrologium*, J. Dubois & G. Renaud (eds), *Édition pratique de Bède, de l'Anonyme lyonnais et de Florus* (Paris, 1976); F. Lifshitz trans., 'Bede, *Martyrology*', in *Medieval Hagiography: An Anthology*, T. Head (ed.) (London, 2001).

Bede, *Opera Didascalica*, C. W. Jones (ed.), *CCSL* CXXIIIA (Turnhout, 1975).

Bede, *Opera Homilectica*, D. Hurst (ed.), *CCSL* CXXII (Turnhout, 1955), 1–378; L. T. Martin & D. Hurst trans., *Bede the Venerable: Homilies on the Gospels*, 2 vols. (Kalamazoo, 1991).

Bede, *Vita Sanctae Cuthberti Metrica*, W. Jaager (ed.), *Bedas metrische Vita Sancti Cuthberti* (Palaestra, 198; Leipzig, 1935).

Bede, *Vita Sanctae Cuthberti Prosaica*, B. Colgrave (ed.), *Two Lives of Saint Cuthbert* (Cambridge, 1940), 142–307.

Bede, *Vita Sancti Felicis*, J. A. Giles (ed.), *Venerabilis Bedae Opera*, 4 (London, 1843-44), 174–202.

Bede, *Libri II De Arte Metrica et De Schematibus et Tropis – The Art of Poetry and Rhetoric*, C. B. Kendall trans. (Saarbrücken, 1991).

Boniface, *Bonifatii Epistolae*, Tangl (ed.) (Berlin, 1916); E. Emerton trans., *The Letters of Boniface* (New York, 1940).

Calendar of St Willibrord, H. A. Wilson (ed.), HBS, 55 (London, 1918).

Cicero, *De Inventione*, H. M. Hubbell (ed.) (London, 1949).

Cicero, *De Oratore*, K. Kumaniecki (ed.) (Leipzig, 1969); J. M. May & J. Wisse trans., *Cicero: On the Ideal Orator* (Oxford, 2001).

Eddius Stephanus, *Vita Sancti Wilfridi*, B. Colgrave (ed.), *The Life of Bishop Wilfrid by Eddius Stephanus* (Cambridge, 1927).

English kalendars before A.D. 1100, F. Wormald (ed.), HBS, 72 (London, 1934).

Eusebius, *Life of Constantine*, E. C. Richardson trans., in *A Select Library of Nicene and Post-Nicene Fathers* (Oxford, 1890).

Felire Oengussi celi de: The Martyrology of Oengus the Culdee, W. Stokes (ed.), HBS, 29 (London, 1905).

Felix, *Vita Sancti Guthlaci*, B. Colgrave (ed.), *Felix's Life of St Guthlac* (Cambridge, 1956).

Gesta Sanctorum Patrum Fontanellensis Coenobii, F. Lohier & R. P. J. Laporte (eds) (Paris, 1935); also *Gesta Abbatum Fontanellensium*, S. Loewenfeld (ed.) (Hanover, 1886).

Gildas, *De Excidio Britonum*, M. Winterbottom (ed.), *Gildas: The Ruin of Britain and Other Works* (London, 1978).

Gregory the Great, *Dialogues*, A. de Vogue & P. Autin (eds), 3 vols. (Paris, 1978–80).

Gregory the Great, *Regulae Pastoralis Liber*, PL 77 (Paris, 1896), 13–128.

Gregory of Tours, *Liber Historiarum X*, B. Krusch & W. Levison (eds), *MGH: SRM*, I/I (1951).

Hilary, *Vita Sancti Honorati*, *PL, 50*.

Isidore, *Etymologiarum siue originum*, W. M. Lindsey (ed.) (OCT, 1911); also, *Isidorus Hispalensis: Etymologiae II*, P. K. Marshall (ed.), *Etymologies Book II: Rhetoric* (Paris, 1983).

Isidore, *Historia Gothorum Vandalorum Sueborum*, T. Mommsen (ed.), *MGH: AA* XI (1894), 267–303; K. B. Wolf trans., *Isidore of Seville, History of the King of the Goths*, in *Conquerors and Chronicles of Early Medieval Spain* (Liverpool, 1990), 81–110.

Jerome, *Ad Innocentium Presbyterum de Septies Percussa*, in *Jerome: Select Letters*, F.A. (Wright) trans. (London, 1954).

Le Martyrology d'Usuard: Texte et Commentaire, J. Dubois (ed.) (Brussels, 1965).

Liber Pontificalis, L. Duschesne & C. Vogel (eds), *Le Liber Pontificalis, Texte, introduction et commentire*, 3 vols. (Paris, 1886–92); R. Davis trans., *The Book of the Pontiffs* (Liverpool, 1989/2000 rev.edn).

Martyrologium Hieronymianum, H. Quentin & H. Delehaye (eds), *Acta Sanctorum*, November, II.2 (Brussels, 1931).

Martyrology of Tallaght, R. I. Best & H. J. Lawlor (eds), HBS, 68 (London, 1931).

Orosius, *Historiarum Aduersum Paganos libri VII*, C. Zangemeister (ed.), *CSEL*, V (Vienna, 1882), 1–600; R. J. Deferrari trans., *Paul Orosius – The Seven Books of History Against the Pagans*, Fathers of the Church, 50 (Washington, 1964).

Passio et miracula sancti Eadwardi Regis et Martyris, C. E. Fell (ed.), *Edward, King and Martyr*, Leeds Texts and Monographs, New Series 3 (Leeds, 1971).

Paulinus of Nola, *Epistolae*, J. Hartel (ed.), *CSEL*, 29 (Vienna, 1894).

Possidius, *Vita Augustini*, PL 32.

Prudentius, *Peristaphanon Liber*, in *Prudentius*, H. J. Thomson trans, vol. II (London, 1949).

Pseudo-Cyprianus, *De duodecim abusiuis saeculi*, CSEL iii. 3 (Vienna).

Rufinus-Eusebius, *Die Kirchengeschichte*, E. Schwartz & T. Mommsen (eds), *Eusebius Werke*, 2.2, *Die griechischen christlichen Schriftsteller* (Leipzig, 1903–09); H. J. Lawlor & J. E. L. Oulton trans., *Eusebius –The Ecclesiastical History and the Martyrs of Palestine* (London, 1927).

Simeon of Durham, *Historia de Sancto Cuthberto*, T. Arnold (ed.), *Symeonis Monachi Opera Omnia*, 1 (London, 1885); T. J. South (ed.) *Historia de sancto Cuthberto* (Cambridge, 2002)

Simeon of Durham, *Historia Regum*, T. Arnold (ed.), *Symeonis Monachi Opera Omnia*, 2 (London, 1885).

Symeon of Durham, Libellus de Exordio atque Procursu istius hoc est Dunhelmensis Ecclesie, D. Rollason (ed.), (Oxford, 2000).

Venantius Fortunatus, *Vita Sanctae Radegundis*, liber 1, B. Krusch (ed.), *MGH: SRM*, 2 (Hanover,1888).

Vita Glodesindae, Vita Antiquior, in *Acta Sanctorum*, July 25, 198–224.

Vita Sanctae Balthildis, version 'A', B. Krusch (ed.), *MGH: SRM*, 2 (Hanover, 1888).

Vita Sanctae Genovifae, in *Acta Sanctorum*, January 3, 137–53.

Vita Sanctae Geretrudis, version 'A', B. Krusch (ed.), *MGH: SRM*, 2 (Hanover, 1888).

Vita Sancti Fursei, B. Krusch (ed.), *MGH: SRM*, 4 (Hanover, 1902).

Secondary Sources

Albertson, C., *Anglo-Saxon Saints and Scholars* (Fordham, 1967).

Alter, R., *The Art of Biblical Narrative* (London,1981).

Auerbach, E., *Literary Language & its Public in Late Latin Antiquity and in the Middle Ages* (London, 1965).

Bäuml, F. H., '*Scribe et Impera*: Literacy in Medieval Germany', *Frankia*, 24/1 (1997), 123–32.

Bitel, L. M., *Isles of the Saints: Monastic Settlement and Christian Community in Early Ireland* (New York, 1990).

Blair, P. H., 'The Historical Writings of Bede', in *La Storiografia Altomedievale*, Settimone di Studio, XVII (Spoleto, 1970), 197–221.

Blair, P. H., 'The *Moore Bede*', in *Early English Manuscripts in Facsimile*, IX (Copenhagen, 1959).

Blair, P. H., *The World of Bede* (Cambridge, 1970).

Bonner, G., 'St. Cuthbert at Chester-le-Street', in *St Cuthbert, His Cult and His Community to AD 1200*, G. Bonner *et al.* (eds) (Woodbridge, 1989).

Bonner, G. (ed.), *Famulus Christi: Essays in the Commemoration of the Thirteenth Centenary of the Birth of the Venerable Bede* (London, 1976).

Bonner, G. *et al.* (eds), *St. Cuthbert, His Cult and His Community to AD 1200* (Woodbridge, 1989).

Bonner, S. F., *Roman Declamation in the Late Republic and Early Empire* (Liverpool, 1969).

Brooks, N., *The Early History of the Church of Canterbury* (Leicester, 1984).

Brown, G. H., *Bede the Venerable* (Boston, 1987).

Brown, G. H., *Bede the Educator* (Jarrow, 1996).

Brown, G. H., 'The Dynamics of Literacy in Anglo-Saxon England', in *Textual and Material Culture in Anglo-Saxon England*, D. Scragg (ed.) (Cambridge, 2003), 183–212.

Brown, J. C., 'Writing Power and Writing-Power: The Rise of Literacy as a Means of Power in Anglo-Saxon England', *Medieval Perspectives*, 15 (2000), 42–56.

Brown, M. P., *In the beginning was the Word: Books and Faith in the Age of Bede* (Jarrow, 2002).

Brown, P., 'Relics and Social Status in the Age of Gregory of Tours', in *Society and the Holy in Late Antiquity* (London, 1982), 222–50.

Brown, P., *The Body and Society: Men, Women and Sexual Renunciation in Early Christianity* (London, 1988).

Brown, P., *The Cult of Saints – Its Rise and Function in Latin Christianity* (London, 1981).

Brown, P., 'The Rise and Function of the Holy Man in Late Antiquity', in *Society and the Holy in Late Antiquity* (London, 1982), 103–52.

Brown, P., 'The Notion of Virginity in the Early Church', in *Christian Spirituality – Origins to the Twelfth Century* (London, 1989), 427–43.

Bullough, D. A., 'The Missions to the English and Picts and their Heritage (to c.800)', in *Die Iren und Europa im Früheren Mittelatter,* H. Lowe (ed.) (Stuttgart, 1982), I.

Bullough, D. A., *Hagiographie, cultures et societes, ive – xiie siecles* Études Augustiniennes (Paris, 1981), 339–59.

Burrus, V., 'Word and Flesh – The Bodies and Sexuality of Ascetic Women in Christian Antiquity', *Journal of Feminist Studies in Religion,* 10 (1994).

Cameron, A., *Christianity and the Rhetoric of Empire: The Development of Christian Discourse* (Oxford, 1991).

Campbell, J., *Essays in Anglo-Saxon History* (London, 1986).

Campbell, J., 'Elements in the Background to the Life of St Cuthbert and His Early Cult', in *St Cuthbert, His Cult and His Community to AD 1200*G. Bonner *et al.* (eds) (Woodbridge, 1989), 3–20.

Chadwick, H. M., *Studies in Anglo-Saxon Institutions* (Cambridge, 1905).

Chadwick, H. 'Theodore, the English Church and the monothelete controversy', in *Archbishop Theodore: Commemorative Studies on his Life and Influence,* M. Lapidge (ed.) (Cambridge, 1995)

Chaney, W., *The Cult of Kingship in Anglo-Saxon England* (Manchester, 1970).

Charles-Edwards, T., *Early Christian Ireland* (Cambridge, 2000).

Clanchy, M., *From Memory to Written Record: England 1066–1307* (Oxford, 1993, 2nd edn)

Clark, E. A., *Women in the Early Church* (Minnesota, 1983).

Clarke, M. L., *Rhetoric at Rome: A Historical Survey* (London, 1996 rev. edn).

Clayton, M., *The Cult of the Virgin Mary in Anglo-Saxon England* (Cambridge, 1990).

Clemoes, P., *The Cult of St Oswald on the Continent* (Jarrow, 1983).

Coats, G. W.(ed.), *Saga, Legend, Tale, Novella, Fable: Narrative Forms in Old Testament Literature, Journal for Study of the Old Testament*, Supplement series, 35 (1985).

Coleman, J. *Ancient and Medieval Memories: Studies in the Reconstruction of the Past* (Cambridge, 1992).

Colgrave, B., 'Bede's Miracle Stories', in A. Hamilton Thompson, *Bede, His Life, Times and Writings* (London, 1935), 201–29.

Collins, R., *Early Medieval Europe 300–1000* (London, 1991).

Cowdrey, H. E. J., 'Bede and the "English People"', *Journal of Religious History,* vol. II (1981), 501–23.

Cramp, R., *Wearmouth and Jarrow Monastic Sites* (Swindon, 2005)

Croke, B. & Emmett, A. M. (eds), *History and Historians in Late Antiquity* (Oxford, 1983).

Cubitt, C., *Anglo-Saxon Church Councils, 650–850* (London, 1995).

Cubitt, C., 'Sites and sanctity: revisiting the cult of murdered and martyred Anglo-Saxon royal saints', *Early Medieval Europe*, 9 (2000), 53–83.

Deferrari, R. J., trans., *Early Christian Biographies* (Washington, 1952).

Delehaye, P. H., *The Legends of the Saints – An Introduction to Hagiography*,V. M. Crawford trans. (London, 1907).

Delehaye, H., *Cinq Leçons sur la méthode hagiographique*, Société des Bollandistes, Subsidia Hagiographica, 21 (Brussels, 1934).

De Vegvar, C. N., 'Saints and Companions to Saints: Anglo-Saxon Royal Women Monastics in Context', in *Holy Men and Holy Women: Old English Prose Saints' Lives and their Context*, P. E. Szarmach (ed.) (New York, 1996).

Dubois, J., 'Le martyrologe metrique de Wandelbert', in *AB*, 79 (1961), 257–93.

Dubois, J., *Les Martyrologes du Moyen Age Latin*, Typologie des Sources du Moyen Age Occidental (Turnhout, 1978).

Dubrow, Heather, *Genre* (London, 1982).

Eckenstein, L., *WomanUnder Monasticism* (Cambridge, 1896).

Emmerson, R. K., *Antichrist in the Middle Ages: A Study of Medieval Apocalypticism, Art, and Literature* (Manchester, 1981).

Faivre, A., *The Emergence of the Laity in the Early Church*, D. Smith trans. (New York, 1990).

Farmer, D., *The Age of Bede* (Harmondsworth, 1985).

Fell, C., 'Hild, Abbess of Streonashalch', in *Hagiography and Medieval Literature: A Symposium*, H. Bekker-Nielson *et al.* (eds) (Odense, 1981), 76–99.

Fell, C., 'Saint Ædelflryð: a Historical Hagiographical Dichotomy Revisited', *Nottingham Medieval Studies,* 38 (1994), 19–34.

Fichtenau, H., *Living in the Tenth Century – Mentalities and Social Orders,* P. Geary trans. (London, 1991).

Folz, R., 'Tradition hagiographique et culte de Saint Dagobert, roi des Francs', *Le Moyen Age,* 69 (1963), 17–35.

Folz, R., 'Saint Oswald Roi de Northumbrie – Étude d'Hagiographie Royale', *AB,* 98 (1980), 49–74.

Folz, R., *Les Saints Rois du Moyen Âge en Occident (VIe – XIIIe siecles)* (Brussels, 1984).

Fouracre, P., 'Merovingian History and Merovingian Hagiography', *Past & Present,* 127 (1990), 3–38.

Franklin, A. C., 'Theodore and the *Passio S. Anastasii*', in *Archbishop Theodore: Commemorative Studies on his Life and Influence,* M. Lapidge (ed.) (Cambridge, 1995).

Franklin, C. V., 'Grammar and Exegesis: Bede's *Liber de schematibus et tropis,* in *Latin Grammar and Rhetoric: From Classical Theory to Medieval Practice,* C. D. Lanham (ed.)(London, 2002), 63–91.

Frantzen, A. J., *Desire for Origins: New Language, Old English, and the Teaching Tradition* (London, 1990).

Frantzen, A. J., 'Literature, Archaeology, and Anglo-Saxon Studies: Reconstruction and Deconstruction', in *Sutton Hoo: Fifty Years After,*R. Farell & C. N. de Vegvar (eds), American Early Medieval Studies, 2 (1992).

Geary, P. J., *Before France and Germany: the Transformation of the Merovingian World* (Oxford, 1988).

Geary, P. J., *Phantoms of Remembrance: Memory and Oblivion at the End of the First Millennium* (Princeton, 1994).

Gerberding, R. A., *The Rise of the Carolingians and the Liber Historiae Francorum* (Oxford, 1987).

Gerberding, R. A., 'Review of Walter Goffart's *The Narrators of Barbarian History* (AD 550–800)', *Speculum*, 65 (1990), 674–6.

Genicot, L. (ed.), *Typologie des Sources du moyen âge Occidental* (Turnhout, 1972).

Gilbert, E., 'Saint Wilfrid's Church at Hexham', in *Saint Wilfrid at Hexham*, D. P. Kirby (ed.)(Newcastle, 1974), 81–113.

Gneuss, H., 'The Study of Language in Anglo-Saxon England', in *Textual and Material Culture in Anglo-Saxon England*, D. Scragg (ed.) (Cambridge, 2003),75–105.

Godden, M., 'King Alfred's Preface and the Teaching of Latin in Anglo-Saxon England', *EHR*, 472 (2002), 596–604.

Godfrey, J., 'The Place of the Double Monastery in the Anglo-Saxon Minster System', in *Famulus Christi: Essays in Commemoration of the Thirteenth Centenary of the Birth of the Venerable Bede*, G. Bonner, (ed.) (London, 1976), 344–50.

Goffart, W., *The Narrators of Barbarian History, AD 500–800* (Princeton, 1988).

Goffart, W., 'The *Historia Ecclesiastica*: Bede's Agenda and Ours', *Haskins Society Journal,* 2 (1990), 29–45.

Greenway, D., 'Authority, Conversation and Observation in Henry of Huntingdon's *Historia Anglorum*', *Anglo-Norman Studies,* xviii (1995), 105–22.

Grierson, P., 'Abbot Fulco and the Date of the *Gesta Abbatum Fontanellensium*', *English Historical Review*, lv (1940), 275–84.

Gunn, V., 'Bede and the Martyrdom of St. Oswald', *Martyrs and Martyrologies*, D. Wood (ed.) Studies in Church History, 30 (1993), 57–66.

Gunn, V., 'Transforming Subject Boundaries: the interface between Higher Education teaching and learning theories and subject-specific knowledge', *Arts and Humanities in Higher Education*, 2 (2003), 265–80.

Gurevich, A. J., *Categories of Medieval Culture*, G. L. Campbell trans. (London, 1985).

Gurevich, A., *Medieval Popular Culture: Problems of Belief and Perception*, J. M. Bak & P. A. Hollingsworth trans. (Cambridge, 1988).

Gurevich, A., *A Historical Anthropology of the Middle Ages*, J. Howlett (ed.) (Cambridge, 1992).

Halporn, J. W., 'Literary History and Generic Expectations in the *Passio and Acta Perpetuae*', *Vigiliae Christianae*, 45 (1991), 223–41.

Hamilton Thompson, A. (ed.), *Bede: His Life, Times and Writings* (Oxford, 1935).

Hanning, R. W., *The Vision of History in Early Britain: From Gildas to Geoffrey of Monmouth* (London, 1966).

Harrison, K., *The Framework of Anglo-Saxon History to AD 900* (Cambridge, 1976).

Haywood, P., 'Gregory the Great as "Apostle of the English" in Post-Conquest Canterbury', *Journal of Ecclesiastical History*, 55:1 (2004), 19–57.

Heene, K., 'Audire, Legere, Vulgo: An Attempt to Define Public Use and Comprehensibility of Carolingian Hagiography', in *Latin and the Romance Languages in the Early Middle Ages*, R. Wright (ed.) (Pennsylvania, 1991), 146–63.

Heffernan, T. J., *Sacred Biography: Saints and Their Biographers in the Middle Ages* (Oxford, 1988).

Herbert, M., *Iona, Kells and Derry: The History and Hagiography of Columba* (Oxford, 1988).

Herrin, J., *The Formation of Christendom* (London, 1987).

Herrin, M., 'The transmission and reception of Graeco-Roman mythology in Anglo-Saxon England, 670–800', *ASE*, 27 (1998), 87–103.

Higgitt, J., 'The Dedication Inscription at Jarrow and its Context', *The Antiquaries Journal*, 59 (1979), 343–74.

Hillgarth, J. N., *Christianity and Paganism, 350–750* (Philadelphia, 1985).

Hollis, S., *Anglo-Saxon Women and the Church* (Woodbridge, 1992).

Hughes, K., *Early Christian Ireland: Introduction to the Sources* (London, 1972).

Innes, M . & McKitterick, R., 'The Writing of History', in *Carolingian Culture: Emulation and Innovation*, R. McKitterick (ed.) (Cambridge, 1994), 193–220.

Innes, M., 'Memory, Orality and Literacy in an Early Medieval Society', *Past & Present*, 158 (1998), 1–30.

Jenkins, C., 'Bede as Exegete and Theologian', in *BLTW*, 152–200.

John, E., 'The Social and Political Problems of the Early English Church', *Agricultural History Review,* 18 (1970), supplement, 39–63.

Jones, C. W., *Saints' Lives and Chronicles in Early England* (New York, 1947).

Jones, P. F., *A Concordance to the Historia Ecclesiastica of Bede* (Massachusetts, 1929).

Kelly, S., 'Anglo-Saxon Lay Society and the Written Word', in *The Uses of Literacy in Early Medieval Europe,* R. McKitterick (ed.) (Cambridge, 1990), 36–62.

Kemp, E. W., *Canonization and Authority in the Western Church* (London, 1948).

Kendall, C. B., 'Bede's *Historia Ecclesiastica*: The Rhetoric of Faith', in *Medieval Eloquence: Studies in the Theory and Practice of Medieval Rhetoric,* J. J. Murphy (ed.) (Berkeley, 1978), 145–72.

Kirby, D. P., 'Bede's Native Sources for the *Historia Ecclesiastica*', *Bulletin of the John Rylands Library,* 48 (1965), 341–71.

Kirby, D. P. 'Northumbria in the Time of Wilfrid', in Kirby, D. P. (ed.), *Saint Wilfrid at Hexham* (Newcastle, 1974), 1–34.

Kirby, D. P., 'King Ceowulf of Northumbria and the *Historia Ecclesiastica*', *Studia Celtica,* xiv/xv (1979/80), 168–73.

Kirby, D. P., 'Bede, Eddius Stephanus and the "Life of Wilfrid"', *English Historical Review,* 98 (1983), 101–14.

Kirby, D. P., *The Earliest English Kings* (London, 1991).

Kirby, D. P., *Bede's Historia Ecclesiastica Gentis Anglorum: Its Contemporary Setting* (Jarrow, 1992).

Kitchen, J., *Saints' Lives and the Rhetoric of Gender: Male and Female in Merovingian Hagiography* (Oxford, 1998).

Klaniczay, G., *The Uses of Supernatural Power: The Transformation of Popular Religion in Medieval Early-Modern Europe*, S. Singerman trans., K. Margolis (ed.) (Cambridge, 1990).

Knappe, G., 'Classical rhetoric in Anglo-Saxon England', *ASE*, 27 (1998), 5–29.

Koziol, G., *Begging Pardon and Favour: Ritual and Political Order in Early Medieval France* (Ithaca, 1992).

Laistner, M. L. W., 'The Library of the Venerable Bede', in *BLTW*, 237–66.

Lapidge, M., 'The Saintly Life in Anglo-Saxon England', in *The Cambridge Companion to Old English Literature*, M. Godden & M. Lapidge (eds) (Cambridge, 1991), 243–63.

Lapidge, M., *Archbishop Theodore: Commemorative Studies on his Life and Influence* (Cambridge, 1995)

Lapidge, M., *Anglo-Latin Literature 600–899* (London, 1996).

Lapidge, M., 'Textual Criticism and the Literature of Anglo-Saxon England', in *Textual and Material Culture in Anglo-Saxon England*, D. Scragg (ed.) (Cambridge, 2003), 107–36.

Lapidge, M., *The Anglo-Saxon Library* (Oxford, 2006).

Lawrence, C. M., *Medieval Monasticism* (London, 1984).

Leclercq, J., *The Love of Learning and the Desire for God*, C. Misrahi trans., (London, 1978).

Lees, C. & Overing, G., *Double Agents: Women and Clerical Culture in Anglo-Saxon England* (Philadelphia, 2001).

Lerner, G., *The Creation of Patriarchy* (Oxford, 1986).

Levison, W., *England and the Continent in the Eighth Century* (London, 1956).

Loyn, H. R., 'Bede's Kings : A Comment on the Attitude of Bede to the Nature of Secular Kingship', in *Eternal Values in Medieval Life*, N. Crossley-Holland (ed.), *Trivium*, 26 (1991), 54–64.

Markus, R. A., *Bede and the Tradition of Ecclesiastical Historiography* (Jarrow, 1975).

Markus, R. A., 'Chronicle and Theology: Prosper of Aquitaine', in *The Inheritance of Historiography 350–900*, Christopher Holdsworth & T. P. Wiseman (eds) (Exeter, 1986), 31–44.

Markus, R. A., *The End of Ancient Christianity* (Cambridge, 1990).

Markus, R. A., 'Gregory the Great on Kings: Rulers and Preachers in the Commentary on I Kings', in *The Church and Sovereignty c590–1918*, D.Wood (ed.) (Oxford, 1991), 7–22.

Markus, R. A., *Signs and Meanings: World and Text in Ancient Christianity* (Liverpool, 1996).

Martindale, C., *Redeeming the Text: Latin Poetry and the Hermeneutics of Reception* (Cambridge, 1993).

Mayr-Harting, H., *The Venerable Bede, the Rule of Saint Benedict, and Social Class* (Jarrow, 1976).

Mayr-Harting, H., *The Coming of Christianity to Anglo-Saxon England* (London, 3rd edn 1991).

Mayr-Harting, H., 'Bede's Patristic Thinking as an Historian', in *Historiographie im frühen Mittelalter*, A. Scharer & G. Scheibelreiter (eds) (München, 1994), 367–74.

McClure, J., 'Bede's Old Testament Kings', in *Ideal and Reality in Frankish and Anglo-Saxon Society*, P. Wormald, (ed.) (Oxford, 1983), 76–98.

McClure, J., 'Bede and the Life of Ceolfrid', *Peritia*, 3 (1984), 71–84.

McClure, J., 'Bede's *Notes on Genesis* and the Training of the Anglo-Saxon Clergy', in *The Bible in the Medieval World: Essays in Memory of Beryl Smalley*, Studies in Church History, Subsidia 4 (Oxford, 1985),

McCready, W., *Miracles and the Venerable Bede* (Toronto, 1994).

McCulloh, J. M., 'Historical Martyrologies in the Benedictine Cultural Tradition', in *Benedictine Culture 750–1050*, W. Lourdaux & D. Verhelst (eds), *Medievalia Lovanensia*, series 1/studio xi (Leuven, 1983), 114–31.

McKitterick, R., *The Carolingians and the Written Word* (Cambridge, 1989).

McKitterick, R., 'The Audience for Latin Historiography in the Early Middle Ages: Text Transmission and Manuscript Dissemination', in *Historiographie im frühen Mittelalter*, A. Scharer & G. Scheibelreiter (eds) (München, 1994), 96–114.

McLaughlin, E., 'Women, Power and the Pursuit of Holiness in Medieval Christianity', in *Feminist Theology – A Reader*, A. Loades (ed.) (London, 199), 94–120.

McNamara, J. A., 'The Need to Give: Suffering and Female Sanctity in the Middle Ages', in *Images of Sainthood in Medieval Europe,* R. Blumenfeld-Kosinski & T. Szell (eds) (New York, 1991).

Meyendorff, J., *Imperial Unity and Christian Divisions – The Church 450–680 AD* (New York, 1989).

Meyvaert, P., *Bede and Gregory the Great* (Jarrow, 1964).

Meyvaert, P., 'Bede the Scholar', in *Famulus Christi*, G. Bonner (ed.) (London, 1976), 40–69.

Mitchell, K., 'Saints and Public Christianity in the Historiae of Gregory of Tours', in *Religion, Culture and Society in the Early Middle Ages – Studies in Honour of Richard E. Sullivan,* T. F. X. Noble & J. J. Contreni (eds) (Kalamazoo, 1987), 77–94.

Morse, R., *Truth and Convention in the Middle Ages: Rhetoric, Representation, and Reality* (Cambridge, 1991).

Nelson, J. L., 'Queens as Jezebels: The Careers of Brunhild and Balthild in Merovingian History', in *Medieval Women,* D. Baker (ed.) (Oxford, 1978), 31–77.

Nelson, J. L., 'Women and the Word in the Earlier Middle Ages' in *Women in the Church,* W. J. Sheils & D. Wood (eds), Studies in Church History, 27, (Oxford, 1990), 53–78.

Nicholson, J., '*Feminae Gloriosae*: Women in the Age of Bede', in *Medieval Women,* D. Baker (ed.) (Oxford, 1978), 15–29.

O'Croínín, D., 'Rath Melsigi, Willibrord, and the Earliest Echternach Manuscripts', *Peritia,* 3 (1984), 17–49.

O'Sullivan, D., 'Space, silence and shortages on Lindisfarne. The archaeology of asceticism', in *Image and Power in the Archaeology of Early Medieval Britain: Essays in Honour of Rosemary Cramp*, H. Hamerow & A. MacGregor (eds) (Oxford, 2001), 33–52.

Palmer, A., *Prudentius on the Martyrs* (Oxford, 1989).

Parkes, M. B., 'Rædan, areccan, smeagan: how the Anglo-Saxons read', *ASE*, 26 (1997), 1–16.

Petersen, J. M., 'Dead or Alive? The Holy Man as Healer in East and West in the Late Sixth Century', *Journal of Medieval History*, 9 (1983), 91–8.

Ray, R., 'Bede's *Vera lex Historiae*', *Speculum*, 55 (1980), 1–21.

Ray, R., 'What do we Know About Bede's Commentaries?', *Recherches de Théologie ancienne et médiévale*, 49 (1982), 5–20.

Ray, R., 'The Triumph of Greco-Roman Rhetorical Assumptions in Pre-Carolingian Historiography', in *The Inheritance of Historiography 350–900*, C. Holdsworth & T. P. Wiseman (eds) (Exeter, 1986), 67–84.

Ray, R., *Bede, Rhetoric and the Creation of Christian Culture* (Jarrow, 1997).

Reynolds, L. D. *et al.*, *Texts and Transmission: A Survey of Latin Classics* (Oxford, 1983).

Reynolds, S., *Medieval Reading: grammar, rhetoric and the classical text* (Cambridge, 1996).

Richter, M., *Medieval Ireland – The Enduring Tradition* (London, 1988).

Ricoeur, P., 'History and Rhetoric', in *The Social Responsibility of the Historian*, F. Bedarida (ed.) (Oxford, 1994), 7–23.

Ridyard, S. J., *The Royal Saints of Anglo-Saxon England* (Cambridge, 1988).

Roberts, M., *Poetry and the Cult of the Martyrs: The Liber Peristephanon of Prudentius* (Ann Arbor, 1993).

Rollason, D. W., *The Mildrith Legend: A Study in Early Medieval Hagiography in England* (Leicester, 1982).

Rollason, D. W., 'The Cults of Murdered Royal Saints in Anglo-Saxon England', *ASE*, 11 (1983), 1–22.

Rollason, D. W., *Saints and Relics in Anglo-Saxon England* (Oxford, 1989).

Rollason, D. W., 'Hagiography and Politics in Early Northumbria', in *Holy Men and Holy Women – Old English Prose Saints' Lives and Their Context*, P. E. Szarmach (ed.) (New York, 1996), 96–114.

Roper, M., 'The Donation of Hexham', in *Saint Wilfrid at Hexham*, D. P. Kirby (ed.) (Newcastle, 1974), 169–171.

Roper, M., 'Wilfrid's Landholdings in Northumbria', in *Saint Wilfrid at Hexham*, D. P. Kirby (ed.) (Newcastle, 1974), 61–79.

Rosenthal, J., 'Anglo-Saxon Attitudes: Men's Sources, Women's History', in *Medieval Women and the Sources of Medieval History*, J. Rosenthal (ed.) (London, 1990).

Salisbury, J. E., *Church Fathers, Independent Virgins* (London, 1991).

Schaefer, U., '*Ceteris Imparibus*: Orality/Literacy and the Establishment of Anglo-Saxon Literate Culture', in *The Preservation and Transmission of Anglo-Saxon Culture*, P. E. Szarmach & J. T.

Rosenthal (eds), *Studies in Medieval Culture* XL (Kalamazoo, 1997), 287–312.

Schneider, D. B., 'Anglo-Saxon Women in the Religious Life: A Study of the Status and Position of Women in an Early Medieval Society', Unpublished PhD Thesis (Cambridge, 1985).

Schulenberg, J. T., 'Female Sanctity: Public and Private Roles, c.500–1100', in *Women and Power in the Middle Ages*, M. Erler & M Kowaleski (eds) (London, 1988), 102–25.

Schulenberg, J. T., 'Saints' Lives as a Source for the History of Women', in *Medieval Women and the Sources of Medieval History*, J. Rosenthal (ed.) (London, 1990), 285–320.

Scragg, D. (ed.), *Textual and Material Culture in Anglo-Saxon England* (Cambridge, 2003).

Sharpe, R., 'Some Problems Concerning the Organization of the Church in Early Medieval Ireland', *Peritia,* 3 (1984), 230–70.

Simpson, L., 'The King Alfred/Cuthbert Episode in the *Historia sancto Cuthberto:* Its Significance for Mid-Tenth Century English History', in *St. Cuthbert, Cult & Comm.*, 397–411.

Sims-Williams, P., 'Continental Influence at Bath Monastery in the Seventh Century', *ASE,* IV (1975), 1–11.

Sims-Williams, P., *Religion and Literature in Western England, 600–800,* Cambridge Studies in Anglo-Saxon England, 3 (Cambridge, 1990).

Smith, J., 'The Hagiography of Hucbald of St. Amand', *Studi Medievali,* 35 (1994), 517–42.

Smyth, A., *Warlords and Holy Men* (London, 1984).

Sot, M., *Gesta Episcoporum, Gesta Abbatum,* Typologie des sources (Turnhout, 1981).

Stancliffe, C., 'Kings Who Opted Out', in *Ideal and Reality in Frankish and Anglo-Saxon Society,* P. Wormald *et al.* (eds), (Oxford, 1983) 154–76.

Straw, C., *Gregory the Great: Perfection in Imperfection* (London, 1988).

Stock, B., *The Implications of Literacy: Written Language and Models of Interpretation in the Eleventh and Twelfth Centuries* (Princeton, 1983).

Thacker, A. T., 'The Social and Continental Background of Early Anglo-Saxon Hagiography', D.Phil (Oxford, 1976).

Thacker, A. T., 'Some Terms for Noblemen in Anglo-Saxon England, c650–900', in *Anglo-Saxon Studies in Archaeology and History,* 2, D. Brown *et al.* (eds), *BAR* British Series 92 (1981), 201–36.

Thacker, A. T., 'Bede's Ideal of Reform', in *Ideal and Reality in Frankish and Anglo-Saxon Society,* P. Wormald *et al.* (eds) (Oxford, 1983), 130–53.

Thacker, A. T., 'Lindisfarne and the Origins of the Cult of St. Cuthbert', in *St. Cuthbert, Cult & Comm.,* 103–22.

Thacker, A. T., 'Monks, Preaching and Pastoral Care in Early Anglo-Saxon England', in *Pastoral Care Before the Parish,* J. Blair & R. Sharpe (eds) (Leicester, 1992), 137–70.

Thacker, A. T., '*Membra Disjecta:* The Division of the Body and the Diffusion of the Cult', in *Oswald – Northumbrian King to European Saint,* C. Stancliffe & E. Cambridge (eds) (Stamford, 1995), 97–127.

Thacker, A. T., 'Bede and the Irish', in *Beda Venerabilis: Historian, Monk and Northumbrian*, L. A. J. R. Houwen & A. A. McDonald (eds) (Groningen, 1996), 31–59.

Thacker, A. T., 'Memorializing Gregory the Great: the Origin and Transmission of a Papal Cult in the Seventh and Early Eighth Centuries', *Early Medieval Europe*, 7 (1998), 59–84.

Thiebaux, M., *The Writings of Medieval Women*, 13, series B (New York, 1987).

Thomas, C., *Bede, Archaeology and the Cult of Relics* (Jarrow, 1973).

Thompson, P., 'St Aethelthryth: The Making of History from Hagiography', in *Studies in English Language and Literature: 'Doubt wisely'– Papers in Honour of E. G. Stanley*, M. J. Toswell & E. M. Tyler (eds) (London, 1996).

Van Caenegem, R. C., *Guide to the Sources of Medieval History* (Amsterdam, 1978).

Wallace-Hadrill, J. M., 'Gregory of Tours and Bede: Their Views on the personal Qualities of Kings', *Frühmittelatterliche Studien*, 2 (1968), 31–44.

Wallace-Hadrill, J. M., *Early Germanic Kingship in England and on the Continent* (Oxford, 1971).

Wallace-Hadrill, J. M., *The Frankish Church* (Oxford, 1983).

Wallace-Hadrill, J. M, *The Barbarian West 400–1000* (Oxford, 1985).

Wallace-Hadrill, J. M., *Bede's Ecclesiastical History of the English People – A Historical Commentary* (Oxford, 1988).

Wallace-Hadrill, J. M., ' Bede and Plummer', originally in *Early Medieval History* (Oxford, 1975), reprinted in *Comm.,* (Oxford, 1988), xv–xxxv.

Ward, B., *Miracles and the Medieval Mind* (Aldershot, 1987).

Ward, B., *The Venerable Bede* (London, 1990).

Warner, M., *Alone of all her Sex: The Myth and the Cult of the Virgin Mary* (London, 1976).

Weinstein, D. & Bell, R. M., *Saints and Society: The Two Worlds of Western Christendom, 1000–1700* (London, 1982).

Wilmart, A., 'Un Témoin Anglo-Saxon du Calendrier Metrique d'York', *Revue Benedictine,* XLVI (1934).

Wilson, D. (ed.), *The Archaeology of Anglo-Saxon England* (Cambridge, 1976).

Wilson, S. (ed.), *Saints and their Cults: Studies in Religious Sociology, Folklore and History* (Cambridge, 1983).

Wood, I. N., 'Forgery in Merovingian Hagiography', *Falschungen im Mittelatter,* V (1988), 369–84.

Wood, I. N., 'Saint Wandrille and its Hagiography', in *Church and Chronicle in the Middle Ages – Essays Presented to John Taylor*, I. Wood & G. A. Loud (eds) (London, 1991), 1–14.

Wood, I. N., 'Ripon, Francia and the Franks Casket in the Early Middle Ages', *Northern History,* XXVI (1990), 1–19.

Wood, I. N., 'The Mission of Augustine of Canterbury to the English', *Speculum,* 69 (1994), 1–17.

Wood, I. N., *The Merovingian Kingdoms 450–751* (Harlow, 1994).

Wood, I. N., *The Most Holy Abbot Ceolfrid* (Jarrow, 1995).

Wormald, P., 'Bede and Benedict Biscop', in *Famulus Christi*, 141–69.

Wormald, P., 'Bede, Beowulf and the Conversion of the Anglo-Saxon Aristocracy', in *Bede and Anglo-Saxon England*, R. T. Farrell (ed.), BAR 46 (1978), 32–95.

Wormald, P., *Bede and the Conversion of England: The Charter Evidence* (Jarrow, 1984).

Wright, N., *History and Literature in Late Antiquity and the Early Medieval West* (Aldershot, 1995).

Yorke, B. A. E., 'The Vocabulary of Anglo-Saxon Overlordship', in*Anglo-Saxon Studies in Archaeology and History*, D. Brown *et al.* (eds), 2, BAR British Series 92 (1981), 171–200.

Yorke, B. A. E., 'Sisters Under the Skin? Anglo-Saxon Nuns and Nunneries in Southern England', *Reading Medieval Studies,* XV (1989), 95–117.

Yorke, B. A. E., *Kings and Kingdoms of Early Anglo-Saxon England* (London, 1990)

Index